IMAGES
of America

HERCULES

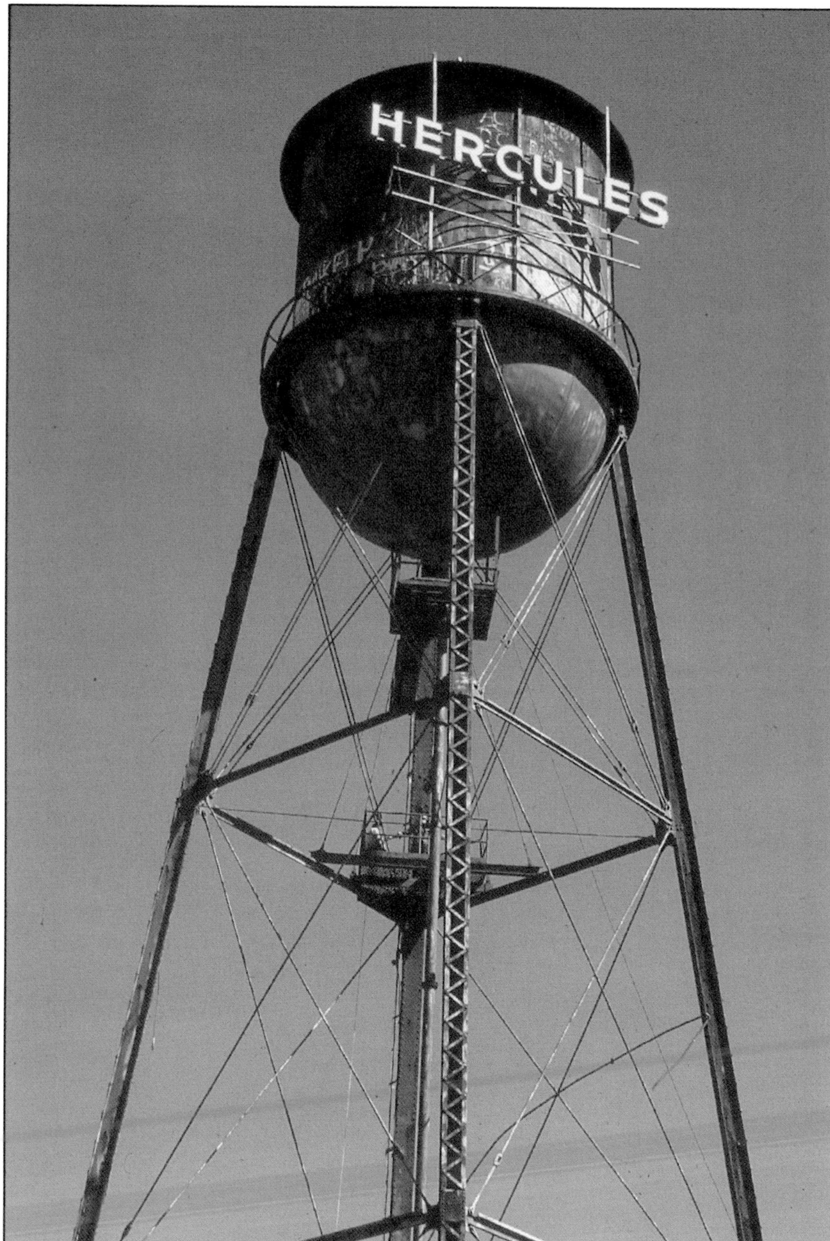

WATER TOWER. The tower, located near San Pablo and Hercules Avenues, was a beacon to motorists traveling on Highway 40. It was built in 1933 at a cost of $10,000 by the Pittsburgh–Des Moines Corporation to provide a water capacity of 100,000 gallons to Hercules Powder. During the blackout years of World War II, the neon-outlined letters were darkened. The tower was in use until 1977. (Courtesy Lynn Fissell.)

ON THE FRONT COVER: CONSTRUCTION CREW, SPRING 1905. This image is one of a series of photographs documenting the major construction project at Hercules, managed by the E.I. du Pont de Nemours Company. The new acid houses these men built at Hercules Point are in the background. (Courtesy M. Wallace and W. Ryder.)

IMAGES
of America

HERCULES

Jennifer Posedel and Stephen Lawton
with the Hercules Historical Society

ARCADIA
PUBLISHING

ISBN 978-0-7385-7440-0

Published by Arcadia Publishing
Charleston, South Carolina

Printed in the United States of America

Library of Congress Control Number: 2010937737

For all general information, please contact Arcadia Publishing:
Telephone 843-853-2070
Fax 843-853-0044
E-mail sales@arcadiapublishing.com
For customer service and orders:
Toll-Free 1-888-313-2665

Visit us on the Internet at www.arcadiapublishing.com

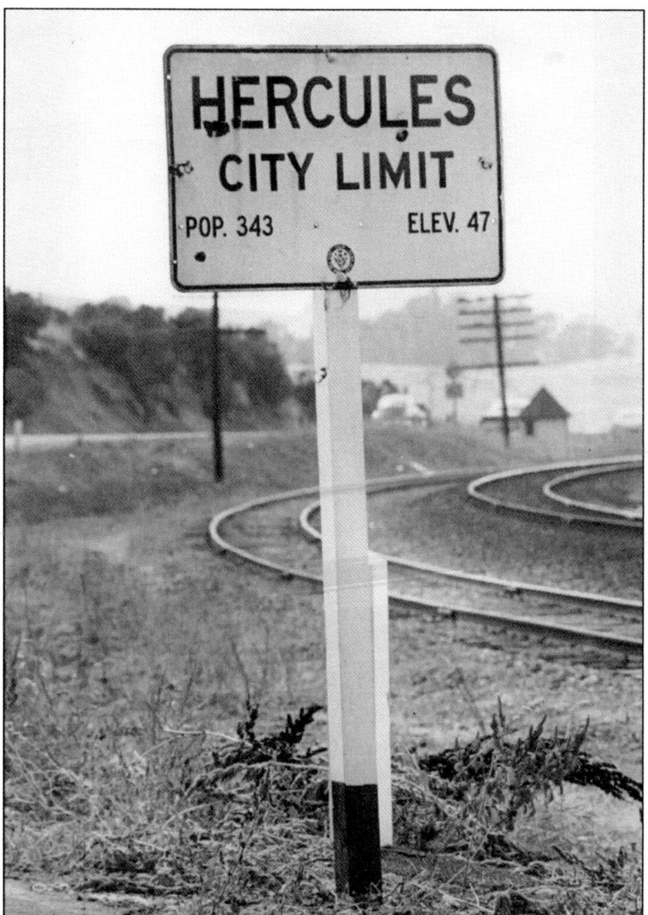

HERCULES SIGN ON STATE ROUTE 4. Although located at a major road and rail gateway to the Bay Area, Hercules was off-limits to all but a few hundred workers and their families. Before residential development commenced in the early 1970s, the explosives factory of Hercules was a hidden, little known place. (Courtesy Hercules Police Department.)

Contents

Acknowledgments

Many individuals and organizations contributed to this book. We are grateful to M. Wallace and W. Ryder for the generous donation of their grandfather Warren Horton McBryde's construction progress photographs and the McBryde family albums. These illustrate the early years of the plant and the family life of a manager. Special thanks go to James Vitak, public relations manager for Ashland Inc., who located and scanned photographs taken for the employee magazine the *Hercules Mixer.* (Ashland Inc. acquired Hercules Incorporated in 2008.) Contributions came from the collections of the California Historical Society, Contra Costa County Historical Society, the Crockett Museum, Drake Property Group/Aegis Financial Corporation, East Bay Regional Park District, Hercules Police Department, Pinole Historical Society, and the Nobel Society. Barry Brown, a Santa Cruz historian, retrieved materials from the Hagley Museum Library in Delaware. William Ingalls, Anita Wennblom Broberg McKee, and Douglas Williams contributed detailed notes to accompany their family photographs. Karana Hattersley-Drayton conducted oral interviews in 1992 of Wilbur Thatcher, Manuel Pavon, Edwin Gray, and Mary Lucid.

Members of the Hercules Historical Society who participated in the development of this book are Lynn Fissell, Susan Keeffe, Stephen Lawton, Edgar Pankey, Pat Patton, Bob Polacchi, Darrel Jay Tucker, and Jeff Wisniewski. Lynn Fissell coordinated outreach and acquisitions. Darrel Jay Tucker handled logistics. Jennifer Posedel did the research and layout for the book and wrote the captions. Stephen Lawton wrote the narrative.

Numerous other individuals loaned photographs and shared memories, including Kristina Warren Barncard, John Bender, Robert Bender, George E. Bradbury, Don Browning, John Cadigan, Donna Payne Cope, John Darke, Graig Dias, Ernest Fawcett, Lynn Fissell, John Harder, Sue Harryman, LaVonne Harrison, Darlene Hasenpflug, Michele LeFebvre, Dr. Joseph Marriotti, Brenda Montano, Robert Morris, Keith Olsen, Barbara Pearce, Pat Perkins, Russ Perkins, Marilyn Bennett Ponting, Dorothy (Mrs. Frank) Potts, Helen Poulos, Bill Prather, Margaret Faria Prather, Robert Reedy, Gigi Reloj, Jeff Rubin, Dan Russell, Walt Seidl, the late Fred Sill Jr., Tom Stewart, Peter Supino, Sharon Taylor, Nancy M. Tooker, Sharon Parshall Townsend, Barbara Woodfield, Pam Dorway Worley, and Chuck Zeiss. Thank you all.

Introduction

Hercules is the name of a settled place occupying the watershed of Refugio Creek, in Contra Costa, California. Hercules was also the name of a hero in Greek mythology and the brand name of an industrial product, dynamite. How this name and this place came together unfolds an important story of the global Industrial Revolution of the 19th century. It is also the earliest story of California-born technological innovation. Hercules, California, is therefore a place of significance in mankind's mastery of energy, particularly the energy of chemical explosives, which is fundamental to every aspect of our lives today.

The story of explosives begins with black powder, used by the world's major civilizations for six centuries. Until about 1840, it was the only known explosive substance. Production of this mixture of potassium nitrate (as saltpeter), sulfur, and carbon (as charcoal) is straightforward and moderately dangerous. Raw materials are pulverized and mixed. The resulting mixture is then rolled or pressed into cakes. The cakes are broken into grains for final polishing, drying, and blending for specific applications, such as blasting or munitions. For safety, production was in small batches, typically located close to the points of use. Rudimentary black powder mills, operated by hardy proprietors, served local markets such as a mining district or a munitions factory. With neither economies of scale nor incentives for innovation, explosives manufacture was a pre-industrial enterprise.

The 1849 California Gold Rush was also a pre-industrial enterprise. Thousands of miners blasted away at the Sierra foothills, and railroad men began carving out graded routes. California, still a remote outpost, became an important new market for black blasting powder.

California's miners and railroad builders needed increasing supplies of black powder at affordable prices. For a time, demand was satisfied with seaborne shipments from the powder mills of the eastern United States and Europe. However, by the late 1850s the eastern mills shifted production to the military in anticipation of the Civil War. As the Union and Confederacy plunged into war, black powder became a strategic material and shipments were embargoed. Californians grew desperate for their vital black blasting powder. In October 1863, the collector of the Port of San Francisco telegraphed the secretary of war in Washington, DC, that unless powder was sent promptly, the Union would receive no more California gold.

John H. Baird, a forty-niner from Kentucky, saw the opportunity to produce black powder in California. In 1861 he led a group of investors to raise capital of $100,000 and incorporate the California Powder Works. A suitable site was selected on the San Lorenzo River, outside Santa Cruz, near a paper mill. With ample waterpower and forests for construction timber and charcoal, the site was separated from the town but enjoyed access to a wharf in the Santa Cruz harbor.

By 1864, with factory equipment procured from the East, the first black powder mill in the West was in operation. It relied on Chinese laborers and saltpeter shipped from India (and later nitrate of soda from Chile). Employing up to 275 workmen, the California Powder Works was for many years the principal industry of Santa Cruz and the sole source of black powder in California. But after only four years, it faced a formidable competitor possessing a new chemical technology.

Nitroglycerine, a chemical compound, was the first "high explosive" that explodes by detonation instead of burning. Italian chemist Ascanio Sobrero discovered this unstable, sensitive liquid in the 1840s. Production requires mixing glycerin into a blend of nitric and sulfuric acids. The mixing operation produces heat, which can cause a runaway explosive reaction if not controlled. Special acid-resistant vessels, often fashioned from lead, are required to handle the corrosive acids.

Nitroglycerine can produce explosive velocities many thousands of times greater than black powder. Despite Sobrero's warnings, harnessing the power of nitroglycerine was an irresistible challenge for men of vision and industry willing to risk death. By the 1860s, nitroglycerine had moved from scientific curiosity to a new technology.

Charles Crocker, one of the "Big Four" owners of the Central Pacific Railroad, brought the power of nitroglycerine to California. He had taken on the greatest engineering challenge of the century. Beginning in 1863, he marshaled the men, money, and equipment to build the transcontinental railroad eastward from Sacramento. By early 1867, more than 10,000 Chinese laborers were at the difficult and dangerous work of digging, blasting, and grading the route. But at the summit, Crocker's men fell behind schedule. Using black powder, the Chinese could advance the face of Tunnel Number Six through the solid granite at a rate of only 1.18 feet per day. The success of the entire enterprise hinged on completing the 1,659-foot tunnel that year.

Crocker brought English chemist James Howden to the tunnel site. Howden set up a simple nitroglycerine factory, using an old kettle beneath a shed roof supported by four posts. Mixing the chemicals, he worked alone, surrounded by red flags. He taught the Chinese how to handle and use nitroglycerine for blasting. In November, the first train rolled through the summit tunnel.

That same year, Swedish scientist Alfred Nobel obtained the first of many patents showing how nitroglycerine could be tamed for practical use by impregnating it in clay or other material, known as "dope." This new product, dynamite, was versatile, reliable, and relatively safe to transport. Unlike black powder, dynamite was a patented chemical product. Because dynamite production required scientific understanding, technical expertise, and capital investment in large, sophisticated factories, it was to call forth one of the earliest recognizably modern industries.

The American cradle of this new industry was to be San Francisco. In 1868, Nobel sold the exclusive US patent for the manufacture and sale of dynamite to the Giant Powder Company, which immediately constructed the first American commercial dynamite factory in San Francisco's Rock House Canyon, now Glen Park. It was destroyed in an 1869 explosion. Operations soon recommenced on a 100-acre site in the sand dunes south of Golden Gate Park.

The men of California Powder Works immediately saw the competitive threat to their black powder business. They needed a product to compete with Giant's Nobel-patented dynamite. In 1869, with the transcontinental railroad completed, James Howden returned to San Francisco with a reputation as one of its best chemists. Funded by California Powder Works, he proceeded to set up a nitroglycerine factory on a site on the southeast corner of Golden Gate Park.

Howden's product used mealed black powder from the Santa Cruz factory as the dope to absorb the nitroglycerine. This formulation was cleverly trade-named "Black Hercules," invoking the mythical hero of great strength who could slay "Giants." Giant Powder immediately sued to protect its patent, ultimately losing at the Supreme Court in 1880. Bitter feelings between the men of the two firms persisted for years.

California Powder Works was well capitalized and a strong competitor to Giant Powder. It continued research and development of new dynamite formulations, marketed using the Hercules trade name. Sales increased under the direction of general manager Joseph Powning. By 1879, however, explosions in the San Francisco factories made obvious the need to move production away from the expanding population.

Giant Powder erected its third dynamite factory in 1879 at Fleming Point, north of the Ocean View district of west Berkeley, on a site now used as a racetrack. In 1881, the newly incorporated Safety Nitro Powder Company built its own dynamite factory on Point Conchal, now known as Point Pinole. Later, after an explosion destroyed its Fleming Point plant, Giant consolidated with Safety Nitro and moved its plant to Point Pinole in 1892.

In 1878, the men of California Powder Works looked farther north and east in Contra Costa—the "opposite coast," across the bay from San Francisco—for a new factory site. They found an ideal site just east of the town of Pinole, at the mouth of the valley of Refugio Creek.

Refugio is one of several creeks draining the low hills of Contra Costa. Its watershed, covering an area of about five square miles, meets San Pablo Bay a few miles west of the Carquinez Strait. Eastward, the Carquinez Strait is the water gateway to the interior of California. Westward, 40 percent of all the waters of California flow through the Carquinez to the Pacific Ocean at the Golden Gate. San Pablo Bay is part of the 1,600-square-mile San Francisco Bay estuary, the largest on the Pacific coast of the Americas.

Today, the San Francisco Bay estuary is the center of a globally important metropolis, the home of seven million people. Two hundred fifty years ago, the estuary was the center of an almost unimaginably different landscape, the home of about 10,000 people living in a complex, subtle, and remarkably stable Stone Age culture. Native people dwelled along Pinole and Refugio Creeks for thousands of years.

The Carquinez Strait marked the northern extent of territory occupied by natives in a cultural grouping later named Ohlone. The Ohlone comprised about 40 territorial groups, or tribelets, each distinguished by language and culture. The Karkin tribelet, and perhaps the Huchiun tribelet, occupied the lands around the Carquinez, encompassing the adjacent valleys of Refugio and Pinole Creeks.

During the time of the Ohlone, the Bay was much larger, ringed with vast marshes of pickleweed, cordgrass, and tule, and teeming with wildlife. The Ohlone lived in permanent upland villages and temporary camps along the shore. One of those camps, a little village of tule huts, stood at the mouth of Pinole Creek.

In March 1772, the men and women of the Ohlone village on Pinole Creek were astonished and frightened at the sight of Spanish men on horseback. Father Juan Crespi and Don Pedro Fages led this first exploration party. Soon, the Ohlone lands were the dominion of Mission San Francisco de Asis (Dolores), established in 1776. Soldiers took the Ohlone people away from their ancestral land to the missions.

The kindly intentions of the missionaries resulted only in misery and death for the Ohlone. Their society and culture was demolished by strict, often harsh treatment, changes in diet, and infection with European diseases. In a few decades, their lifeways were obliterated; their population decimated. Americans would later murder the few survivors.

But the decimation of the natives also meant the failure of the Spanish mission system. By 1822, California was ruled by Mexico. Along the Carquinez, the grasslands and oak woodlands were still full of deer, elk, and grizzly bears, but soon would be destroyed by the running of livestock and the plowing of fields. On Pinole Creek, the little Ohlone village of tule huts vanished. By 1835, the village of Rancho San Pablo was settled a few miles southwest.

The failed missions yielded their land claims to soldiers and ranchers. In 1824, Ignacio Martinez, comandante of the Presidio of San Francisco, petitioned for title to the lands extending from Pinole Creek eastward along the Carquinez Strait to Alhambra Creek. By 1841, Martinez was selling cattle to Swiss immigrant John Sutter for his New Helvetia settlement near today's Sacramento. Seven years later, Sutter made the discovery sparking the Gold Rush. In 1848, the war with Mexico concluded and California was ceded to the United States.

Ignacio Martinez died in 1848, leaving Rancho El Pinole to be divided among his heirs. The pastoral life of ranchers and farmers slipped away before an onslaught of seekers and settlers. Two such immigrants came for Sierra Nevada gold but instead found their fortunes at Rancho El Pinole. English surgeon Dr. Samuel Tennant married a Martinez heir, daughter Rafaela. He platted the blocks of the town of Pinole. In 1854, Portuguese sailor Bernardo Fernandez arrived and established a shipping trade between San Francisco and Pinole. He bought the bay front lands from Dr. Tennant. His 1894 mansion still overlooks the bay today.

In 1878, not far from where the Ohlone had met the Spaniards seeking their empire, the landowners of Pinole met the men of California Powder Works, seeking land for their dynamite factory. Just 30 years after Tennant arrived in Pinole, new enterprises were born in San Francisco to produce the new high explosives. Indeed, these men were inventing the very idea of an industrial organization based on scientific innovation, capital investment, and branded products.

Their new factory for Hercules dynamite would soon occupy the lower Refugio Valley. The site was centered on a station of the Northern Railway, a line constructed in 1878 by two of the Central Pacific's Big Four to connect Oakland with Martinez and beyond to Tracy. The railroad station was named Powning in honor of the general manager of California Powder Works.

Upon Powning's retirement in 1894, the station was renamed Hercules. The name of the product had become the name of the place.

One

California Powder Works

The California Powder Works purchased a 44.94-acre portion of Rancho El Pinole from the Martinez heirs in 1879. Subsequent purchases increased the site to about 3,000 acres, extending two miles up Refugio Valley. By 1881, the first acid plants fed nitroglycerine production lines. In less than 20 years, under the direction of Capt. William Russell Quinan, the Hercules plant became the largest in the world, producing more than half the dynamite made on the West Coast.

The technology of high explosives advanced rapidly. Powerful, reliable, controlled explosive force made possible the extraction of coal and petroleum for energy, and iron ore for steel, at unprecedented scales of effort. Railroads could span continents; the Panama Canal was soon blasted between two oceans. The Hercules plant was a headquarters of innovation in high explosives. Before the turn of the century, the plant was also producing ammonium nitrate and gelatine dynamites, nitroglycerine powder, and nitrocellulose. Nitrocellulose was shipped to the Santa Cruz plant to produce smokeless powder for ammunition.

Transportation was vital. Barges loaded dynamite at a wharf built a half-mile east of Hercules Station. Another "Acid Wharf" extending from the small point of land jutting into the bay handled feedstocks and general freight. In 1899, a second railroad arrived a mile up the valley, providing competition for rail shipments.

Nearby, an oil refinery, a metal smelter, and a sugar refinery joined the Hercules plant to form a belt of industries along the San Pablo Bay and Carquinez Strait.

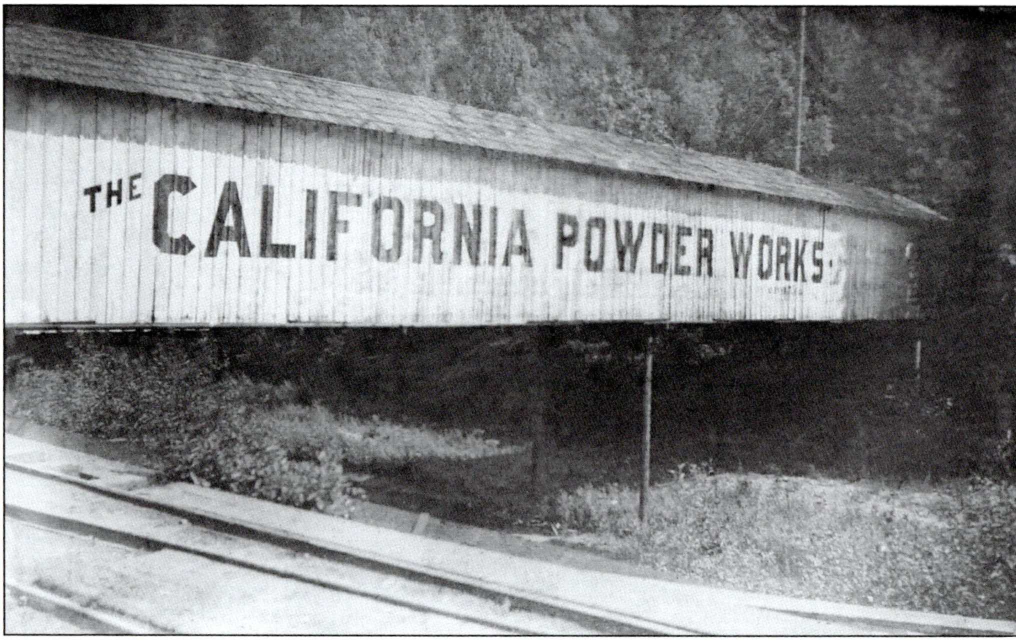

SANTA CRUZ PLANT. California Powder Works manufactured cannon, sporting, and black powders at its plant outside Santa Cruz, which predated the Hercules operation. The covered bridge shown here was built in 1872. Today, the former site of the powder works is part of Paradise Park, a private semi-gated community that can be visited by prior arrangement. (Courtesy the John Carney family collection.)

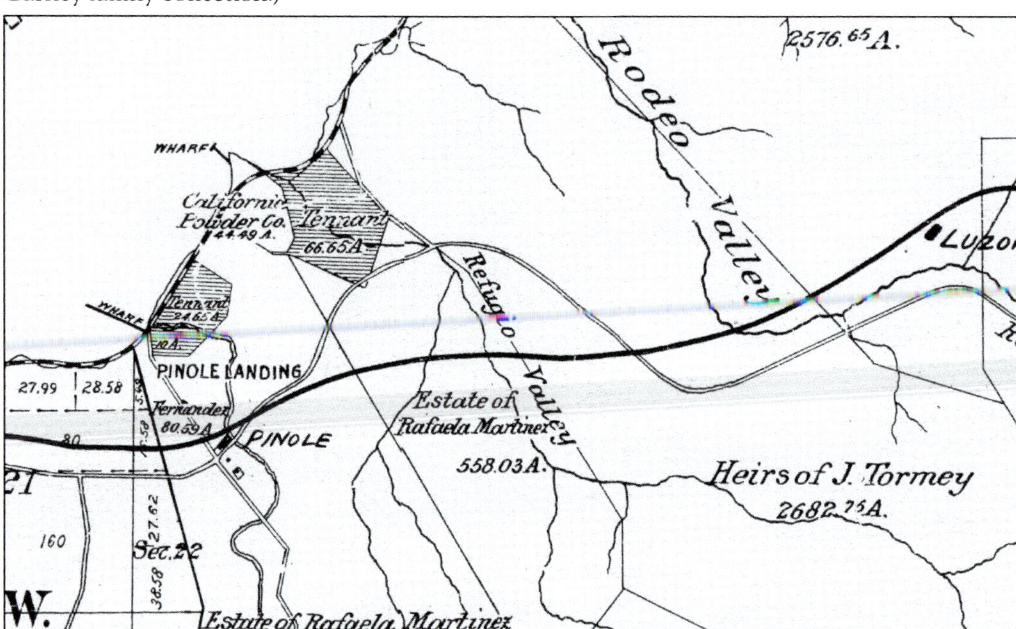

1894 MAP. The California Powder Works at the Hercules location dates from 1879 when a 44.94-acre parcel (incorrectly labeled 44.49 acres on the map) was purchased for $7,500. The property is midway between Pinole, which has a town history dating to 1850, and Rodeo, established in 1890. The company eventually acquired about 3,000 acres. (Courtesy Jennifer Posedel.)

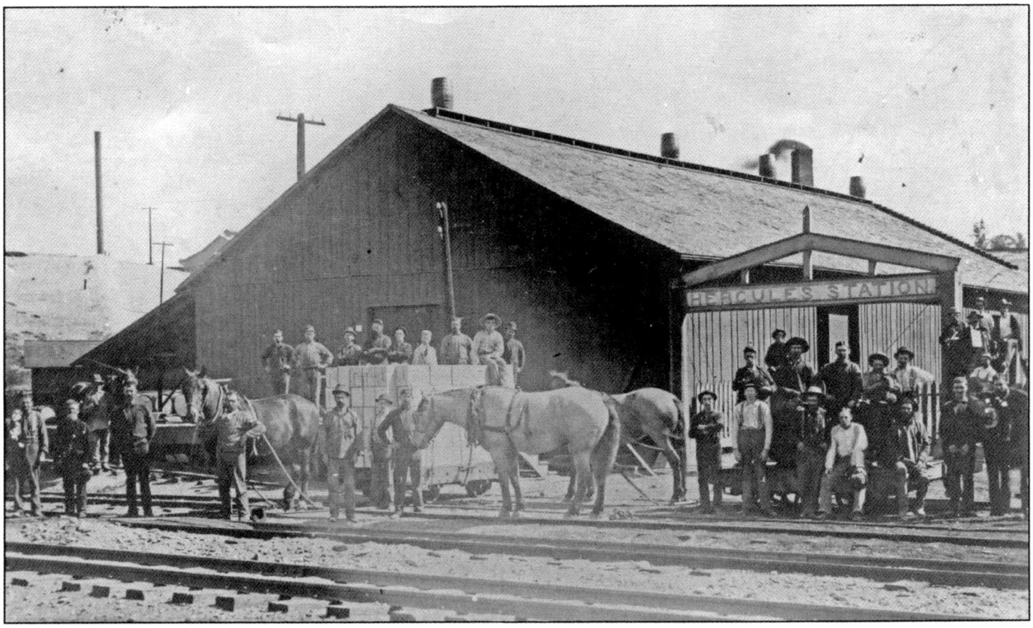

RAIL STATION, 1895. Powning station was on the Northern Railway, along San Pablo Bay. Trains here were operated by Central Pacific Railroad, later the Southern Pacific Railroad. In 1895, this station was renamed Hercules. The unpopulated area with rail and water access was well suited to the manufacture of high explosives. (Courtesy Contra Costa County Historical Society.)

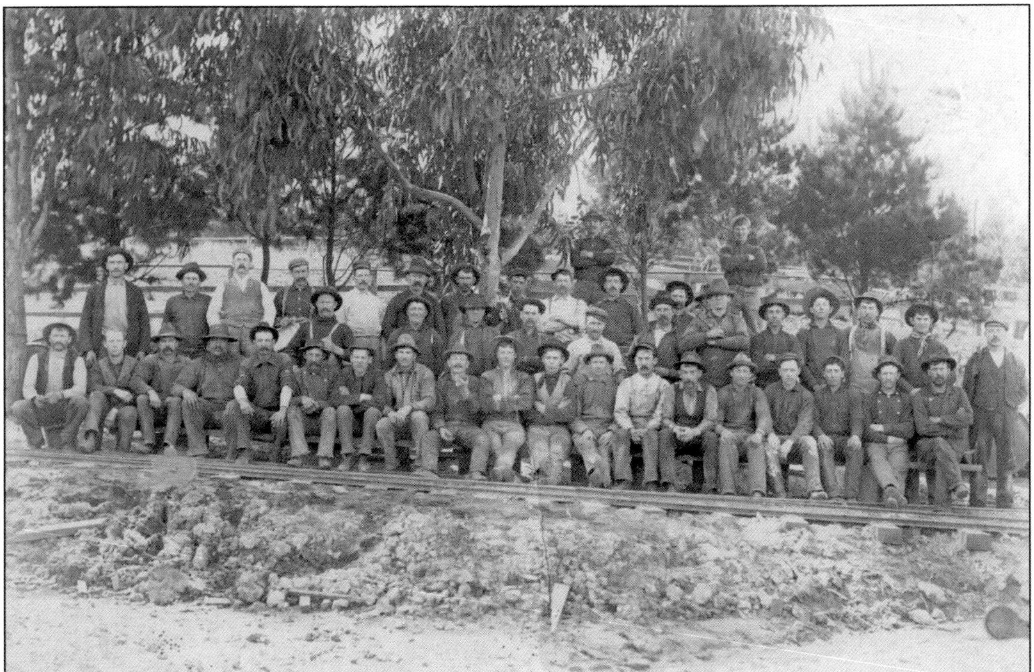

POWDER WORKERS, 1890s. This group posing under eucalyptus trees next to a narrow-gauge track is believed to be employees of the California Powder Works at Hercules. The Logan studio in Oakland took the photograph. (Courtesy Hercules Historical Society.)

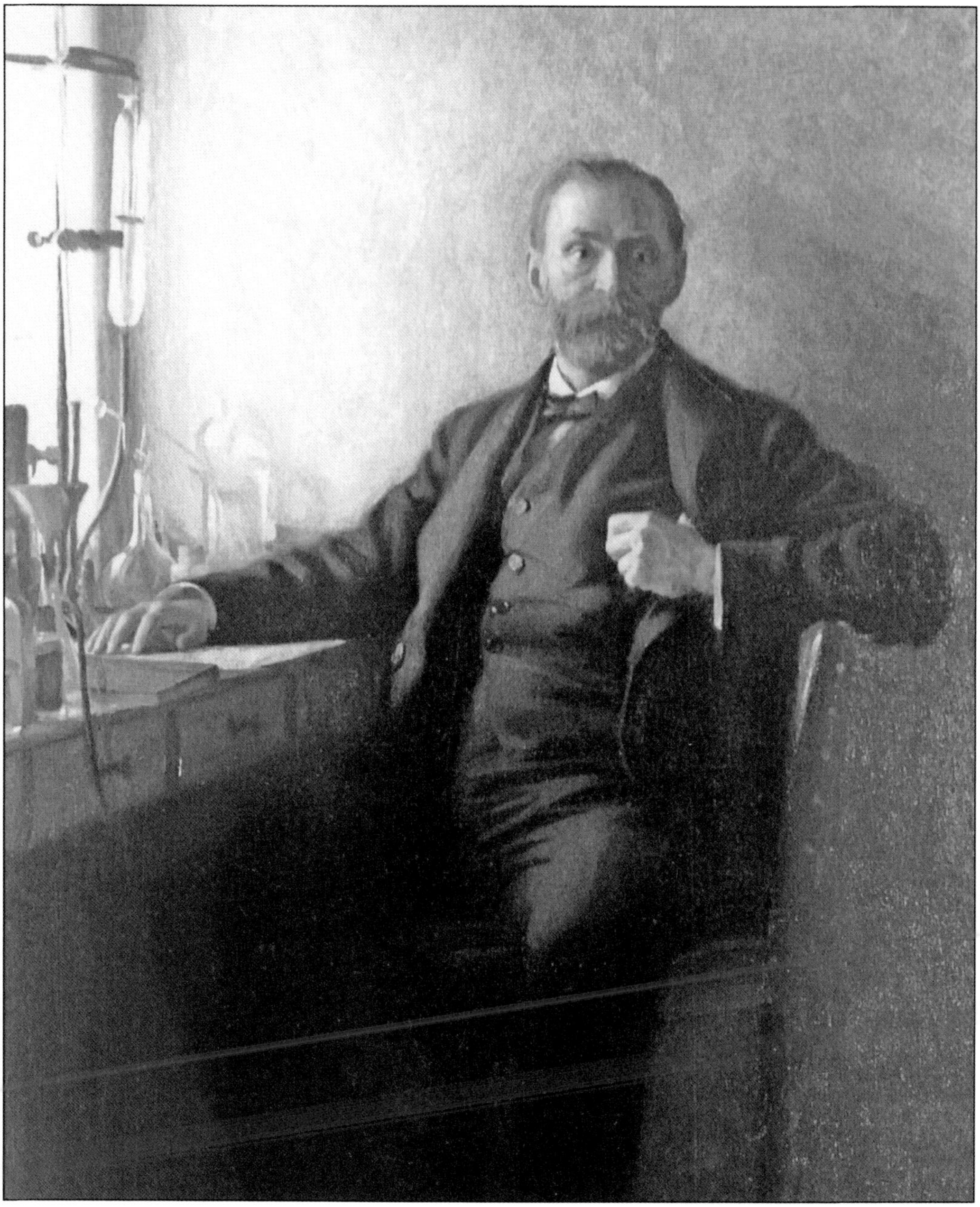

ALFRED NOBEL, 1833–1896. In 1866, Stockholm-born Alfred Nobel discovered a method of stabilizing nitroglycerin by mixing it with an absorbent material. Nobel called the product dynamite, derived from the Greek word for power, *dynamis*. Private teachers in St. Petersburg educated Nobel, the son of a successful industrialist. Although his younger brother Emil was killed in 1864 in an accidental explosion, Nobel continued his work. For safety reasons, he conducted experiments in a boat in the middle of a lake before taking them into the laboratory. Nobel obtained a patent for dynamite in 1867, one of more than 355 patents to his credit. After his death, the Nobel Foundation was established with a $9 million endowment from his estate. Alfred Nobel Drive in Hercules honors his achievements. (© The Nobel Foundation.)

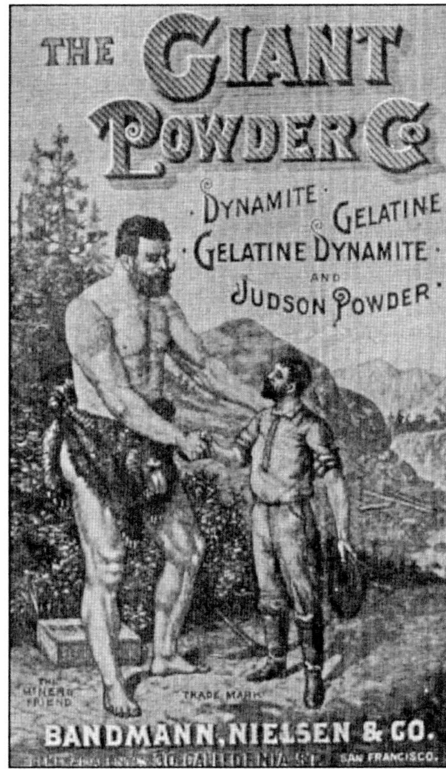

GIANT POWDER ADVERTISEMENT, C. 1884. In 1868, Giant Powder Company of San Francisco obtained a patent for the sole right to manufacture and sell dynamite in the United States. This image illustrates its slogan, "the miner's friend." Giant would eventually join competitor California Powder Works and others in a combination to fix prices and production. (Courtesy Contra Costa County Historical Society.)

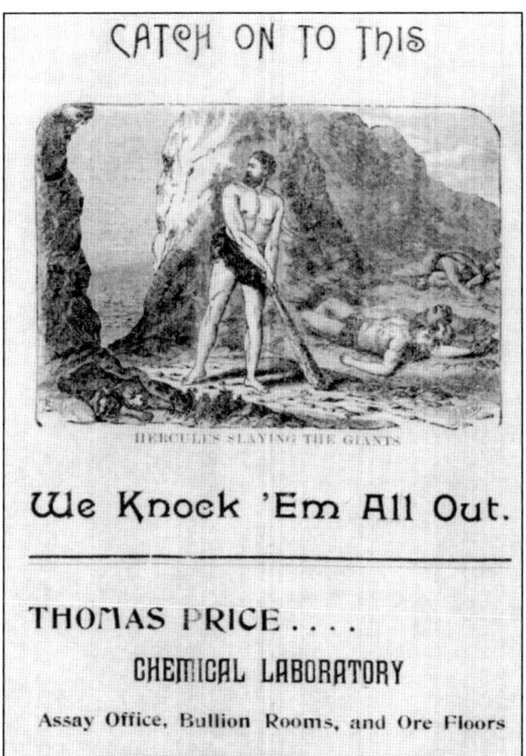

HERCULES POWDER ADVERTISEMENT, 1897. The image of Hercules slaying the giant symbolized the rivalry between the Giant Powder Company and the California Powder Works over the production of dynamite. Although Giant won its 1875 suit for patent infringement, Hercules continued manufacturing dynamite, claiming it had developed a different compound. In 1880, the Supreme Court ruled that the original patents did not apply to the new Hercules formulations. (Courtesy Hercules Historical Society.)

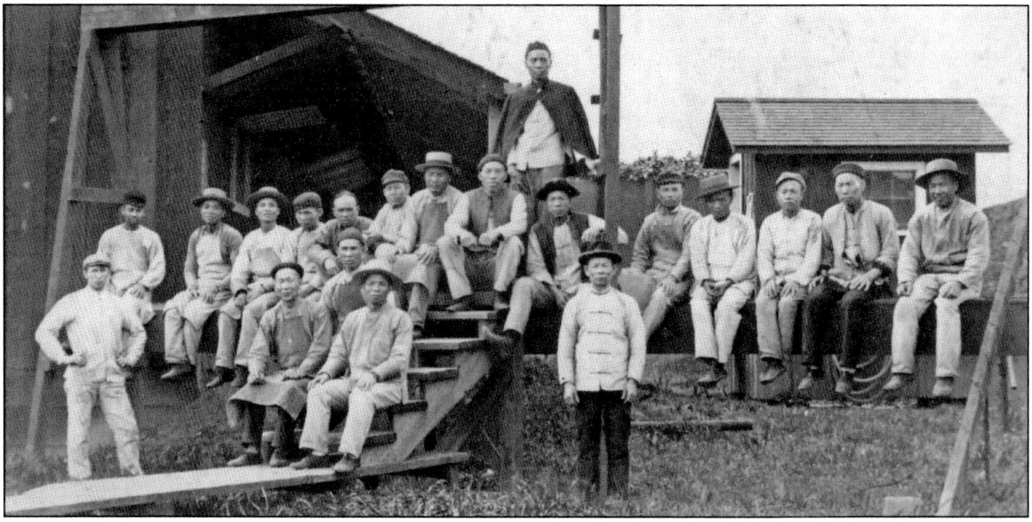

The Outside Men, c. 1900. Chinese workers, who once made up the largest part of the workforce at the California Powder Works, were called "the outside men." The Chinese boss at front center is believed to be Hong Quong, who for a fee, procured labor for the plant and provided lodging and meals for the workers at a waterfront camp. An unnamed white foreman stands to the left. In 1914, the camp was dismantled and the Chinese workers left Hercules. (Courtesy California Historical Society.)

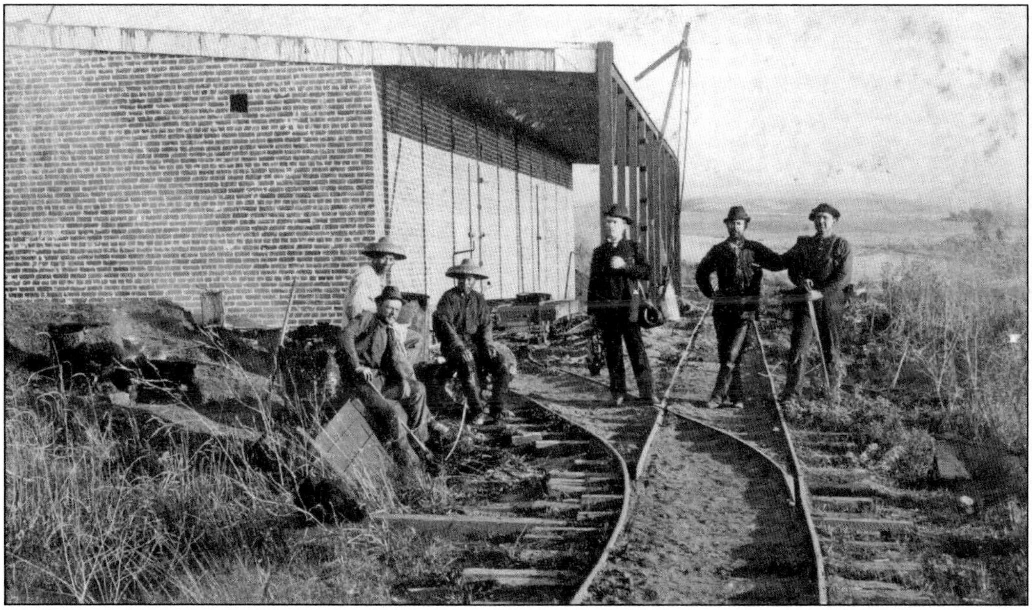

Giant Powder Crew. This view was taken at Point Pinole, where Giant operated following its move from West Berkeley in 1892. Charley Warner, shown at far right, is the only person identified. Note the Chinese workers at left. Most of the 19th century powder mills in California employed Chinese laborers for the low-paying, dangerous work. (Courtesy Contra Costa County Historical Society.)

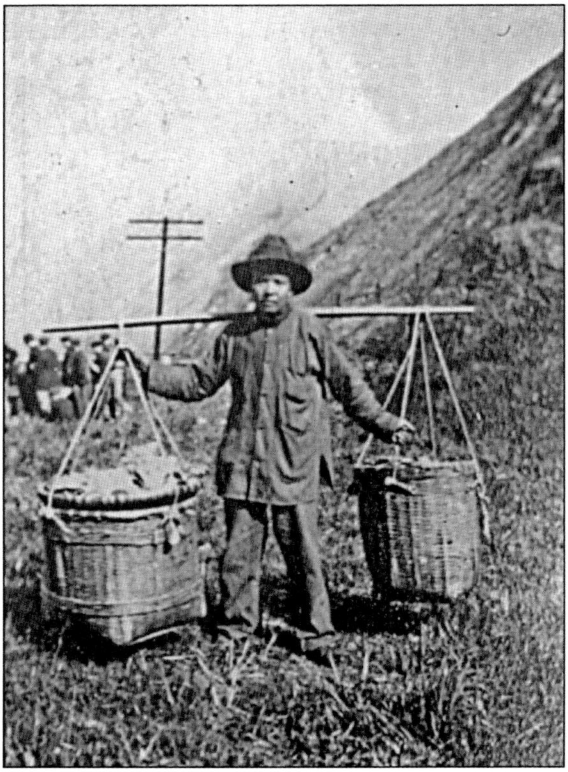

Itinerant Peddler. Shellfish and vegetables were sold in Contra Costa along the bay shore railroad line. Shrimp came from camps on San Pablo Bay at Point Pinole. At Hercules, California Powder Works rented its shoreline to a Chinese man for clam digging. The clams were so plentiful that one person could dig 60 to 100 pounds at each tide. (Courtesy Contra Costa County Historical Society.)

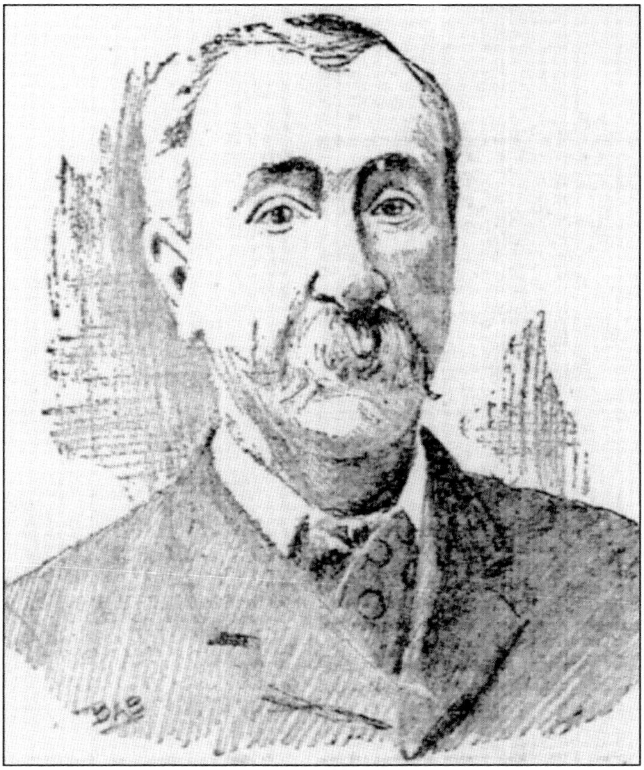

Capt. John McLean, 1896. The foreman at Hercules, employed as a powder man since the 1870s, told the *San Francisco Call* that he could get "swarms" of Chinese workers even after an explosion. "Never was an explosion that we could not fill the places of the lost next morning. Don't you know there are a certain number of men in all communities that like to play with fire." (Courtesy Jennifer Posedel.)

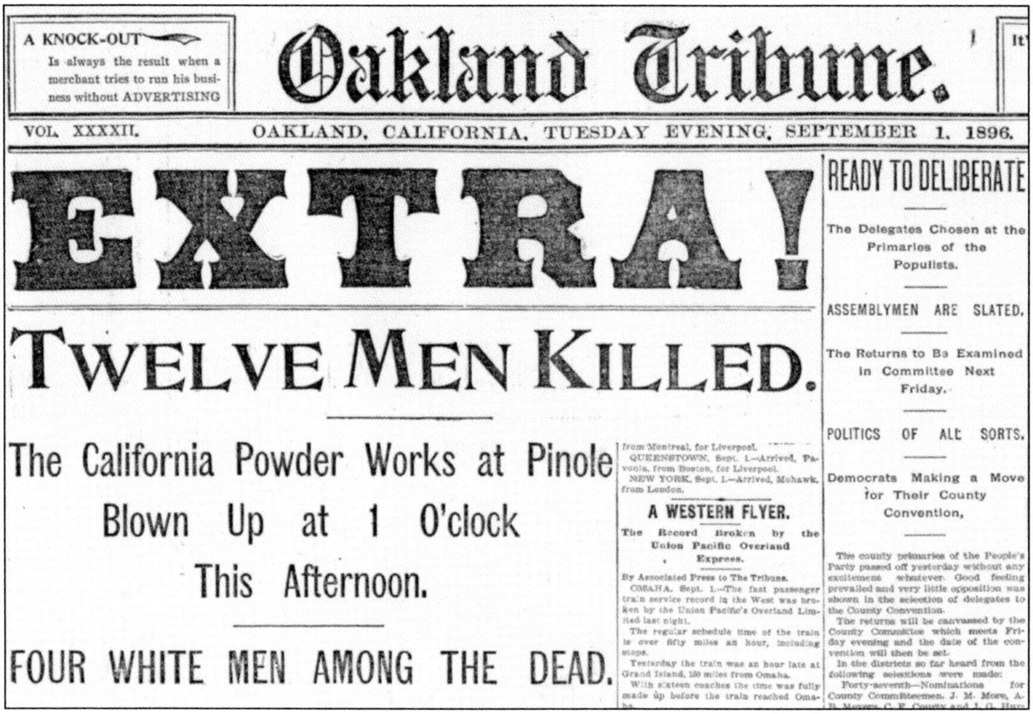

A KNOCK-OUT Is always the result when a merchant tries to run his business without ADVERTISING

Oakland Tribune.

VOL. XXXXII. OAKLAND, CALIFORNIA, TUESDAY EVENING, SEPTEMBER 1, 1896.

EXTRA!

TWELVE MEN KILLED.

The California Powder Works at Pinole Blown Up at 1 O'clock This Afternoon.

FOUR WHITE MEN AMONG THE DEAD.

from Montreal, for Liverpool.
QUEENSTOWN, Sept. 1—Arrived, Pavonia, from Boston, for Liverpool.
NEW YORK, Sept. 1—Arrived, Mohawk, from London.

A WESTERN FLYER.

The Record Broken by the Union Pacific Overland Express.

By Associated Press to The Tribune.
OMAHA, Sept. 1.—The fast passenger train service record in the West was broken by the Union Pacific's Overland Limited last night.
The regular schedule time of the train is over fifty miles an hour, including stops.
Yesterday the train was an hour late at Grand Island, 150 miles from Omaha.
With sixteen coaches the time was fully made up before the train reached Omaha.

READY TO DELIBERATE

The Delegates Chosen at the Primaries of the Populists.

ASSEMBLYMEN ARE SLATED.

The Returns to Be Examined in Committee Next Friday.

POLITICS OF ALL SORTS.

Democrats Making a Move for Their County Convention.

The county primaries of the People's Party passed off yesterday without any excitement whatever. Good feeling prevailed and very little opposition was shown in the selection of delegates to the County Convention.
The returns will be canvassed by the County Committee which meets Friday evening and the date of the convention will then be set.
In the districts so far heard from the following selections were made:
Forty-seventh—Nominations for County Committeemen, J. M. More, A. B. Meyers, C. F. County and J. G. Hur-

EXPLOSION, SEPTEMBER 1, 1896. An *Oakland Tribune* extra edition headlined that 12 men were killed at Pinole. Eight Chinese laborers were among the dead on this September day. The tragedy was recorded in a catalog of earthquakes that registered three separate explosions, the heaviest one being in the mixing house with its 15,000 pounds of dynamite. (Courtesy Hercules Historical Society.)

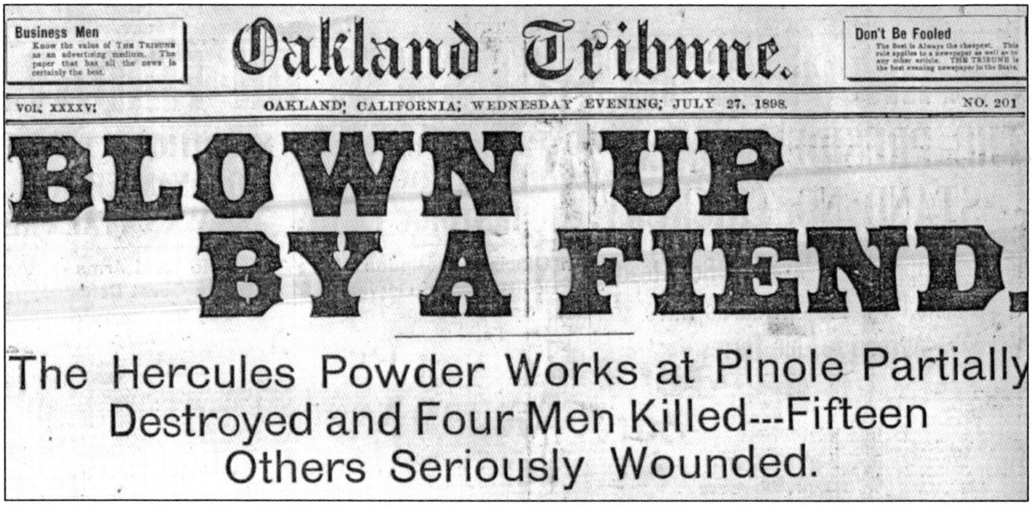

Business Men Know the value of THE TRIBUNE as an advertising medium. The paper that has all the news is certainly the best.

Oakland Tribune.

Don't Be Fooled The Best is Always the cheapest. This rule applies to a newspaper as well as to any other article. THE TRIBUNE is the best evening newspaper in the State.

VOL. XXXXV. OAKLAND, CALIFORNIA, WEDNESDAY EVENING, JULY 27, 1898. NO. 201

BLOWN UP BY A FIEND.

The Hercules Powder Works at Pinole Partially Destroyed and Four Men Killed---Fifteen Others Seriously Wounded.

EXPLOSION, JULY 27, 1898. Explosions always made for sensational news and in 1898 they were heightened by the fear of foreigners or treachery related to the Spanish-American War. On this day, five men were killed in an explosion that occurred while workers were clearing the wreckage from an earlier non-injury blast. As with most other explosions, the cause could not be determined because all evidence was destroyed. (Courtesy Hercules Historical Society.)

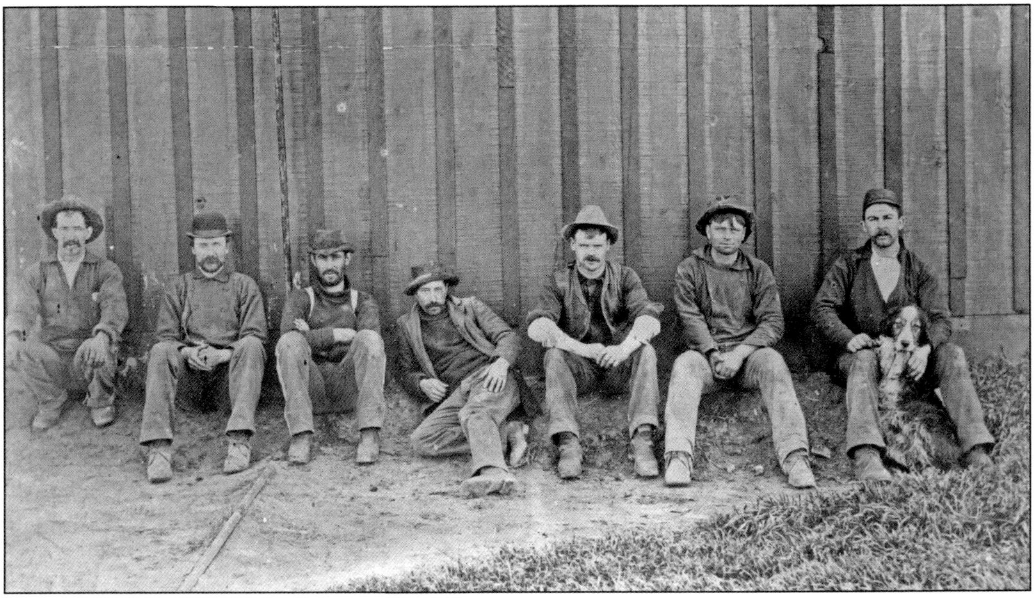

Nitroglycerin House Workers. From left to right are Sam McCabe, Henry Minugh, John Alvarez, Al Humphreys, C. Kendall, Jack Mulholland, and William Munson. Minugh, a chemist and father of six, died in a terrific explosion on May 21, 1895, along with 13 others. Alvarez was killed in 1898, and Mullholland perished in an 1899 explosion. Widow Mary Alvarez received $2,000 from the Ancient Order of United Workmen, the first fraternal order to offer an insurance death benefit. (Courtesy Contra Costa County Historical Society.)

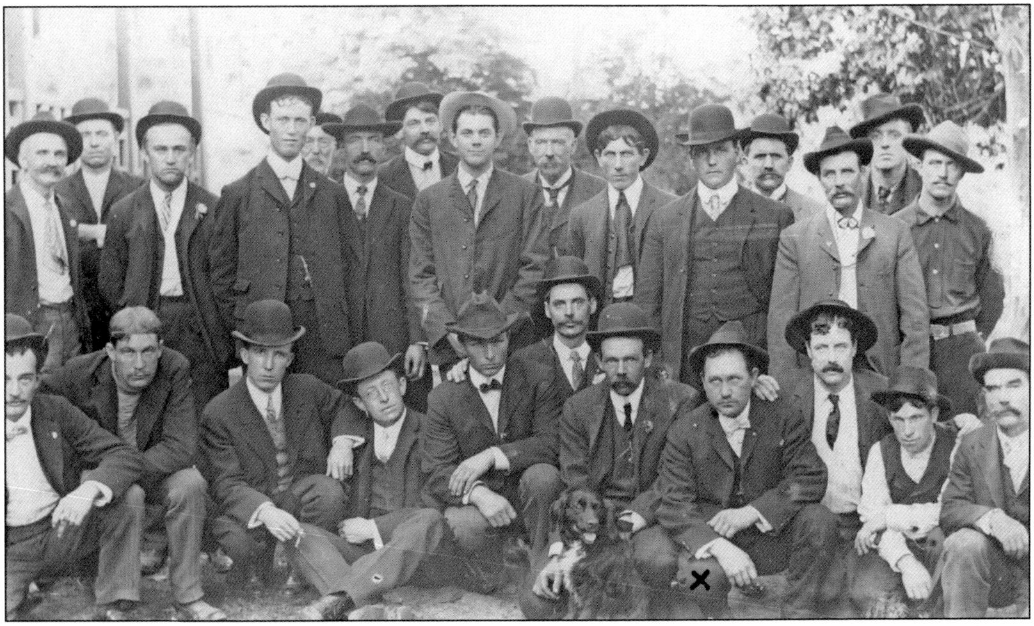

Somber Gathering. These men are believed to have gathered for the funeral of two of the 14 men who perished in the May 1895 explosion. G.B. O'Kerlund is indicated by the "x" on his knee. In the back row, wearing a bowler hat, is plant superintendent Col. William Russell Quinan. The funeral cortege which followed the bodies of two of the victims to Mountain View Cemetery in Oakland was two miles long. (Courtesy of Hercules Historical Society.)

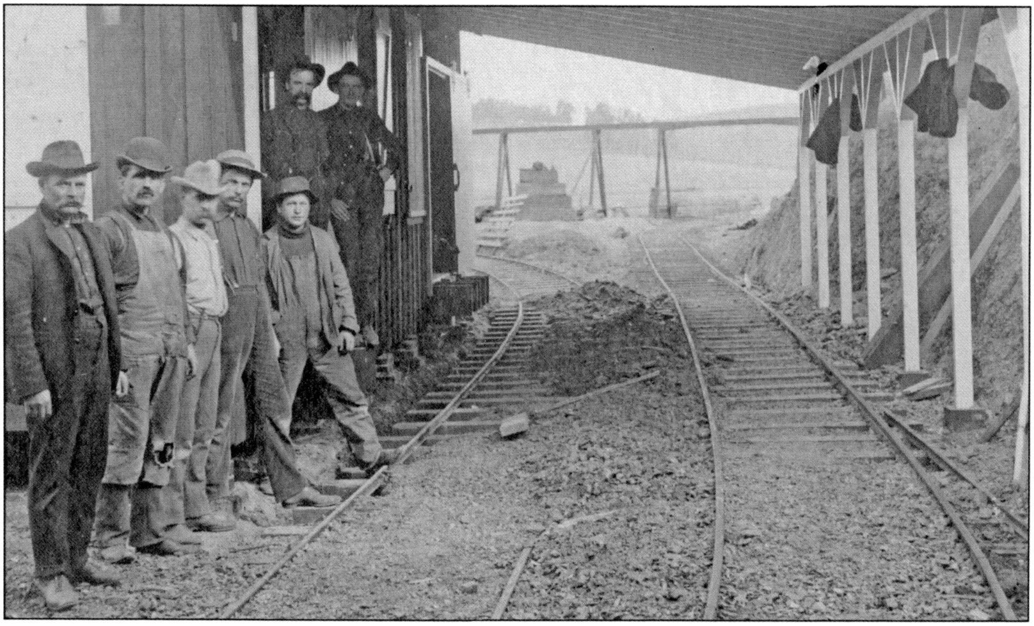

California Powder Workers. The only man identified by name is G.B. O'Kerlund, who has his foot on the narrow-gauge rail. For safety reasons, this building, like others in the plant, was isolated. (Courtesy of Hercules Historical Society.)

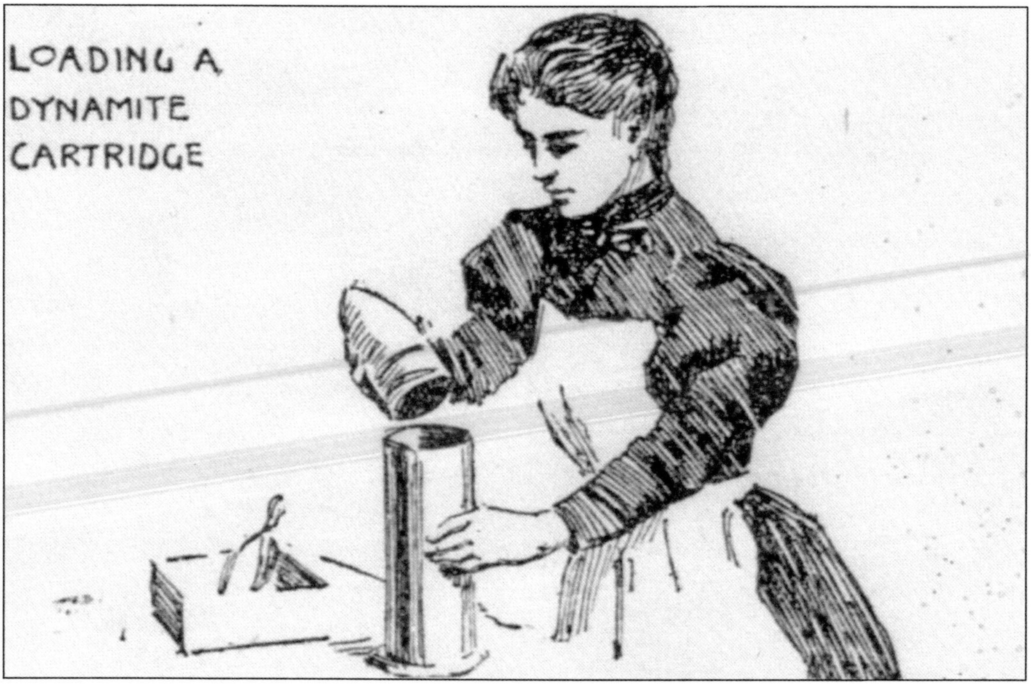

Packing a Dynamite Shell, 1898. A woman is shown working at the Santa Cruz plant. Small groups of women and girls also worked in the gelatin rolling and packing houses at Hercules. A tragedy occurred at the Hercules plant in July 1903 when 16-year-old Mary Woods died in an explosion in the cartridge factory. She and a friend had taken jobs during their summer vacation from school. (Courtesy Library of Congress.)

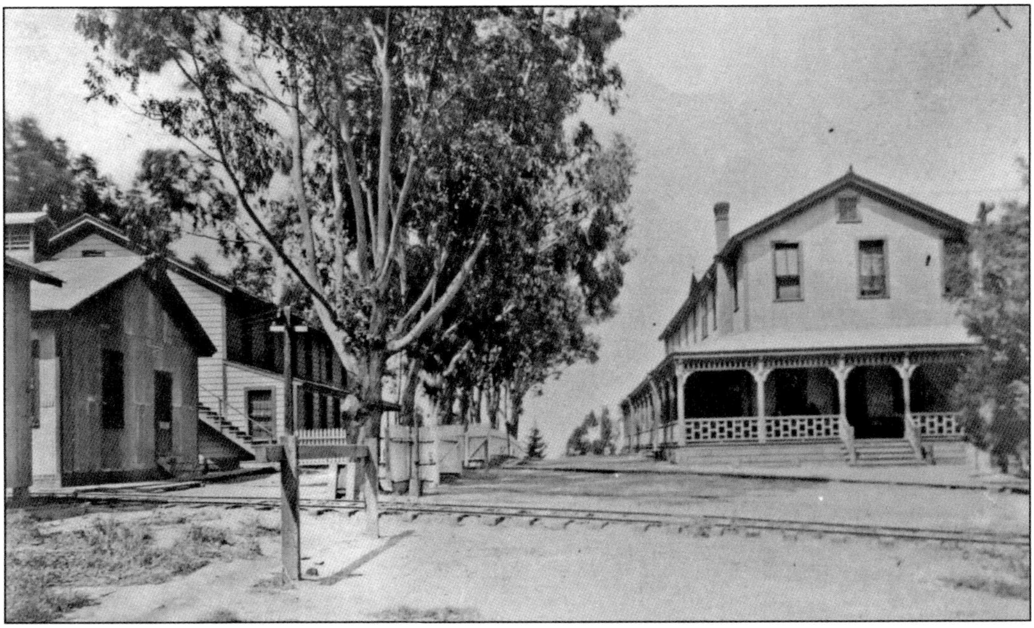

Boarding House. At right is the men's dormitory built in 1899. It replaced a crowded, dimly lit facility in which men rotated shifts for sleeping beds. Prior to the construction of this building, lodgers had to go to San Francisco for a real bath. The clubhouse is behind the boardinghouse, and to its left is a building with a lean-to that may be the town hall shown on page 42. (Courtesy Contra Costa County Historical Society.)

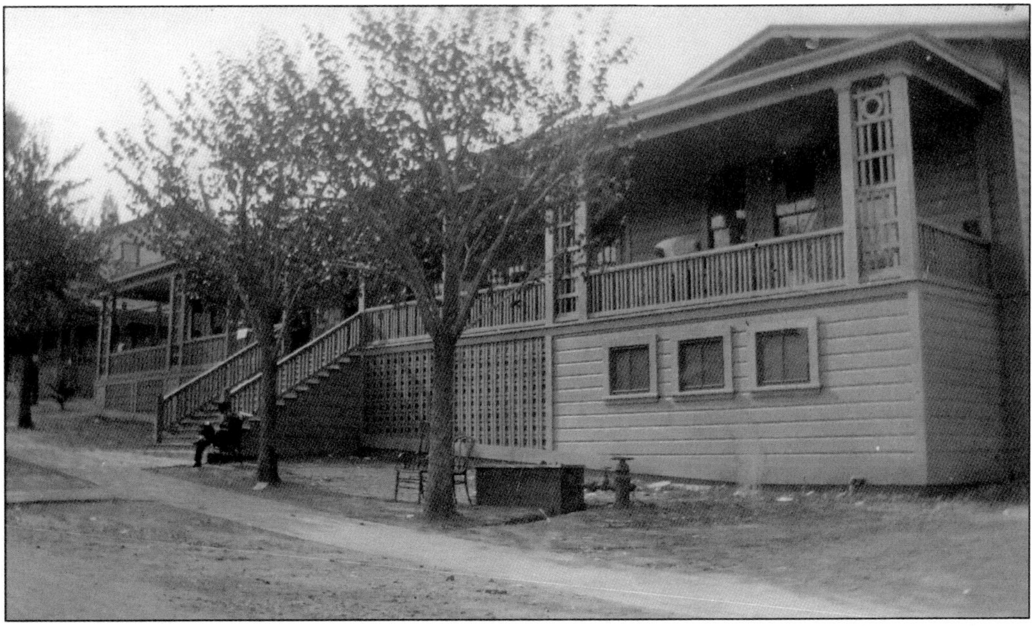

Men's Clubhouse. Although $5,000 was appropriated in 1897 for the club building, completion was delayed by the Spanish-American War. At its 1901 dedication, a dance was held for the 130 members. The men, many of whom were Stanford University graduates, chose cardinal as the club color. On opening night, the porch and grounds were thickly hung with red Japanese lanterns. The boarding house is at left. (Courtesy Contra Costa County Historical Society.)

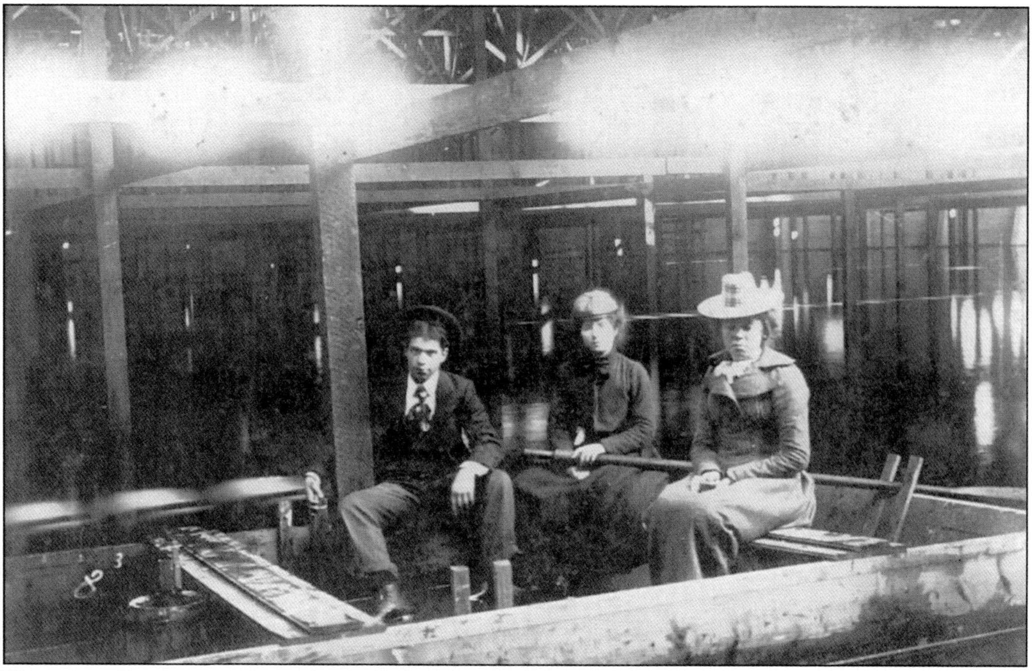

Hercules Reservoir. Seated inside the Hercules plant reservoir located on the Tennant ranch, are, from left to right, M. Lewis; Anastasia Dean, principal at Rodeo School; and Mary Lewis, a Pinole resident who later married John Vincent, a bartender at the First and Last Chance Saloon. The reservoir was constructed during a six-month period in 1899. Today, the ruins of the 10-million gallon tank sit on a hill northwest of Pinole Valley Road and Interstate 80. (Courtesy Dr. Joseph Mariotti.)

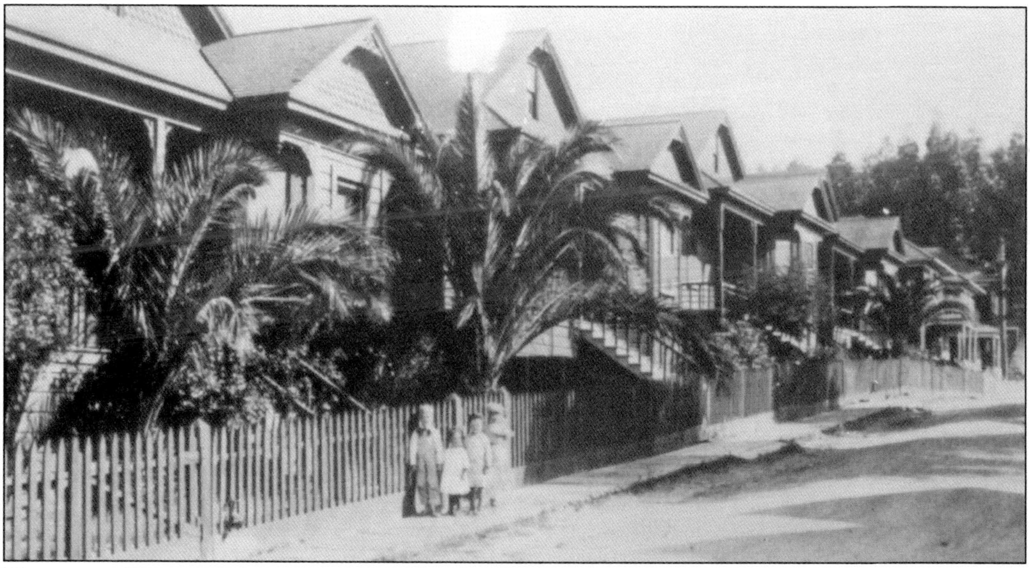

Hercules Village, c. 1912. An unidentified group of children pose on Pinole Street above Santa Fe Avenue. Note the unpaved street and the profusion of palms that were once planted all over the village. Picket fences similar to these were rebuilt on Pinole and Bay Streets during the 1980s restoration of the historic district. (Courtesy Hercules Historical Society.)

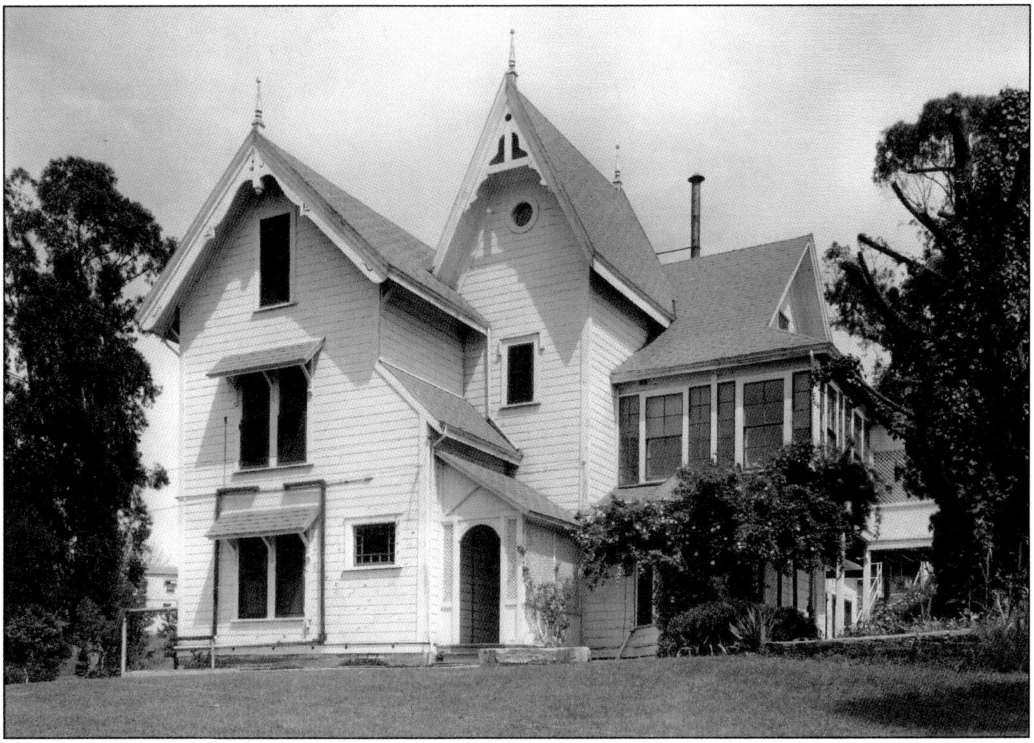

Superintendent's House. This wood-frame house was one of the earliest buildings constructed at Hercules. Steeply pitched asymmetrical roofs, finials, and decorative gable trim with cross bracing characterize the carpenter Gothic style. It is believed to have been the original superintendent's home, built around 1879 and subsequently used for the assistant superintendent and his family before being converted to a bachelors' club. Note the addition of plumbing lines to the exterior wall at left. (Courtesy Ashland Inc.)

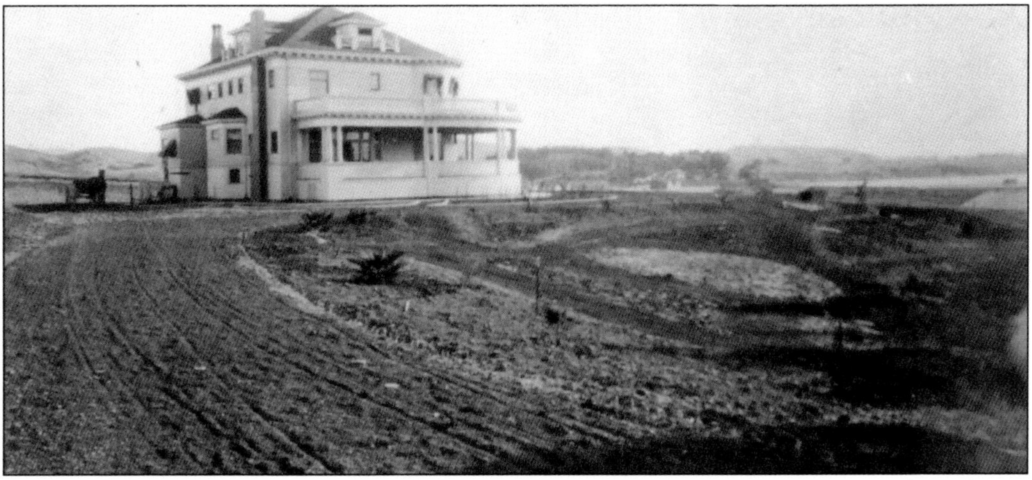

Superintendent's House. Near present-day Railroad Avenue was a new superintendent's house built in 1899. Upstairs were five bedrooms heated by fireplaces. Staff occupied the attic living quarters. In the basement were apartments, a laundry, and large pantry. Interior walls were decorated with alternating strips of redwood paneling and red burlap fabric. Pinole is visible in the distance at far right. (Courtesy Contra Costa County Historical Society.)

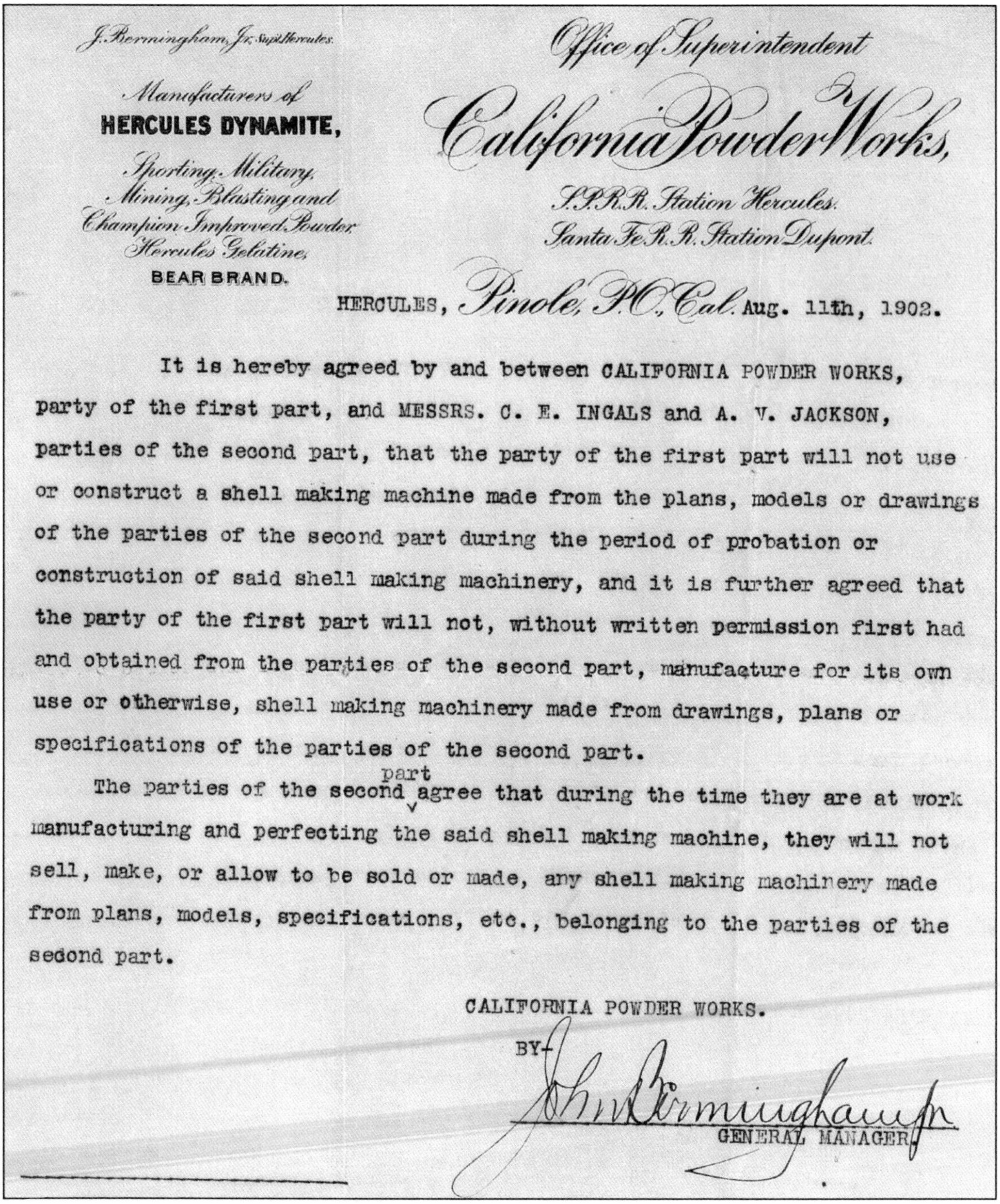

J. Bermingham, Jr. Supt. Hercules.

Manufacturers of

HERCULES DYNAMITE,

Sporting, Military,
Mining, Blasting and
Champion Improved Powder
Hercules Gelatine,

BEAR BRAND.

Office of Superintendent

California Powder Works,

S.P.R.R. Station Hercules.
Santa Fe R.R. Station Dupont.

HERCULES, Pinole, P.O., Cal. Aug. 11th, 1902.

It is hereby agreed by and between CALIFORNIA POWDER WORKS, party of the first part, and MESSRS. C. E. INGALS and A. V. JACKSON, parties of the second part, that the party of the first part will not use or construct a shell making machine made from the plans, models or drawings of the parties of the second part during the period of probation or construction of said shell making machinery, and it is further agreed that the party of the first part will not, without written permission first had and obtained from the parties of the second part, manufacture for its own use or otherwise, shell making machinery made from drawings, plans or specifications of the parties of the second part.

The parties of the second part agree that during the time they are at work manufacturing and perfecting the said shell making machine, they will not sell, make, or allow to be sold or made, any shell making machinery made from plans, models, specifications, etc., belonging to the parties of the second part.

CALIFORNIA POWDER WORKS.

BY John Bermingham Jr

GENERAL MANAGER.

AGREEMENT, 1902. The California Powder Works letterhead lists railroad stations that no longer exist, the Southern Pacific Station at Hercules and the Santa Fe Station at Dupont. In 1902, the company's mailing address was the Pinole post office because there was no post office in Hercules. (Courtesy William Ingalls.)

Two

E.I. du Pont de Nemours Company

After the dynamite patent disputes were settled in the early 1880s, the American explosives industry descended into a fierce trade war. By the mid-1890s, prices had plunged and the producing firms were nearing ruin. To survive, the owners formed cartels and other combinations in restraint of trade. Finally, in 1903, the eastern firm of the du Pont family, which had acquired an initial stake in California Powder Works in 1869, acquired full control of the company and its major competitors, except the Giant Powder Company. Sales continued under the name of California Powder Works until 1906, when Hercules became a Dupont brand. Production continued at the Hercules and Santa Cruz plants, with the sales office in San Francisco.

Dynamite from Hercules played an important role in the response to the great San Francisco earthquake of 1906. Tugs were dispatched by the Army to fetch barges of explosives used in the controversial attempt to stop the ensuing fire.

Following a huge explosion in February 1908, plant manager John Bermingham Jr., son of the former California Powder Works president, was replaced by a Dupont engineer from the East, Charles A. Patterson. Although 24 men had died on his watch, Bermingham's departure was a blow to the men who had worked with him for more than two decades.

In 1907, the United States filed suit against Dupont under the Sherman Antitrust Act. Litigation concluded in 1912 with a final decree ordering Dupont to divest about half of its factory capacity and customers to two new firms, created to provide competition. One of the new firms, Atlas Powder Company, acquired the Giant Powder Company. Giant continued production at its Point Pinole plant until 1960.

The other new firm was to be the Hercules Powder Company.

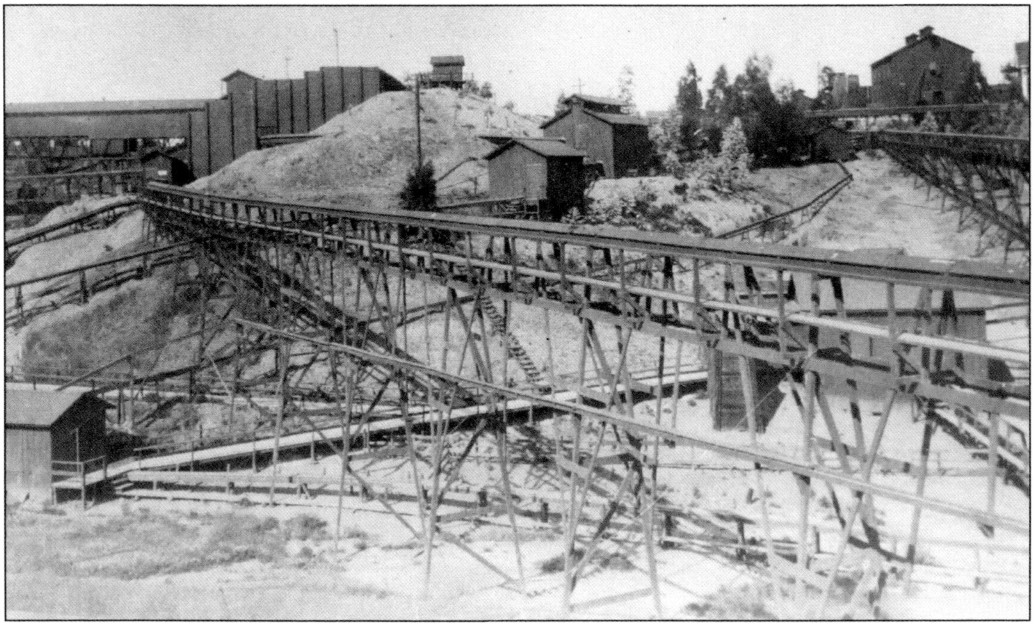

Nitroglycerine Plant Number One. The lead-lined troughs seen in this 1903 view were used to transport materials between buildings. The explosive materials produced here supplied the US Navy guns of the Spanish-American War and, according to the *Oakland Tribune*, enabled it to achieve its victory. During the war, this plant also loaded 75,000 shotgun cartridges daily with smokeless and black powder. (Courtesy Contra Costa County Historical Society.)

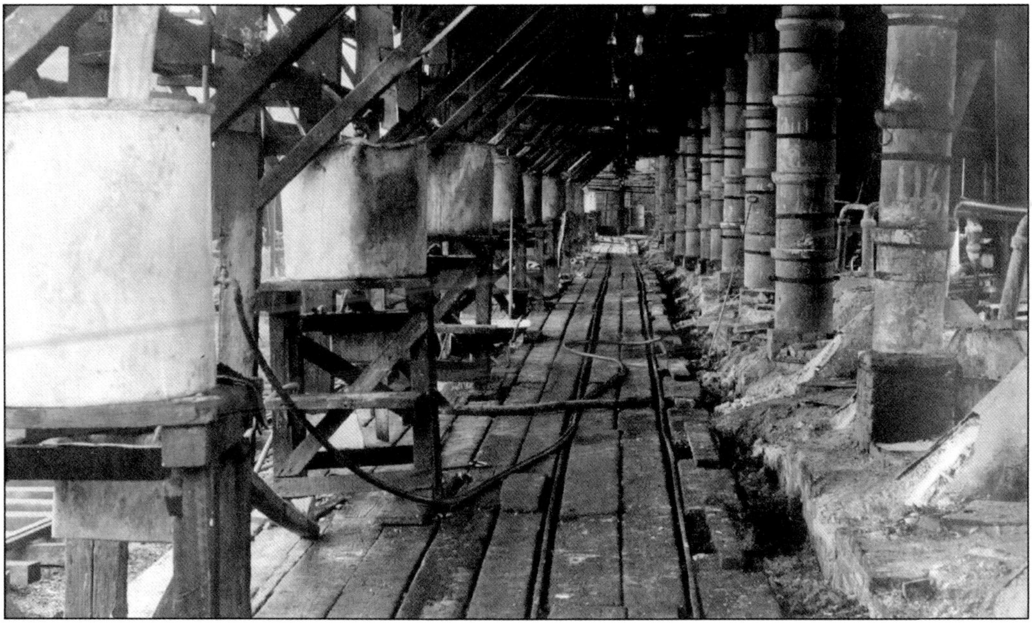

Nitric Acid Works, 1903. Nitric acid is used to make nitroglycerin, a component of dynamite. During the Spanish-American War, 14 tons of sulfur and 1,432 tons of nitrate of soda from Chile were used daily in the manufacture of explosives at Hercules. By 1903, plant superintendent John Bermingham Jr. claimed the acid plant was worn out and losing money. Dupont built new acid facilities in 1905. (Courtesy M. Wallace and W. Ryder.)

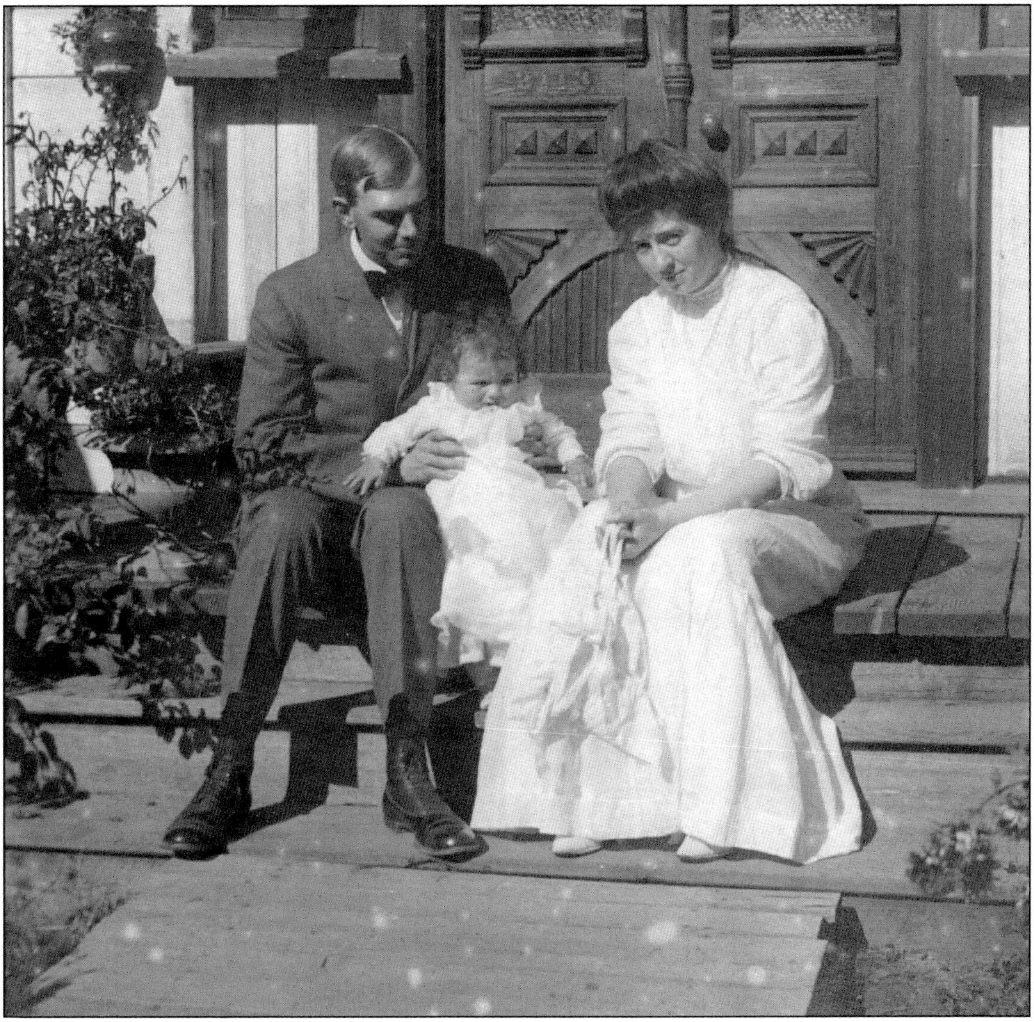

McBryde Family. Warren Horton McBryde and his wife, Abbie, sit with baby Lucile at their Hercules home. In 1905, Dupont sent engineer McBryde to oversee construction of new acid houses. Alabama-born McBryde had served in the US Army Corps of Engineers during the Spanish-American War and afterwards worked on construction projects for several power companies. He was in charge of all maintenance and repairs for Dupont during World War I and held a key engineering position with the corps during World War II. McBryde left Hercules in 1919 for a position at the Crockett sugar refinery. The ambitious, energetic, and progressive McBryde served as president of the Contra Costa Chamber of Commerce, mayor of Hercules, school trustee, and county supervisor, and was a leader in the development of county highways. (Courtesy M. Wallace and W. Ryder.)

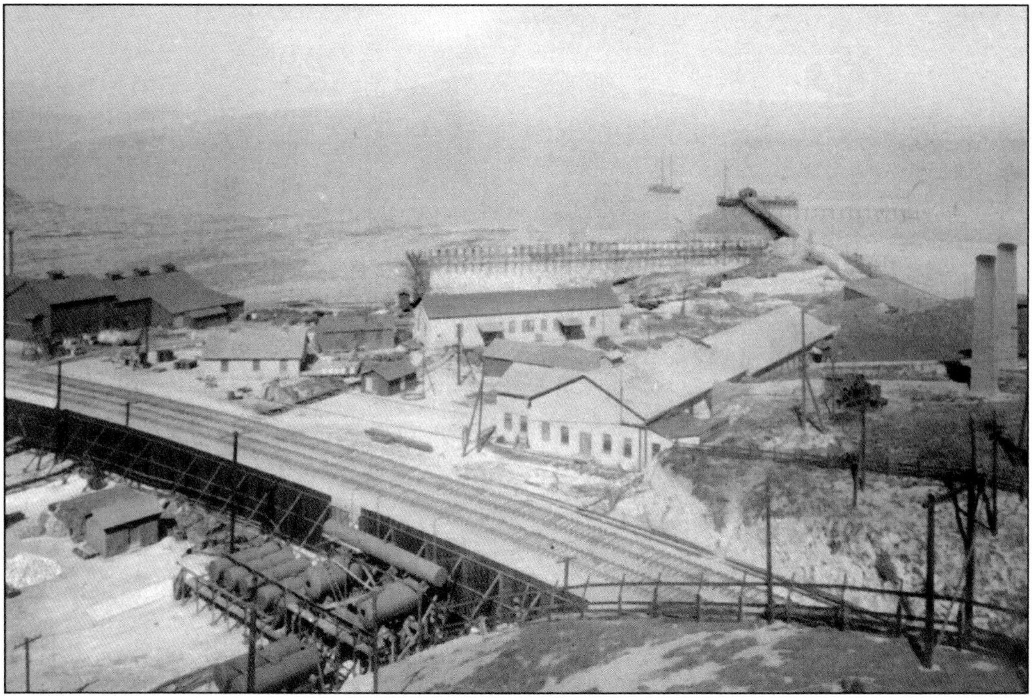

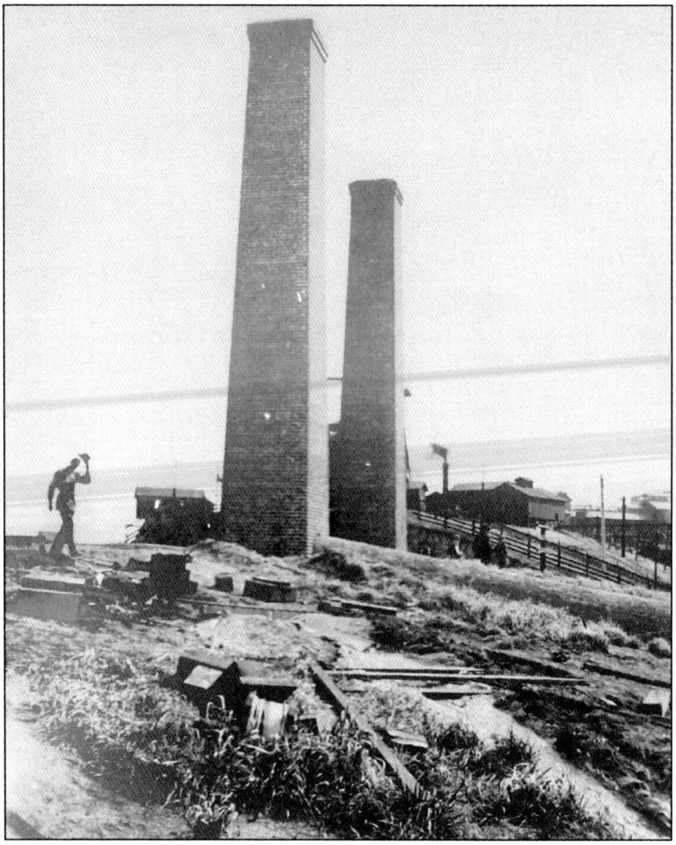

HERCULES POINT, MAY 1, 1905. This view looks north toward San Pablo Bay from the hill where the office and laboratory was located. It was taken shortly before the new acid plant construction began. On the left, blast barriers protect the double track Southern Pacific line that ran through the plant on its northern edge. In the distance, a sailing ship approaches the wharf. (Courtesy Contra Costa County Historical Society.)

DUPONT MODERNIZATION. These two smokestacks were demolished in 1905. The work was under the direction of Dupont, although the plant did not officially adopt the E.I. du Pont de Nemours name until 1907. Dupont is headquartered at Wilmington, Delaware. (Courtesy M. Wallace and W. Ryder.)

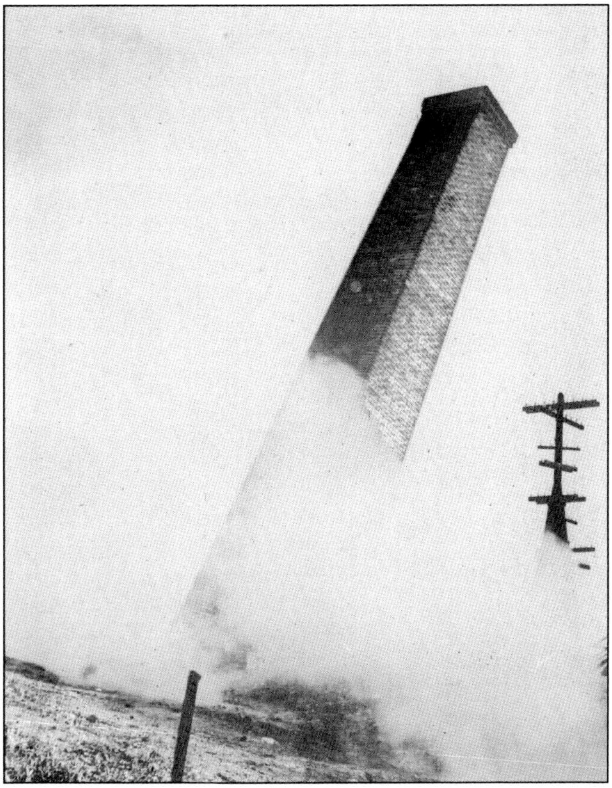

DEMOLITION, 1905. Engineer Warren Horton McBryde's construction photographs included this image of the demolition by explosives of one of the smokestacks. The use of Hercules blasting powder in construction and mining applications far exceeded its military use, even in wartime. One of the witnesses on the left appears to be a boy. Note the reinforced electrical pole. (Both courtesy M. Wallace and W. Ryder.)

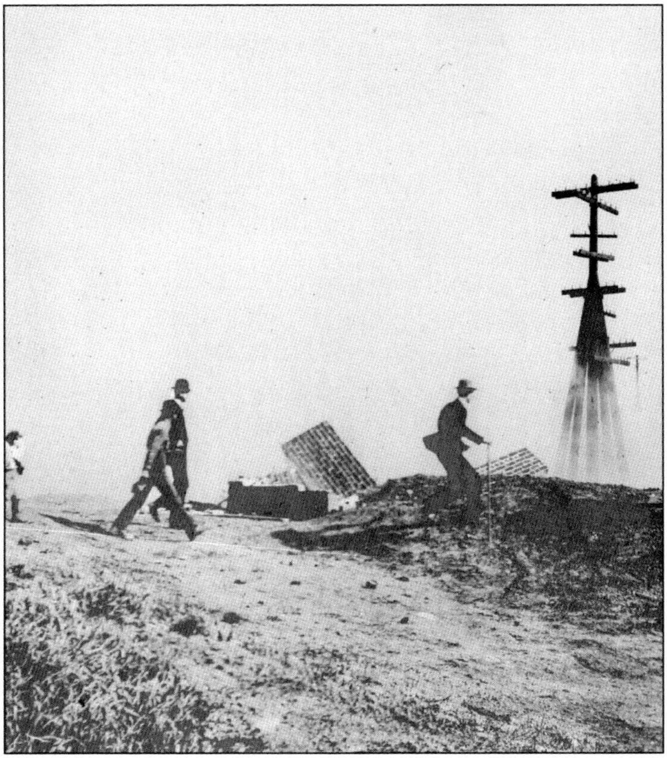

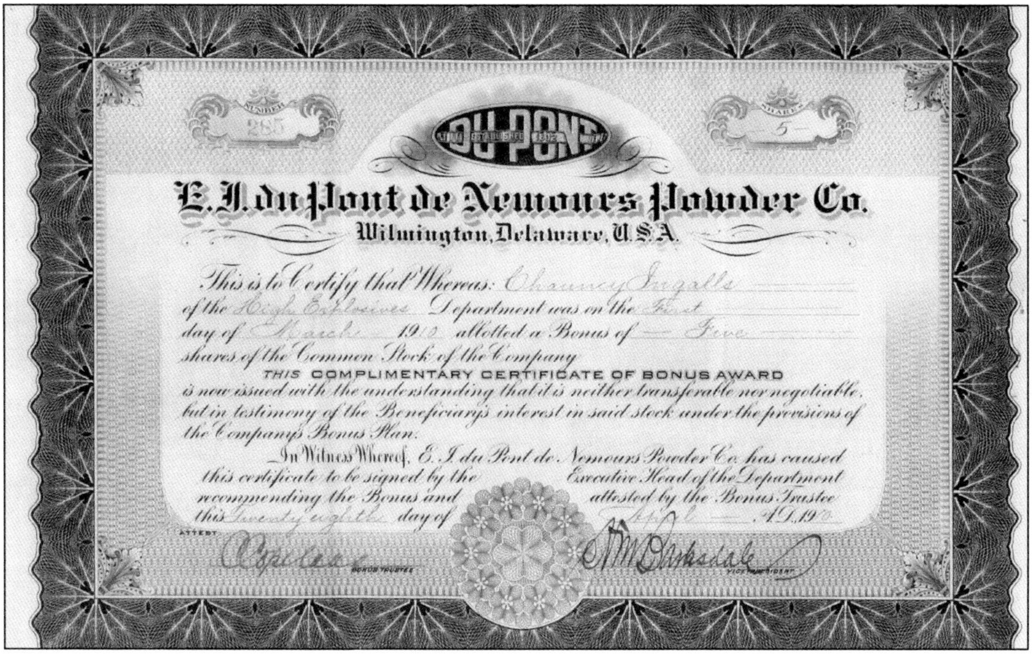

285

5

DU PONT

E. I. du Pont de Nemours Powder Co.
Wilmington, Delaware, U.S.A.

This is to Certify that Whereas: Chauncey Ingalls of the High Explosives Department was on the First day of March 1910 allotted a Bonus of Five shares of the Common Stock of the Company

THIS COMPLIMENTARY CERTIFICATE OF BONUS AWARD is now issued with the understanding that it is neither transferable nor negotiable, but in testimony of the Beneficiary's interest in said stock under the provisions of the Company's Bonus Plan.

In Witness Whereof, E. I. du Pont de Nemours Powder Co. has caused this certificate to be signed by the Executive Head of the Department recommending the Bonus and attested by the Bonus Trustee this Twenty eighth day of April A.D. 1910

ATTEST: Bonus Trustee — Vice President

STOCK BONUS, 1910. Dupont issued five shares of common stock to Chauncey Ingalls as compensation for his co-invention of a shell-packing machine developed in the high explosives department. The Ingalls-Jackson machine had been in development since 1902, when the California Powder Works officially owned the plant. (Courtesy William Ingalls.)

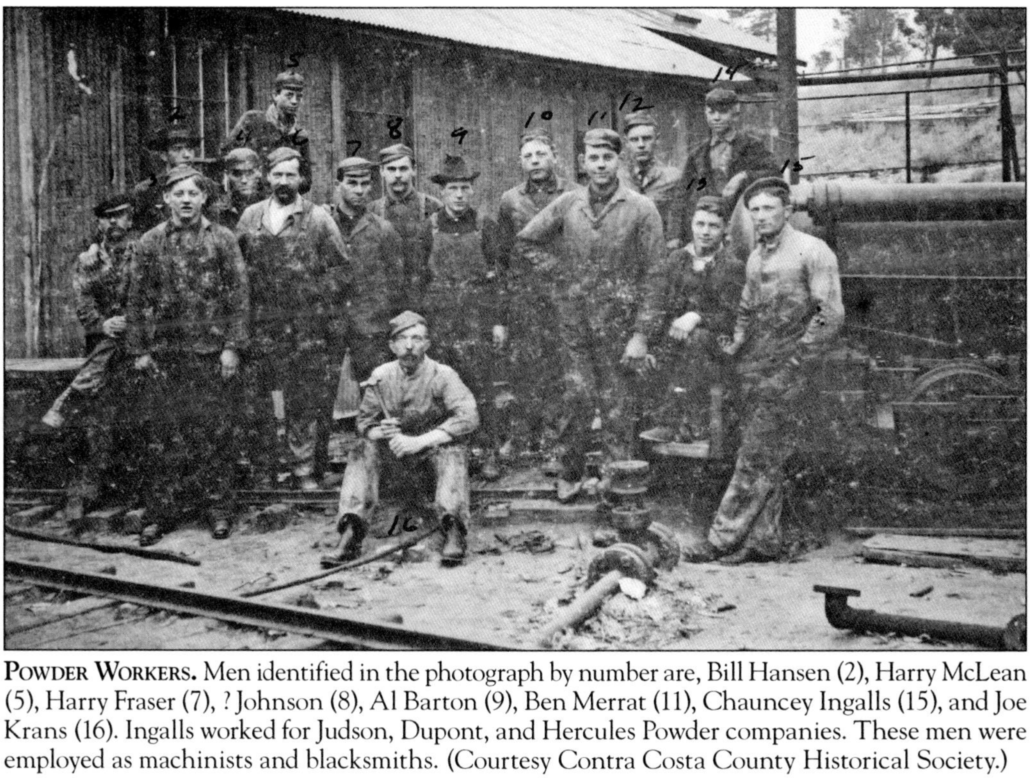

POWDER WORKERS. Men identified in the photograph by number are, Bill Hansen (2), Harry McLean (5), Harry Fraser (7), ? Johnson (8), Al Barton (9), Ben Merrat (11), Chauncey Ingalls (15), and Joe Krans (16). Ingalls worked for Judson, Dupont, and Hercules Powder companies. These men were employed as machinists and blacksmiths. (Courtesy Contra Costa County Historical Society.)

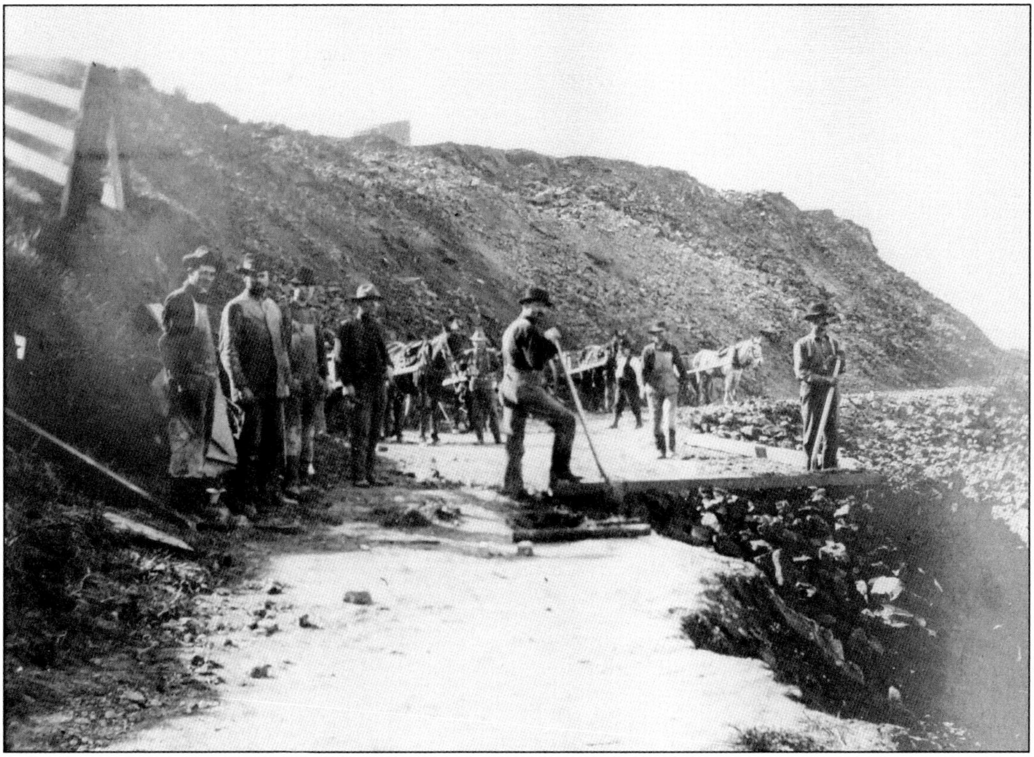

Leveling of Hercules Point, April 1905. Workers using picks and shovels leveled the hill north of the Southern Pacific tracks to create a site for the acid plant. Horses, which were suited to hauling loads across unpaved surfaces, were used in construction at the plant throughout the 1910s. A steam shovel is at work in the image below. Newly constructed narrow-gauge track can be seen at far right. (Both courtesy M. Wallace and W. Ryder.)

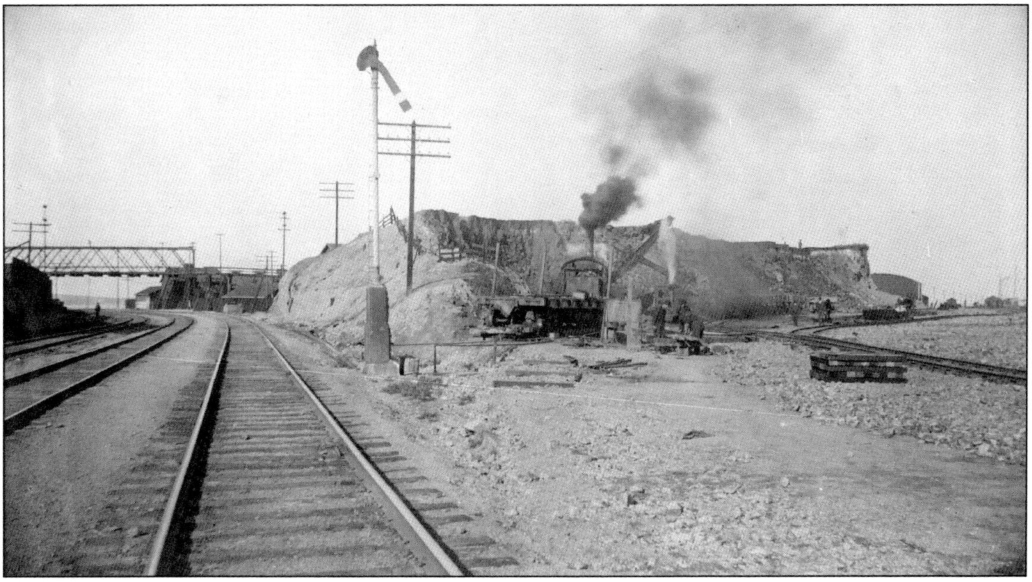

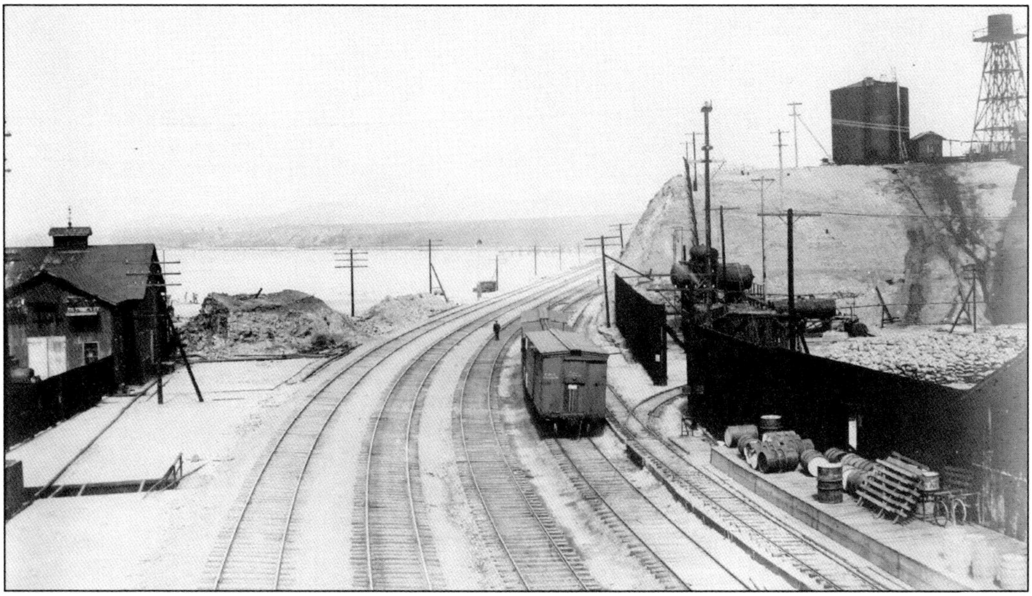

NORTHERN RAILWAY, MAY 3, 1905. The waterfront route was constructed by two of the Big Four owners of the Central Pacific Railroad, which began operating trains over this line in September 1878. The view looks toward Rodeo, with Hercules Point outside the image to the left. The line was consolidated into the Southern Pacific system, then acquired in 1996 by Union Pacific Railroad. From 1899, the Hercules Works was also served by a Santa Fe (now BNSF) line at the Dupont and Herpoco stations. (Courtesy M. Wallace and W. Ryder.)

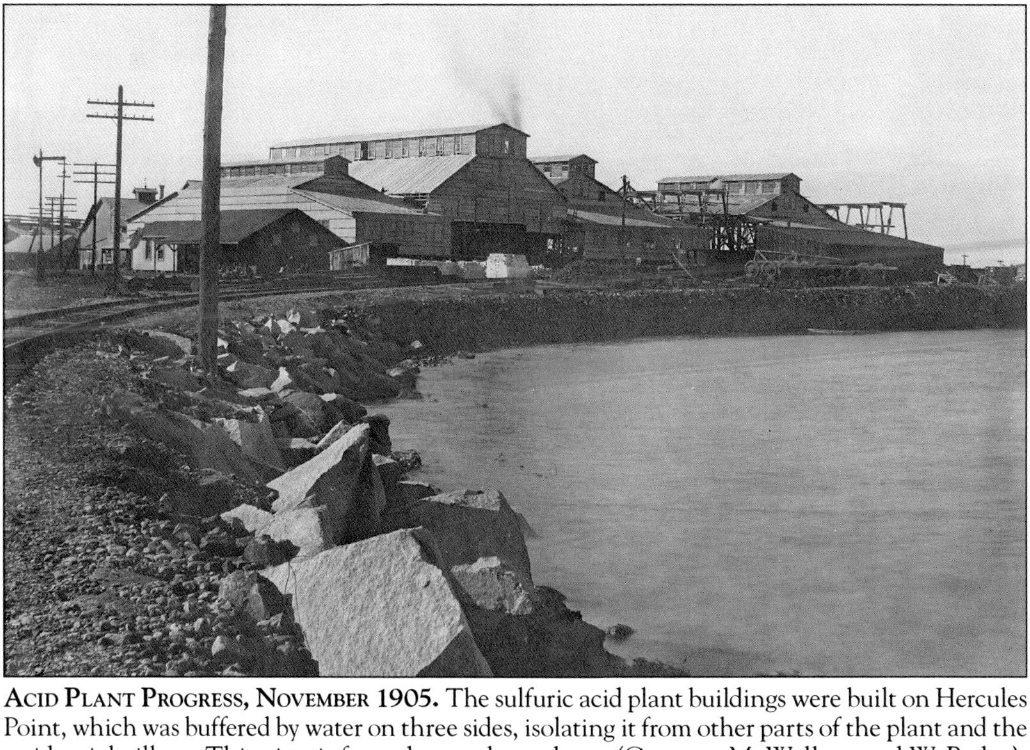

ACID PLANT PROGRESS, NOVEMBER 1905. The sulfuric acid plant buildings were built on Hercules Point, which was buffered by water on three sides, isolating it from other parts of the plant and the residential village. This view is from the northern shore. (Courtesy M. Wallace and W. Ryder.)

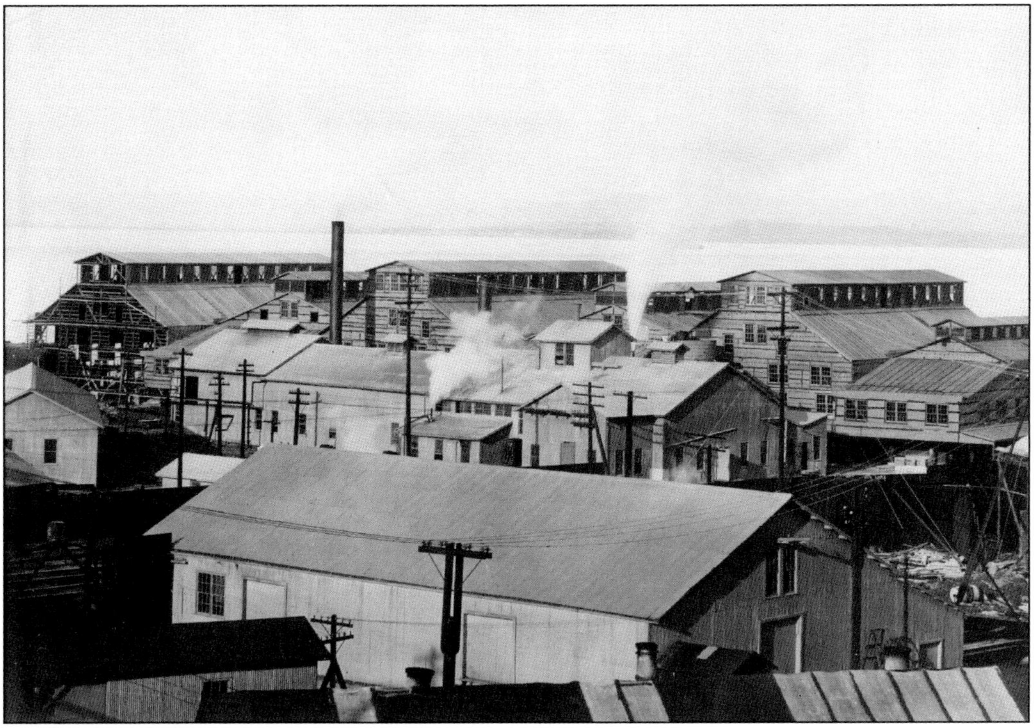

Plant Views, c. 1906. The photograph above was made shortly before completion of the new acid plant buildings at Hercules Point. The postcard image below, made a few months later from a similar vantage point, was printed in Germany for Pinole merchant Theodore W. Woy, who operated a confectionery store on Pinole's Main Street (now San Pablo Avenue). (Above, courtesy M. Wallace and W. Ryder; below, courtesy Jennifer Posedel.)

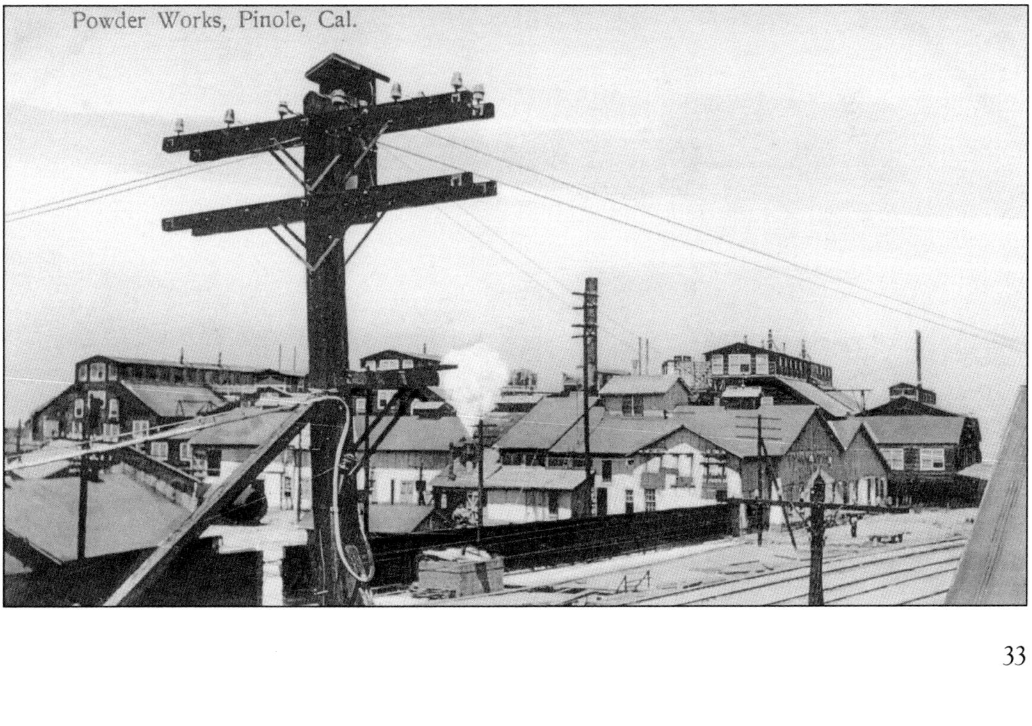

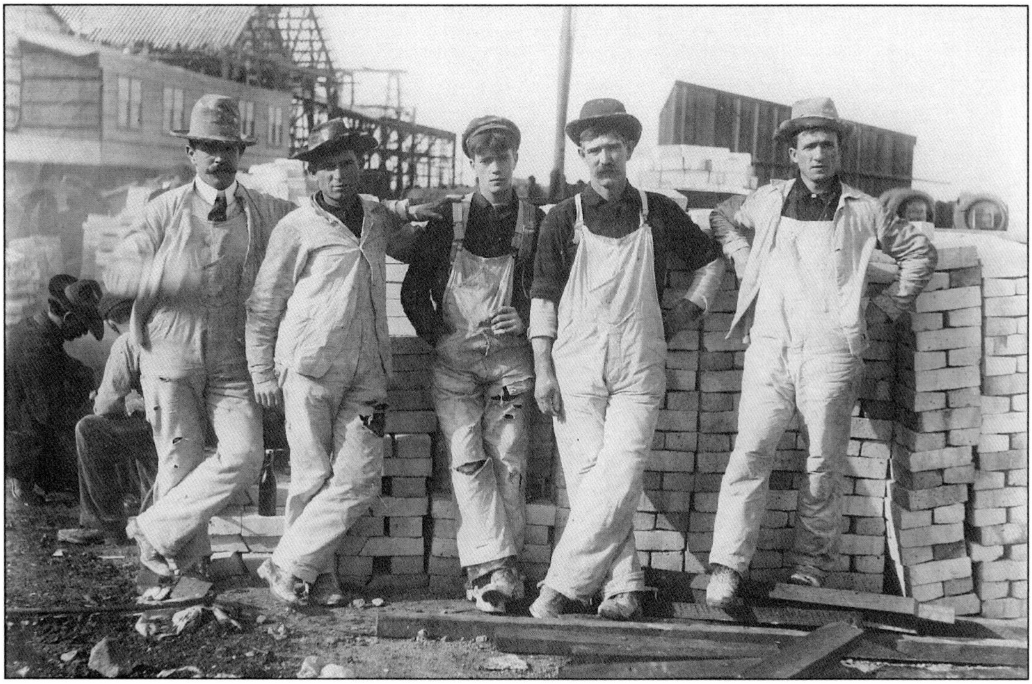

Work Crew, Spring 1905. This image of the building of a new acid plant at Hercules Point is from the series of photographs of the various tradesmen participating in the project. Dupont engineer Warren McBryde managed the project. (Courtesy M. Wallace and W. Ryder.)

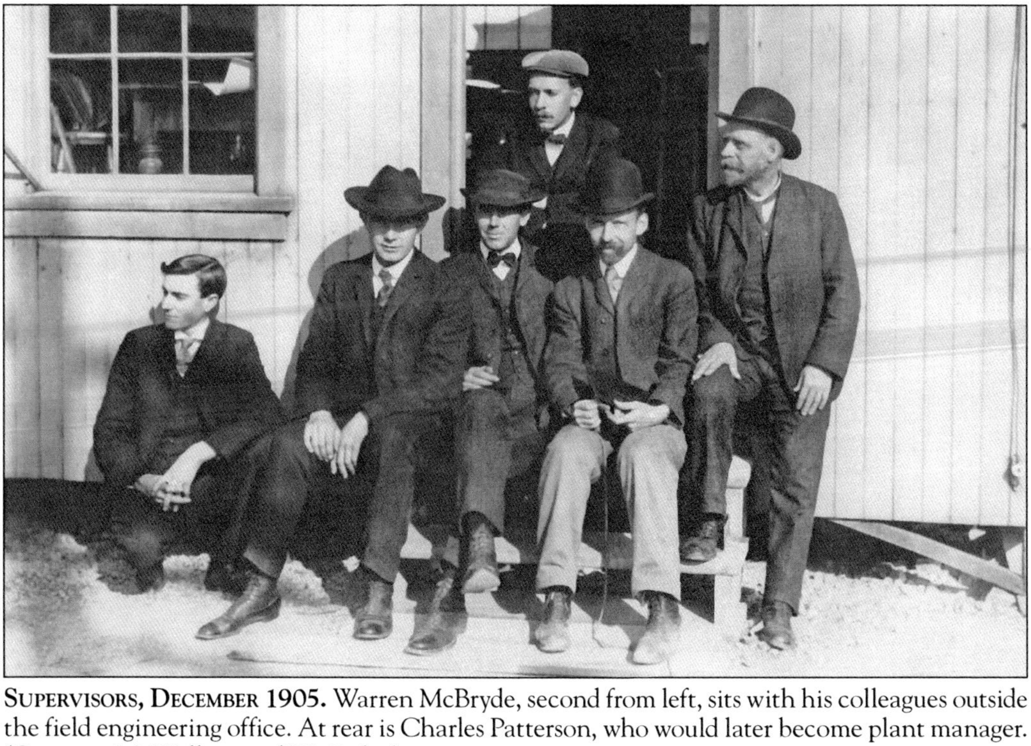

Supervisors, December 1905. Warren McBryde, second from left, sits with his colleagues outside the field engineering office. At rear is Charles Patterson, who would later become plant manager. (Courtesy M. Wallace and W. Ryder.)

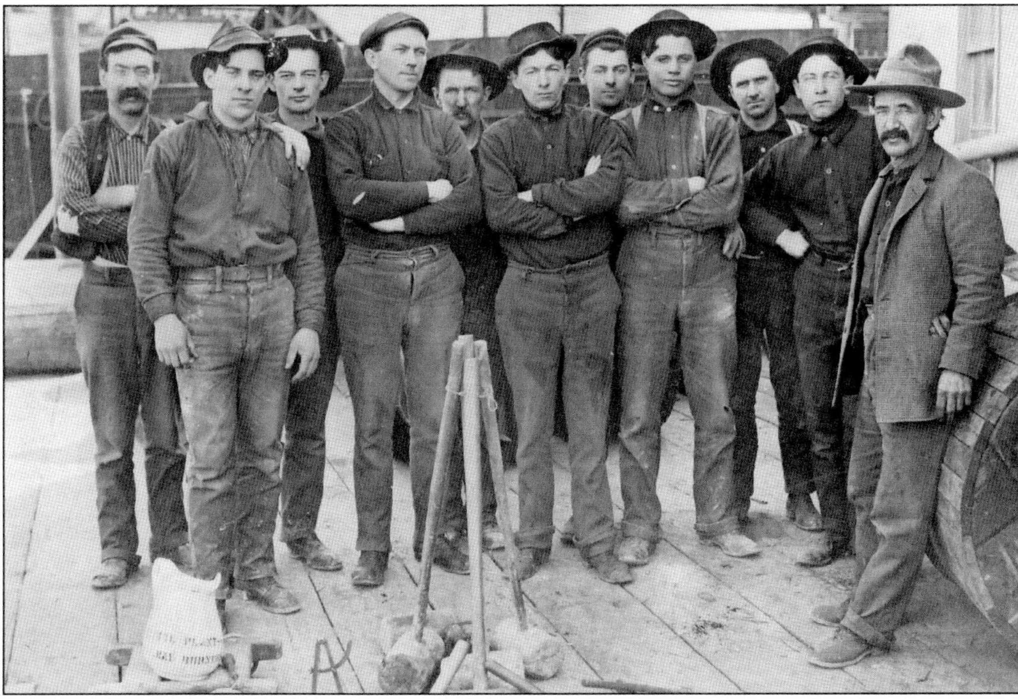

LEAD GANG, C. 1906. Among the men pictured here are Howard Spigelmyer, with a bushy mustache at center rear, and his son Lloyd Howard, fourth from left in the back. They made lead pipes for use in the acid plant. The only strike at the powder works occurred in 1907 when the lead burners walked out, demanding a wage of $5 for an eight-hour day. (Courtesy Sharon Parshall Townsend and Kristina Warren Barncard.)

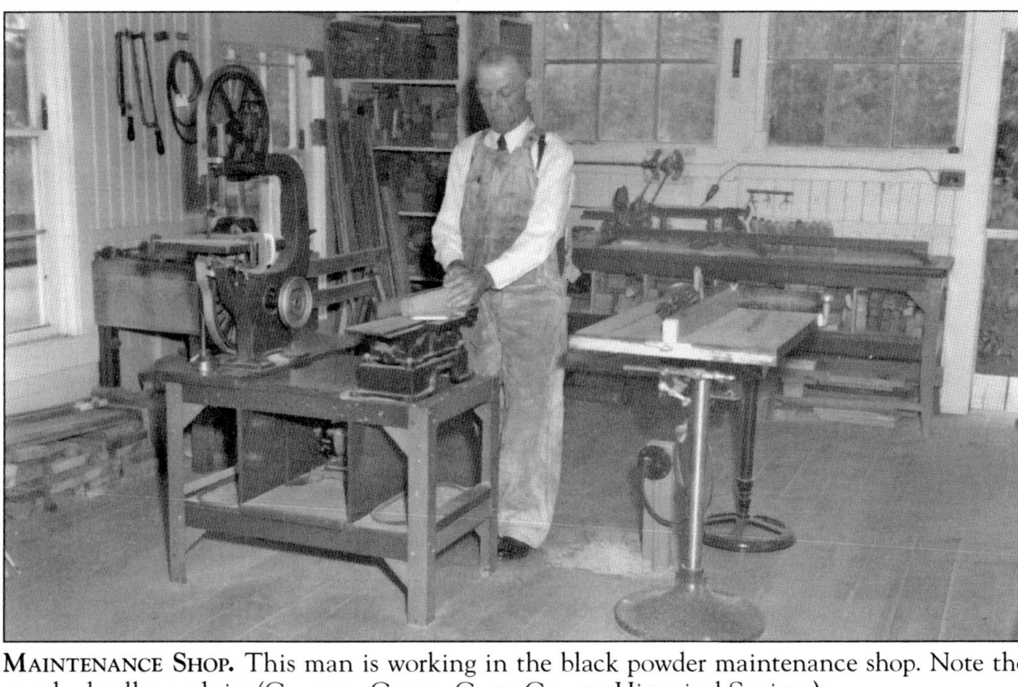

MAINTENANCE SHOP. This man is working in the black powder maintenance shop. Note the starched collar and tie. (Courtesy Contra Costa County Historical Society.)

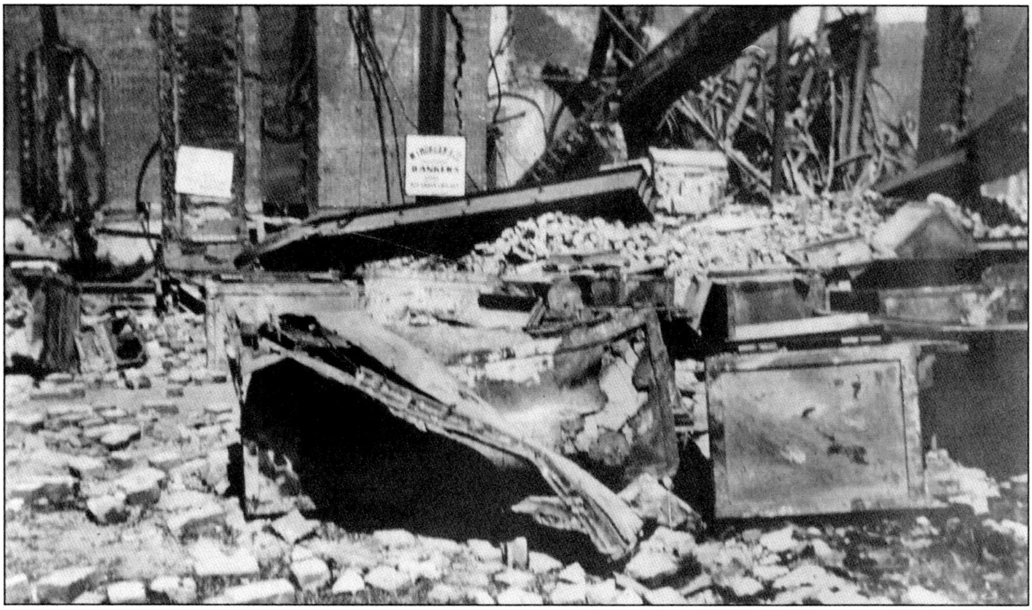

Business Block Ruins, 1906. San Francisco Mayor Eugene Schmitz ordered John Bermingham Jr., superintendent of the California Powder Works at Hercules, to oversee the dynamiting of blocks of buildings in order to halt the spread of fires following the earthquake. The ruins of W.J. Morgan and Company bankers are shown above. Below, safes lay strewn among the rubble. Jack London wrote, "Dynamite was lavishly used, and many of San Francisco's proudest structures were crumbled by man himself into ruins." An official report said Bermingham was "so far under the influence of liquor as to be of no service." Nevertheless, his men took credit for saving the city from complete destruction. Bermingham's men dynamited the area north of Kearney Street, but in the process they ignited 60 fires in the Chinatown-North Beach area. (Both courtesy M. Wallace and W. Ryder.)

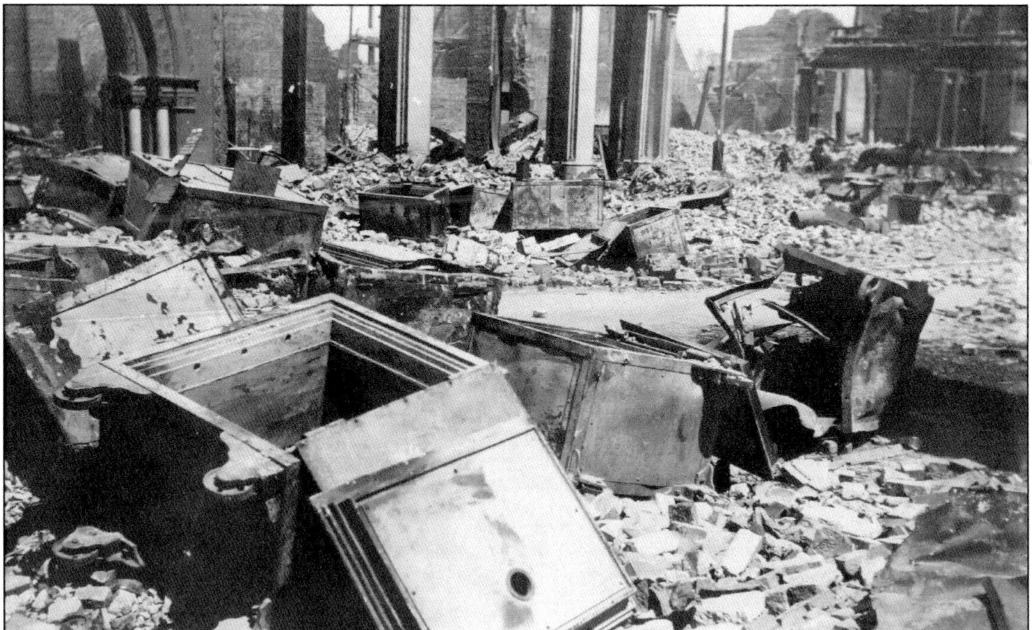

San Francisco Quake Aftermath, 1906. The California Powder Works established an office amid the rubble adjacent to the Henry Cowell Lime and Cement Co. located at Sansome and Washington Streets. A temporary sign on the building indicates that the lime and cement business had moved to Second and Clay Streets, Oakland. Much of the lime used in cement for the rebuilding of San Francisco was provided by this company. (Courtesy M. Wallace and W. Ryder.)

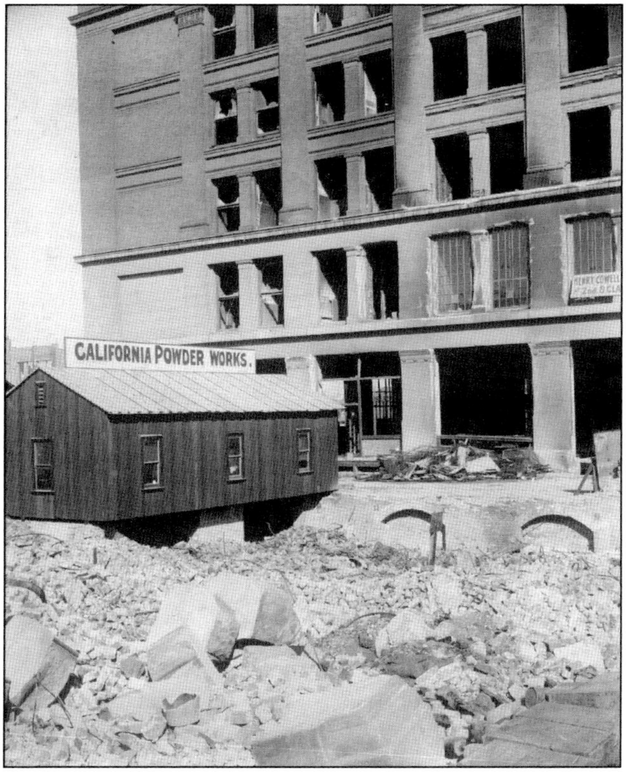

California Powder Works, 1906. Staff members pose outside the hastily constructed San Francisco office of the powder works. California Powder Works also established a temporary office in the East Bay at 2171 Shattuck Avenue in Berkeley. (Courtesy M. Wallace and W. Ryder.)

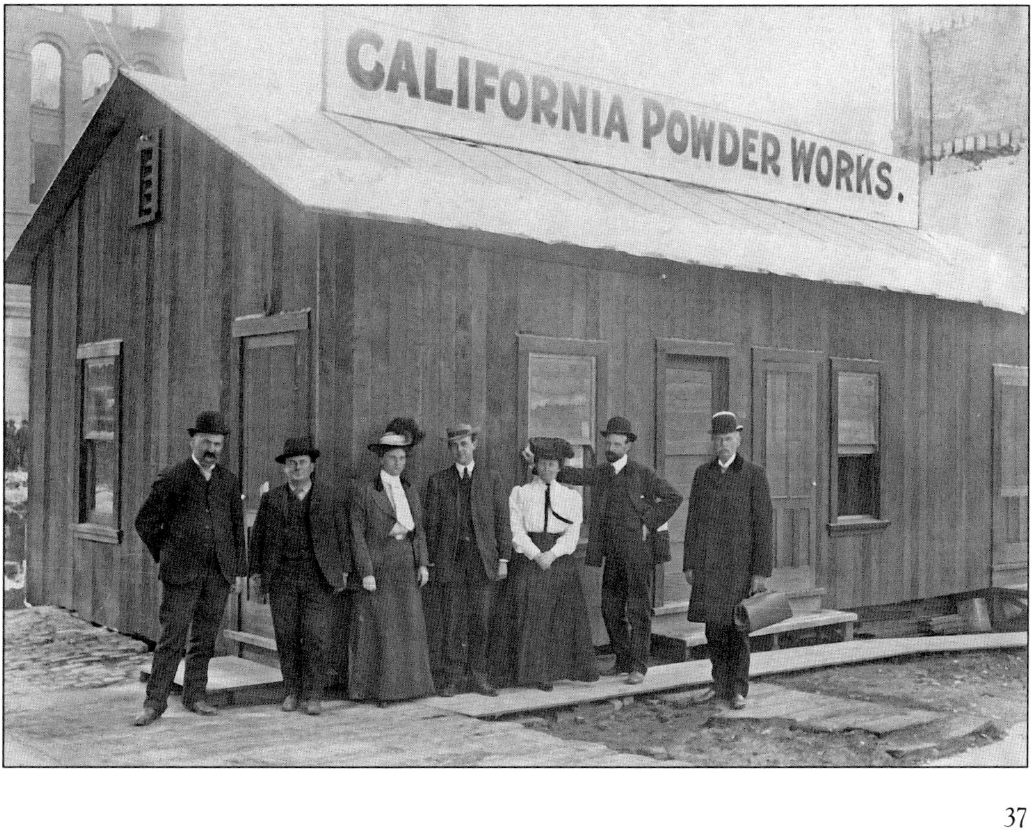

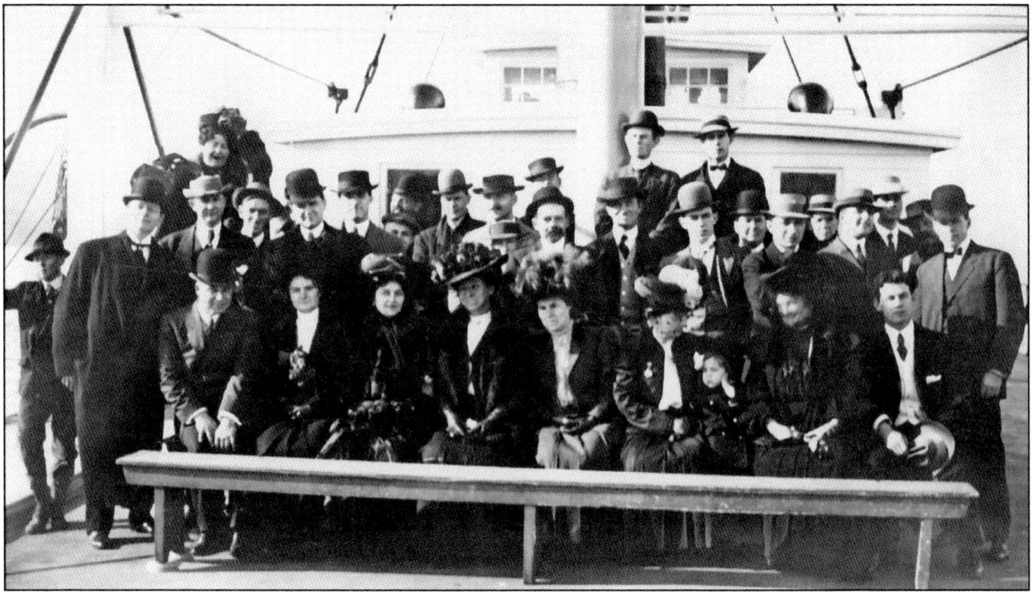

HERCULES STEAMER. Guests are on deck for the trial trip of the *Hercules* on January 11, 1908. When the *Hercules* was commissioned by the powder works, the *San Francisco Call* reported that "vessels meeting it or passing it will stand on little ceremony about yielding the right of way or giving the craft with the strong name a wide berth." (Courtesy M. Wallace and W. Ryder.)

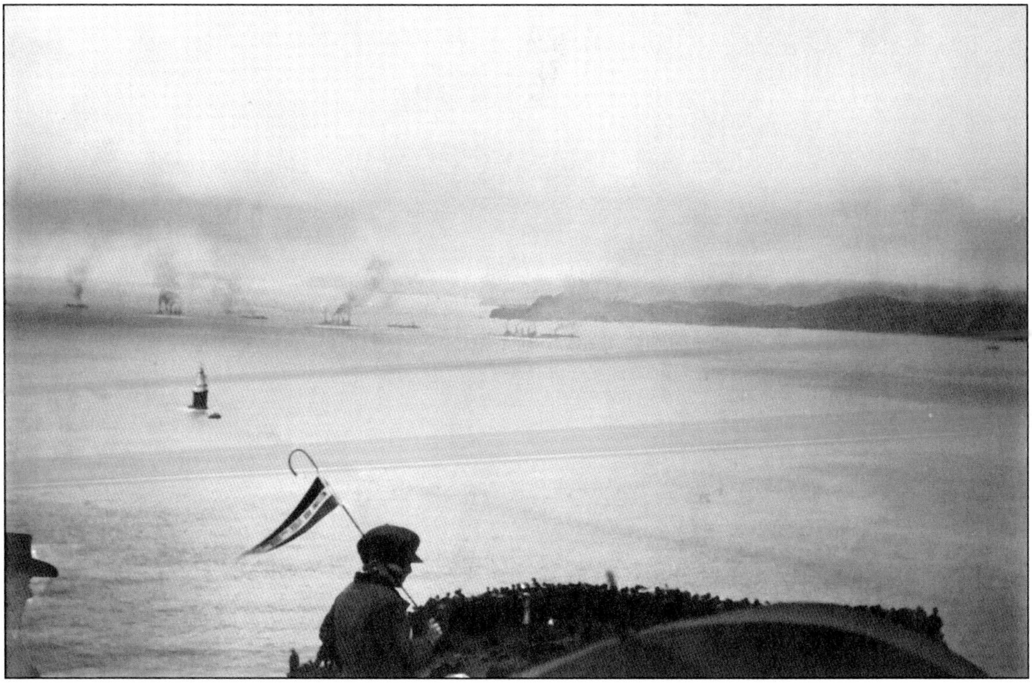

WELCOME OUR FLEET, MAY 1908. The arrival of the Great White Fleet at the Port of San Francisco generated much excitement during its 14-month world cruise. Several battleships are visible in the distance above the boy's pennant. The *Hercules* took school children as young as six on a day-trip to board these warships. Public excursions aboard the *Hercules* included a late evening visit to the illuminated battleships. (Courtesy M. Wallace and W. Ryder)

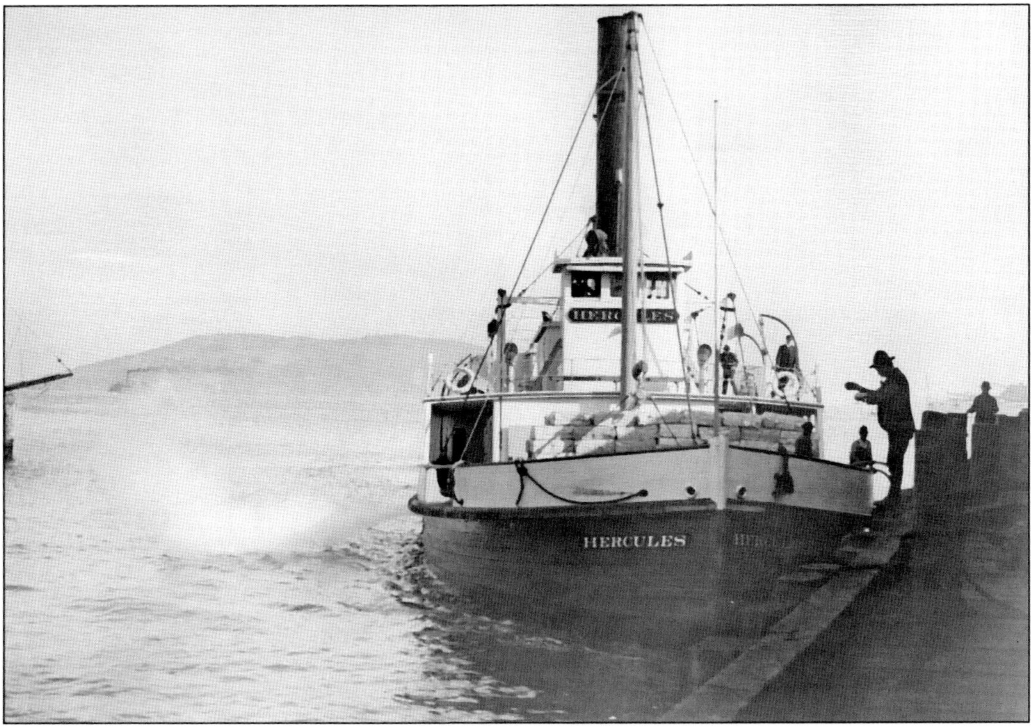

***HERCULES* STERN WHEEL STEAMER.** The *Hercules*, built in 1908 at San Francisco's Risdon Iron Works, transported high explosives. *Hercules* was 160 feet long, 36 feet in beam, and 7 feet deep. It was an oil burner with poppet valve engines of 18 inches diameter and 72 inch stroke. Two Scotch boilers supplied steam. The vessel was capable of carrying about 500 tons of freight while maintaining a speed of 12 miles per hour. (Both courtesy M. Wallace and W. Ryder.)

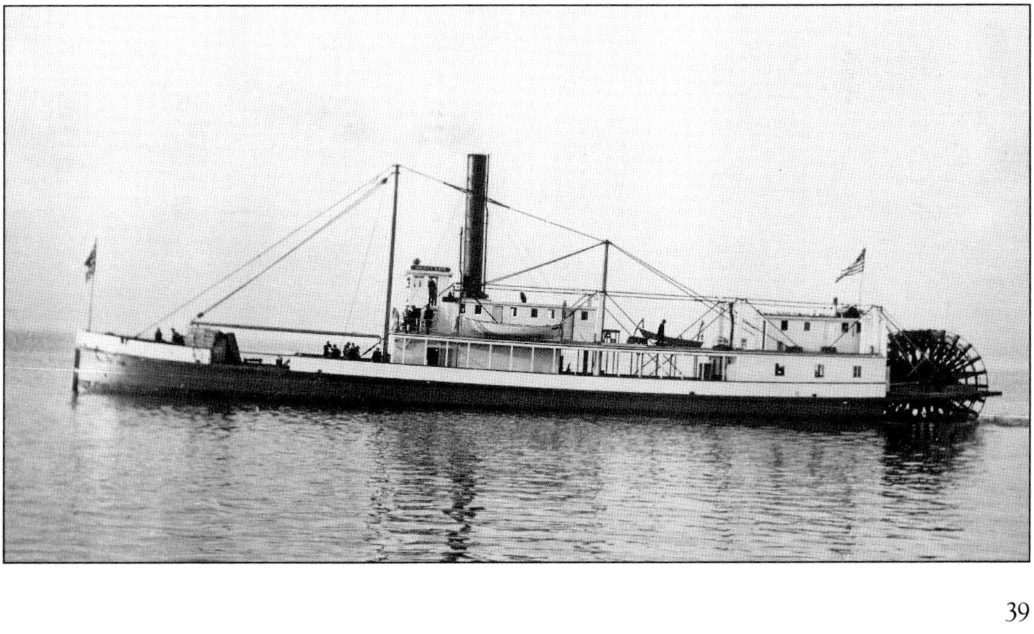

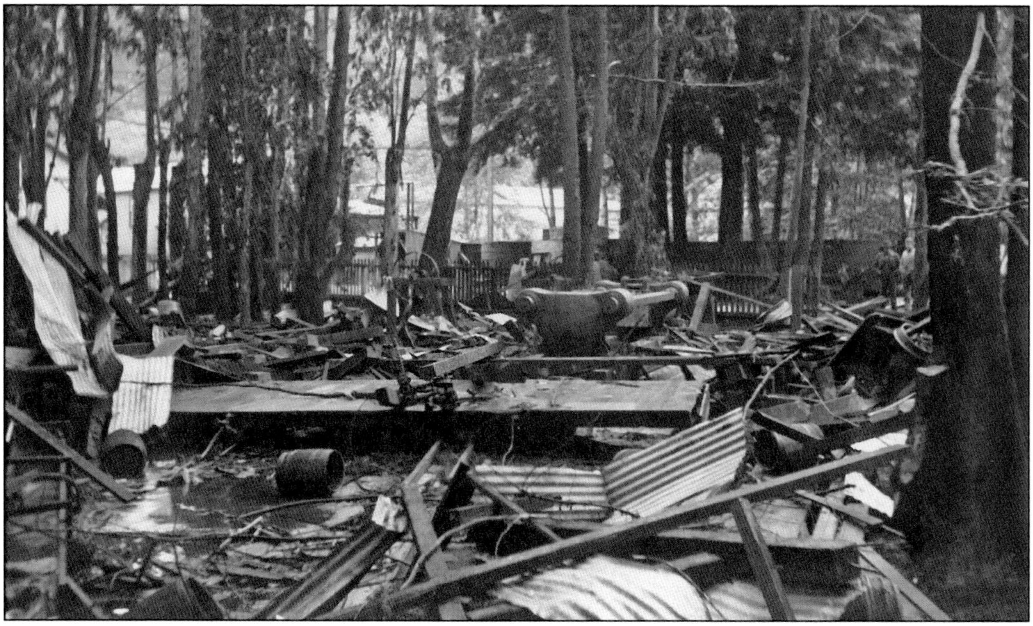

Santa Cruz, June 1907. The black powder press sits amid the rubble of the press house following an explosion of some 12,000 pounds of powder. In 1914, after the assets of this plant were characterized as "vulnerable and underutilized," the black powder line was shut down and the equipment was moved to Refugio Valley at Hercules. Installation was completed in February 1915. (Courtesy M. Wallace and W. Ryder.)

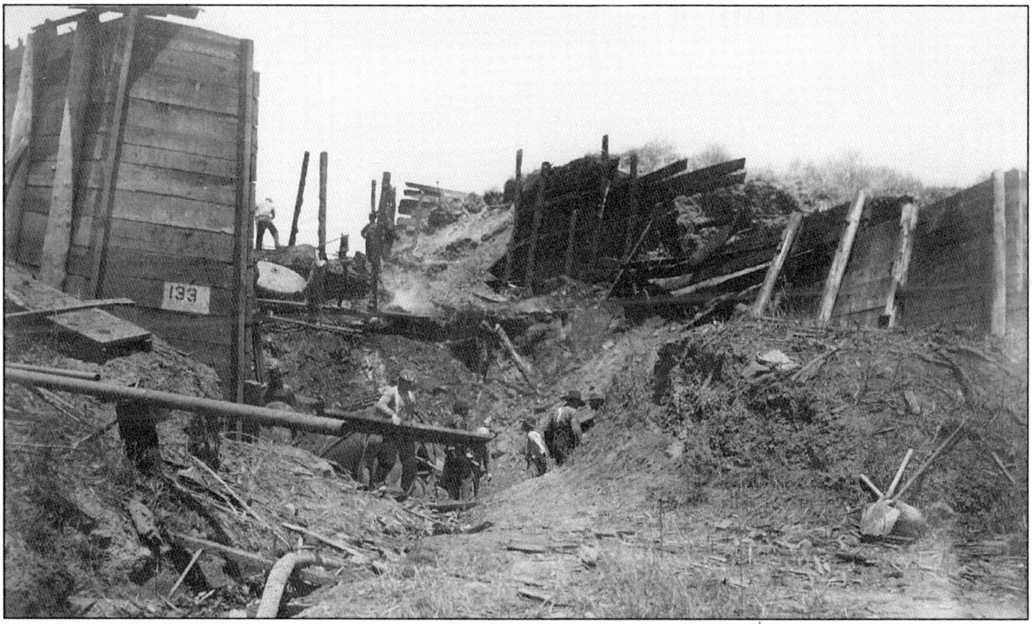

Point Isabel, June 1908. Men clear debris from a crater following an explosion that destroyed the nitroglycerine-mixing house at Dupont's Vigorit plant. All workers had escaped unharmed. Explosions like this rocked the Bay Area. A 1907 explosion at Pinole, thought to be an earthquake, caused a stampede of 700 cannery workers in San Francisco, resulting in many injuries. (Courtesy M. Wallace and W. Ryder.)

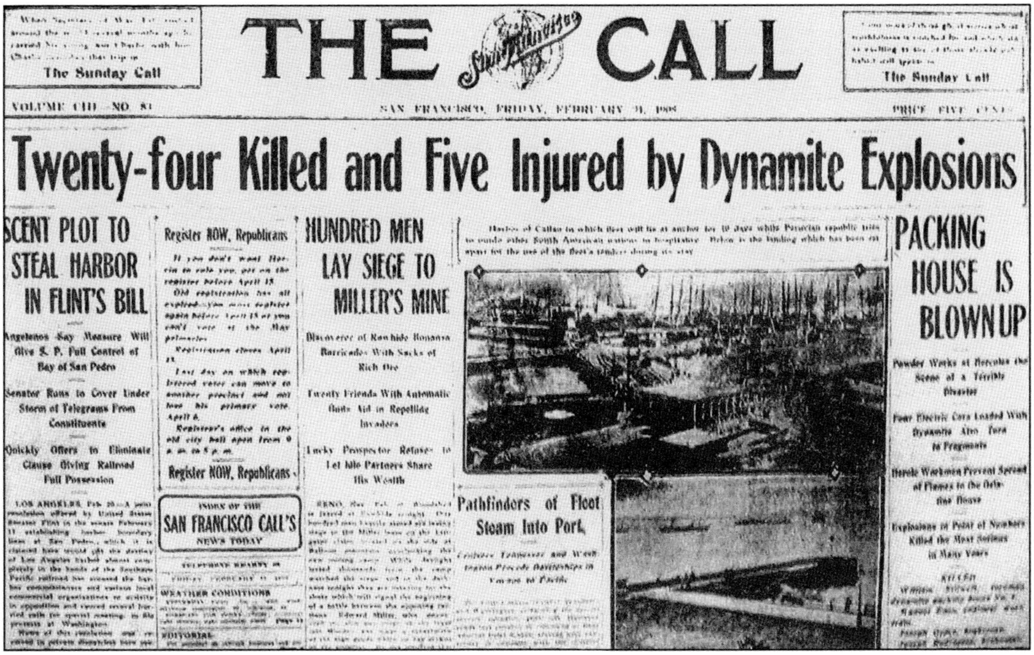

THE CALL

The Sunday Call

Twenty-four Killed and Five Injured by Dynamite Explosions

SCENT PLOT TO STEAL HARBOR IN FLINT'S BILL

Angelenos Say Measure Will Give S. P. Full Control of Bay of San Pedro

Senator Runs to Cover Under Storm of Telegrams From Constituents

Quickly Offers to Eliminate Clause Giving Railroad Full Possession

Register NOW, Republicans

Register NOW, Republicans

SAN FRANCISCO CALL'S NEWS TODAY

HUNDRED MEN LAY SIEGE TO MILLER'S MINE

Twenty Friends With Automatic Guns Aid in Repelling Invaders

Lucky Prospector Refuses to Let Idle Partners Share His Wealth

Pathfinders of Fleet Steam Into Port

PACKING HOUSE IS BLOWN UP

Powder Works at Hercules the Scene of a Terrible Disaster

Four Electric Cars Loaded With Dynamite Also Torn to Fragments

Heroic Workmen Prevent Spread of Flames to the Other Houses

Explosions at Point of Numbers Killed the Most Serious in Many Years

Hercules, February 1908. Twenty Chinese workers were among the 24 dead following an accident at the Quinan packinghouse at Hercules on February 21. An estimated 24,000 pounds of Dupont dynamite exploded, killing every man in the packinghouse and shattering windows all over town. By the time the plant closed seven decades later, some 152 men had perished in explosions and accidents at Hercules. (Courtesy M. Wallace and W. Ryder.)

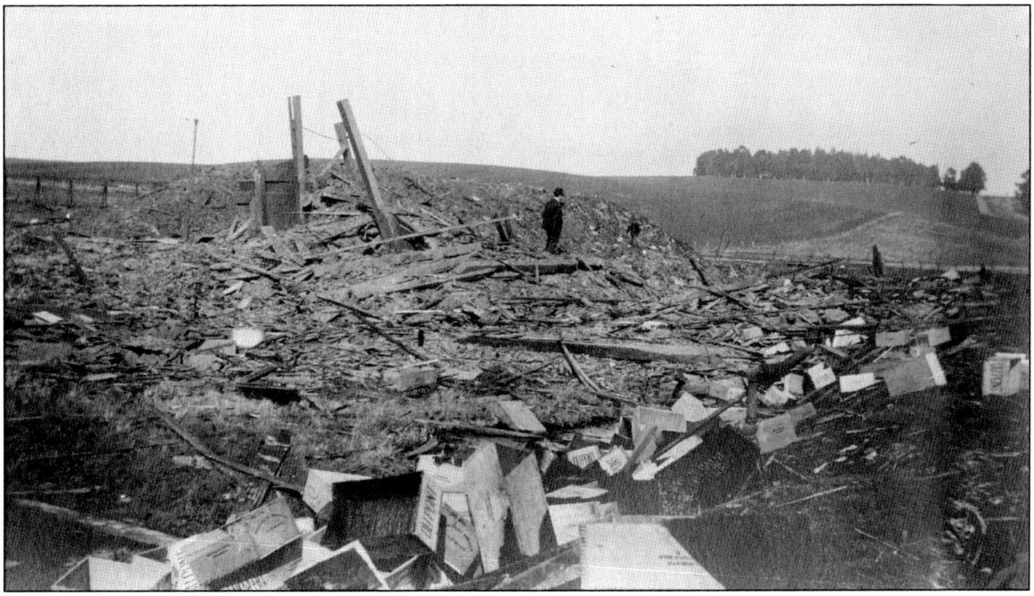

A Terrific Shock. Newspapers around the world reported the 1908 accident. The devastation was so complete that only one of the victims was found, the others being "blown to atoms." Two dozen young women at work in a building 150 yards away were injured by flying debris and were thrown into a panic. Wooden boxes bearing the Dupont trademark litter the scene. (Courtesy Hercules Historical Society.)

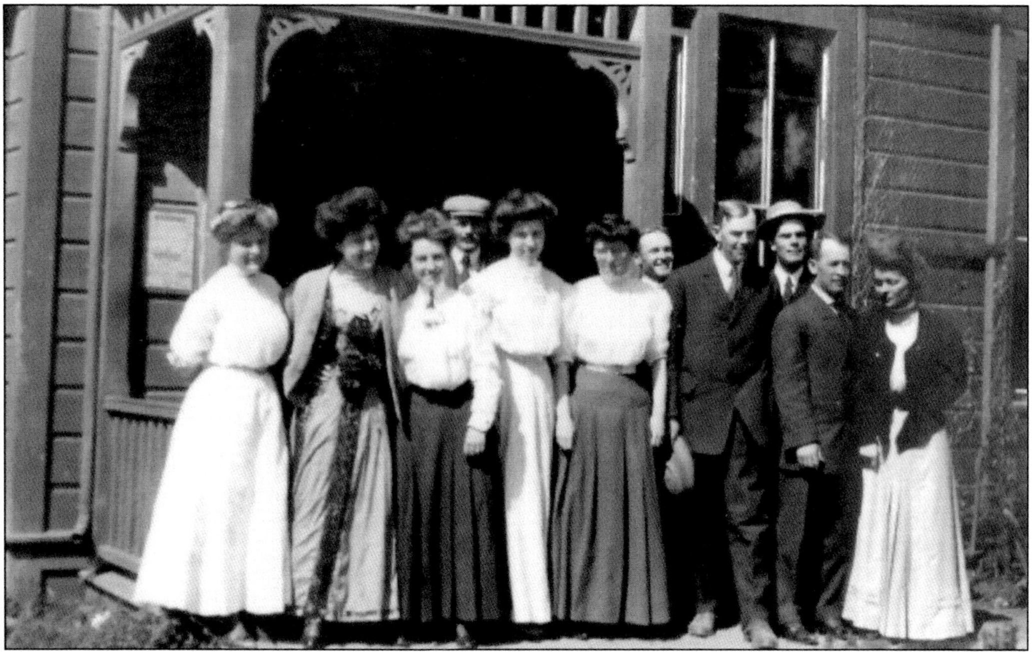

New DuPont Superintendent, April 1908. Superintendent Charles A. Patterson was welcomed at the Hercules town hall. Gathered from left to right are Lucile White, ? MacPherson, ? Hoaxie, Charles A. Patterson, Abbie McBryde, ? Gage, Henry Gage, Warren McBryde, ? Masters, ? Kerfoon, and ? Kerfoon. (Courtesy M. Wallace and W. Ryder.)

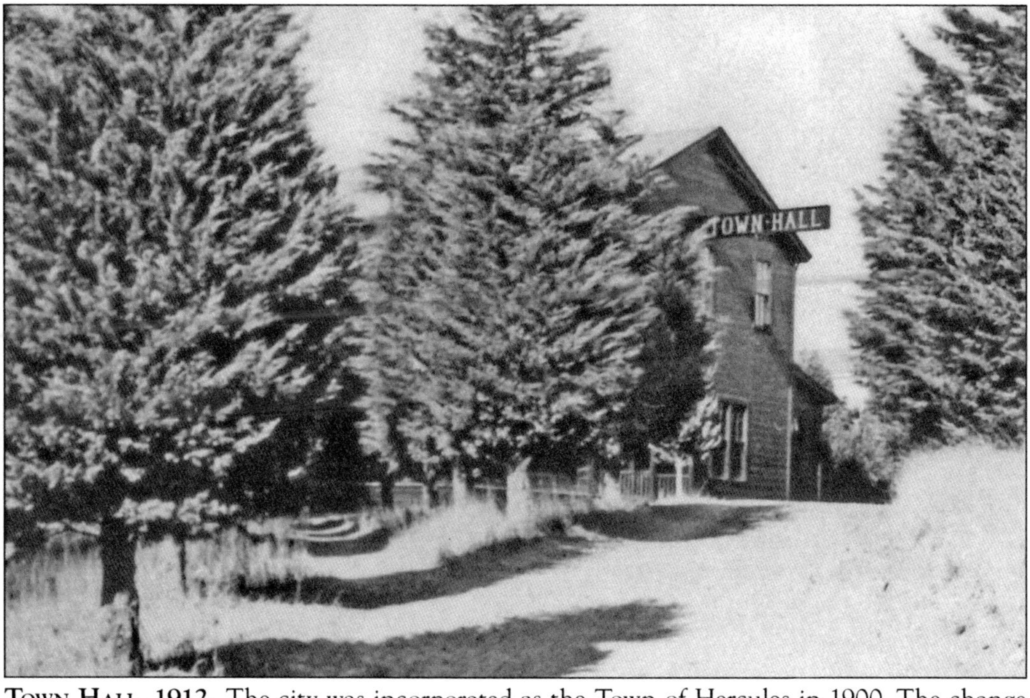

Town Hall, 1912. The city was incorporated as the Town of Hercules in 1900. The change from town to city of Hercules occurred in April 1973, with the adoption of the municipal code for the City of Hercules. (Courtesy Contra Costa County Historical Society.)

Three

Hercules Powder Works

Upon its founding in 1913, the Hercules Powder Company had 11 plants nationwide, including the "Hercules Works" near Pinole.

Dynamite production occurred on the "Flat" of Refugio Valley, in rough buildings of wood and metal, each housing a stage of production from the liquid acids to boxes of finished dynamite. For safety, buildings were set in small clusters or spaced apart; many were sunken behind embankments to direct the force of explosions upwards. Rows of tall eucalyptus trees were planted around the valley to further buffer explosions.

Batches of the dangerous chemicals were moved from one "house" to the next over a network of pipelines, roads, elevated wooden boardwalks, and narrow-gauge lines. Men carefully wheeled 500-pound batches of nitroglycerine in "angel buggies" over the boardwalks. Locomotives powered by compressed air shuttled freight cars up the valley, dipping through a tunnel beneath State Highway 40.

In 1914, the company closed its venerable Santa Cruz powder mill, moving some of its equipment to establish a black powder production line at "Plant B" of the Hercules Works, up the valley from the Flat.

Anticipating World War I, the military placed large orders with Hercules Powder for the newly invented trinitrotoluene (TNT) explosive. By 1918, Hercules Works was the largest TNT plant in America, with 3,000 workers and nine TNT lines producing seven million pounds per month, or one-third of all the TNT used by the United States in the Great War.

Explosives from Hercules Works were used commercially for mining, construction, and agriculture; for civil ammunition; and for the military. Commercial markets were far larger than military contracts. Hercules Powder Company became a large specialty chemical firm, constantly responding to changes in its markets and taking advantage of innovations in chemical technology.

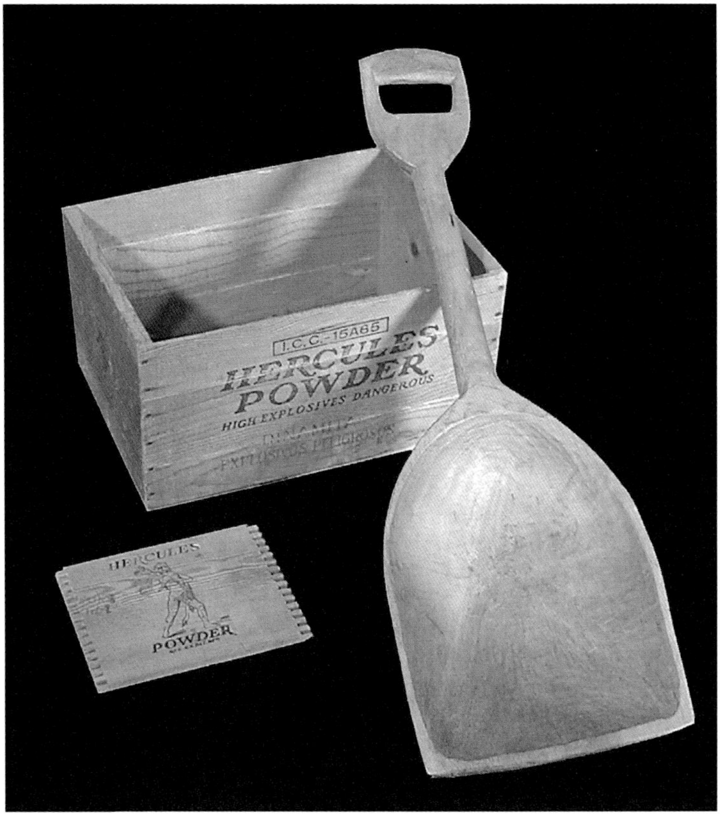

HERCULES ARTIFACTS. The dope house shovel, made of heavily waxed wood, is used in lieu of a metal spade in order to avoid sparks. The late-period dynamite box sits alongside a finger-jointed end panel from an earlier box. As a safety precaution, users were instructed to use only wooden tools and rubber mallets when opening cases and never to use a nail to pry out the sticks of dynamite. (Courtesy Douglas Williams, photographer.)

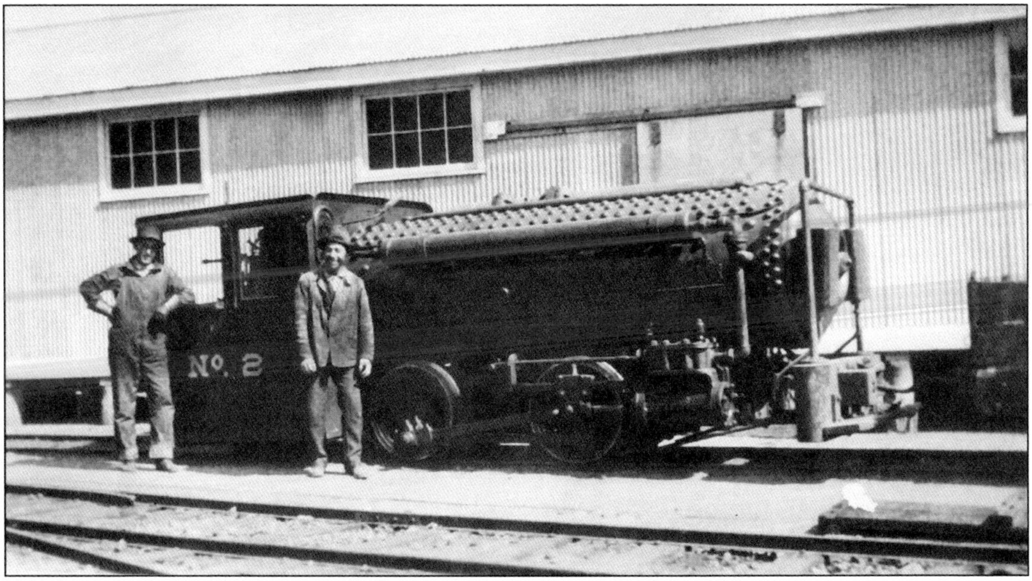

AIR LOCOMOTIVE. Ed Silva (left) and Antone Pereira pose by Engine No. 2, a fireless locomotive, used to transport ingredients and powder. These locomotives, which were also extensively used in mining operations, reduced the fire hazard. Early models had a tank that was charged with steam and hot water from a stationary plant. Gas and electric locomotives replaced the earlier compressed-air models. (Courtesy Contra Costa County Historical Society.)

SYMBOL OF STRENGTH. The official corporate symbol adopted in 1913 was the Greek god Hercules. This statute sat near the Southern Pacific Railroad tracks, which can be seen in the background. The 13-foot-high figure, made of chicken wire and stucco and draped in a lion skin, was said to offend rail passengers. One claim is that owing to the complaints, the statue was dynamited in the late 1920s. Others said it simply fell apart. (Courtesy Ashland Inc.)

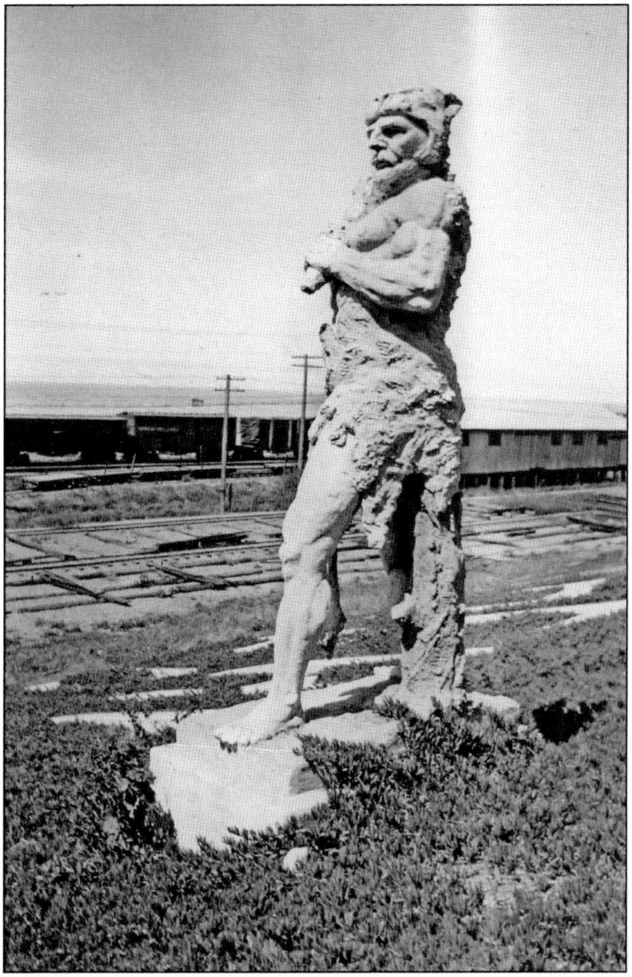

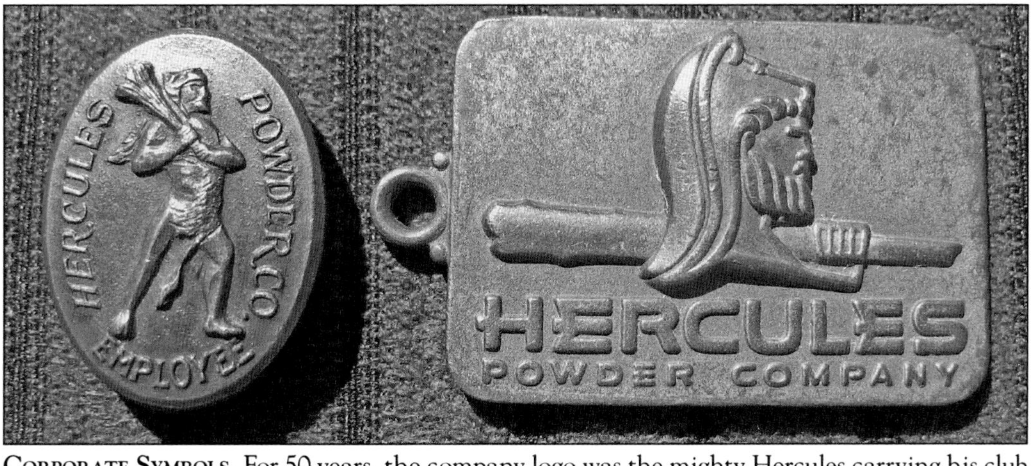

CORPORATE SYMBOLS. For 50 years, the company logo was the mighty Hercules carrying his club as depicted on the employee badge at left. On its 50th anniversary in 1962, the company adopted a new streamlined symbol of "Uncle Herc," represented on the key fob at right. (Courtesy Hercules Historical Society.)

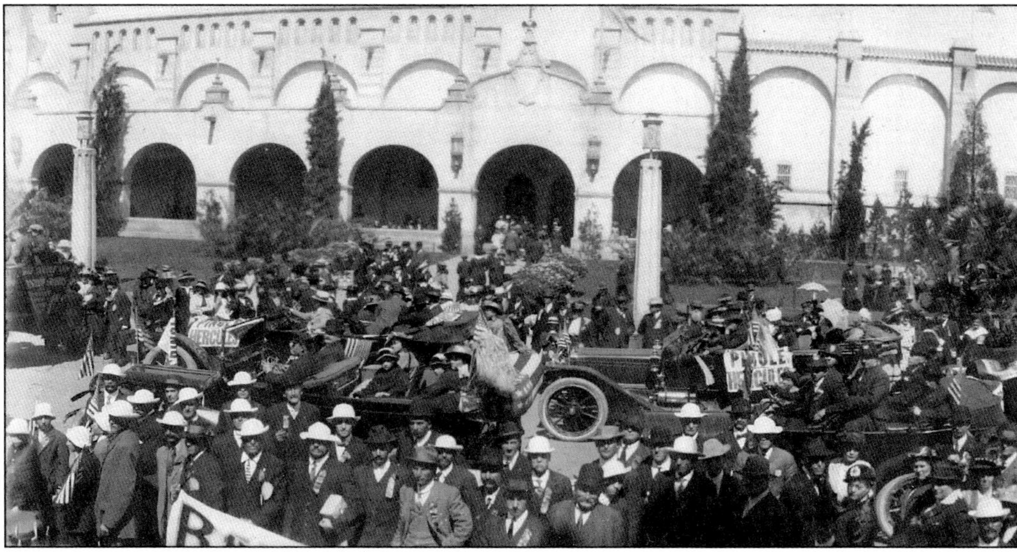

Panama Pacific International Exposition, 1915. Two Pinole-Hercules floats participated in the parade on Contra Costa Day, April 3. Many firms declared a holiday, sending their employees en masse. Direct ferry and special trains took the estimated 10,000 visitors from the county to the exposition that day. This image was made by Cardinell-Vincent, official photographers of the exposition. (Courtesy Contra Costa County Historical Society.)

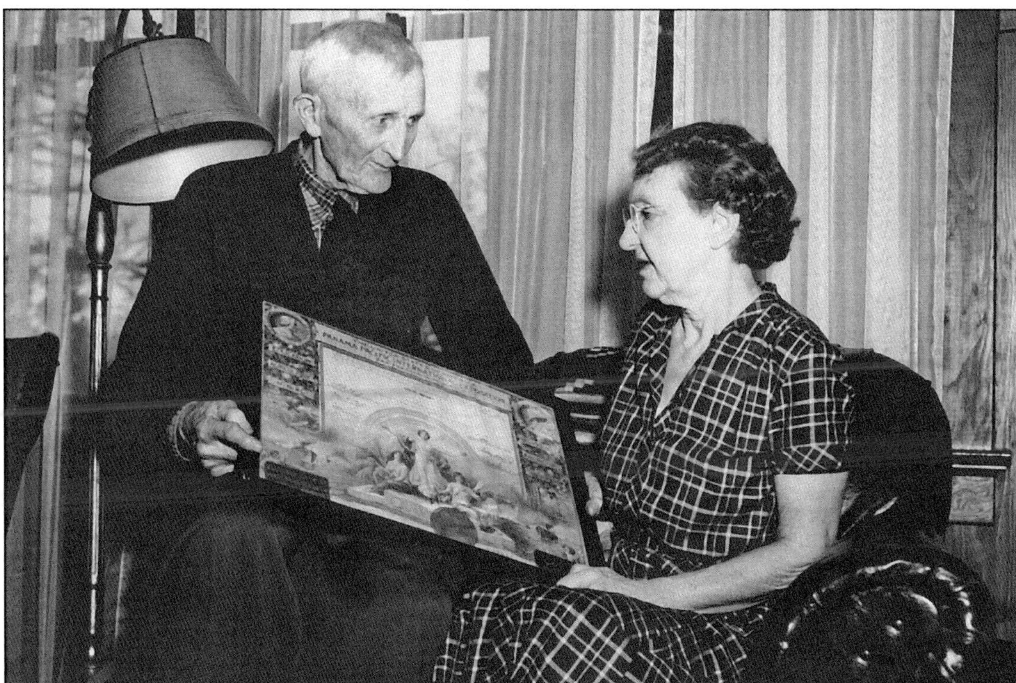

Gold Medal Award. In the 1950s, Chauncey Ingalls and his wife, Stella, display his gold medal certificate from the 1915 Panama Pacific International Exposition. It was for Patent No. 724,104, a machine for making tubular shells. Ingalls had fallen into an empty acid vat in 1916, following which he was granted early retirement with a full pension. Despite the injury to his lungs, he lived until 1956. (Courtesy William Ingalls.)

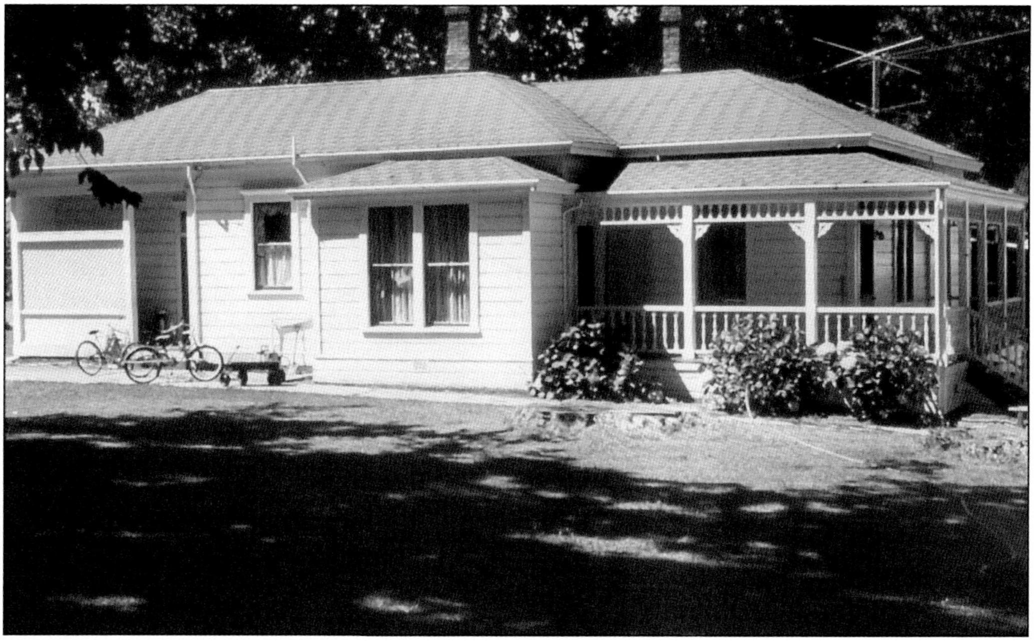

1 Kings Avenue. Senior personnel occupied this home, including Nathaniel Hawthorne, a chemist who supervised the TNT facility. It is said he was a descendant of the author of the same name. This image shows the house after renovations. In the 1970s, the house became Hercules City Hall with a new address on Railroad Avenue. (Courtesy Anita Wennblom Broberg McKee.)

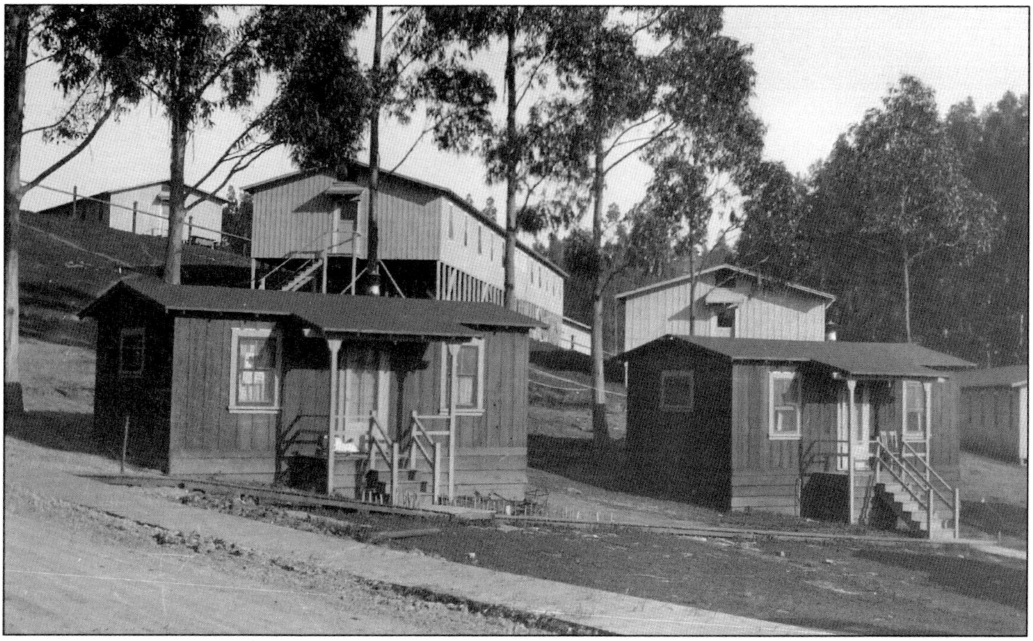

Two-room Bungalows and Dormitories. These buildings were government-built war housing at Hercules. An unprecedented demand for lodging occurred as a result of the expansion of the plant between 1916 and 1918. In a single week in 1918, the company hired 125 carpenters and laborers with an order for 1,400 more. Men were advised to bring a blanket. By the mid-1920s, the workforce had shrunk to 250. (Courtesy Ashland Inc.)

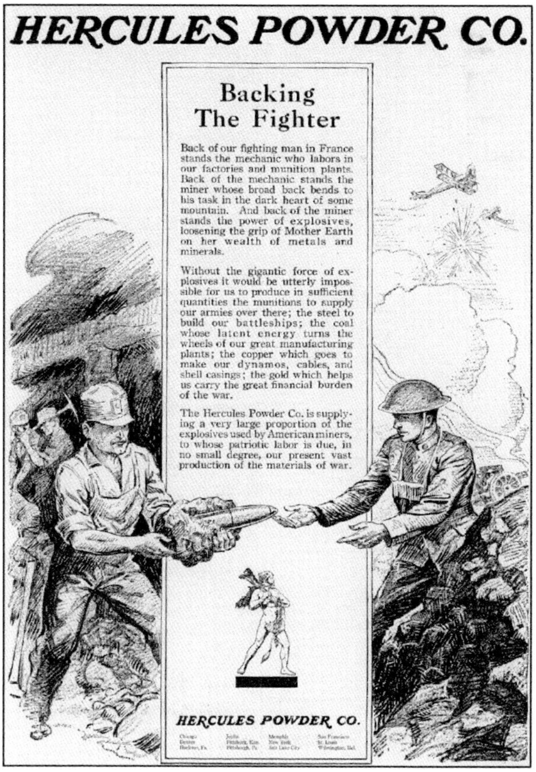

Supplier to War in Europe. Advertisements for the Hercules Powder Company were published in *National Geographic* in 1918, four years after the start of the Great War, now known as World War I. The company touted the use of explosives for mining the ore and coal needed to supply manufacturing plants and shipbuilders. Miners work in the background, providing the raw materials that were needed to produce materials of war.

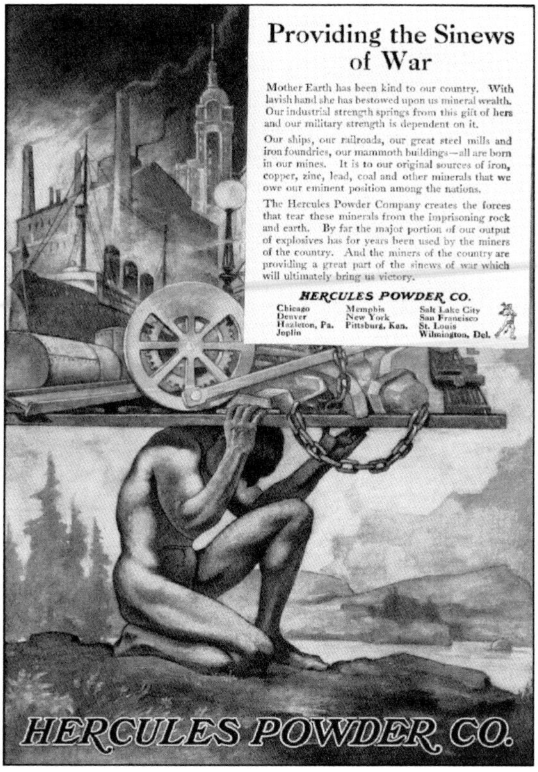

Explosives for Miners. This January 1918 advertisement is characteristic of the beautiful artwork used to illustrate the company's publicity and calendars. The image depicts a man with Herculean strength, holding up the industry of America. (Courtesy John Cadigan.)

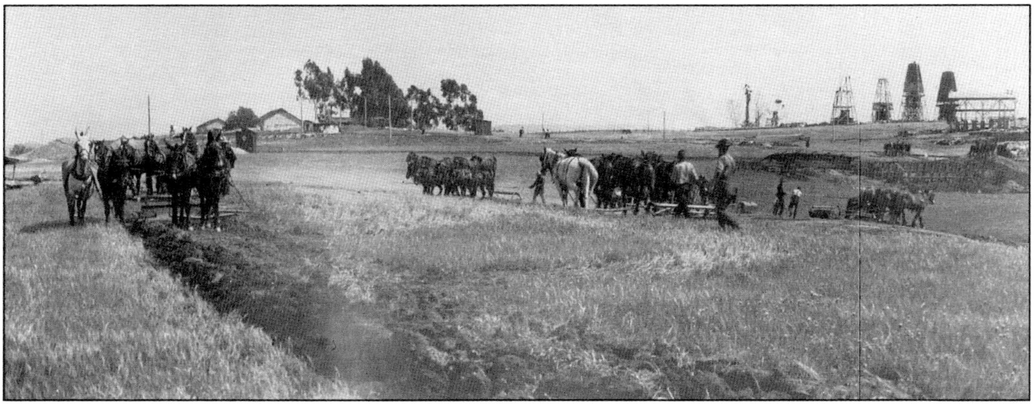

New TNT Units, 1918. Richmond-based architect James Thomas Narbett designed the TNT facility. Narbett had joined the US Army Corps of Engineers and in 1918, the powder company petitioned the US War Department for his services. The image above is dated April 24. These government-paid laborers earned $4 per day. Below is a June 1918 image that looks toward the Rodeo Valley's Indian Peak (at right) from the present-day intersection of Bayfront Boulevard and Railroad Avenue. TNT (trinitrotoluene) is primarily a military explosive used inside bombs and shells. To fulfill war contracts, millions of dollars were invested at Hercules. Six new TNT units were added to five already in operation. (Both courtesy City of Hercules.)

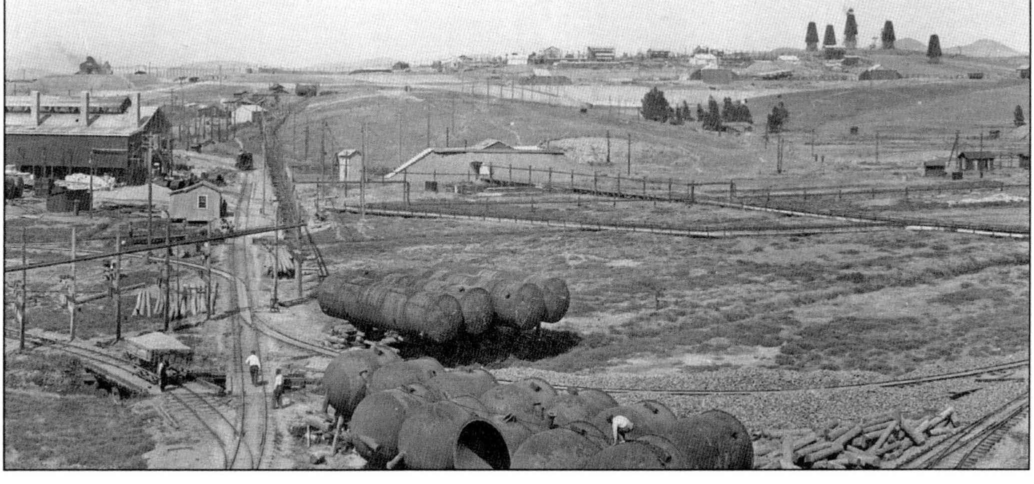

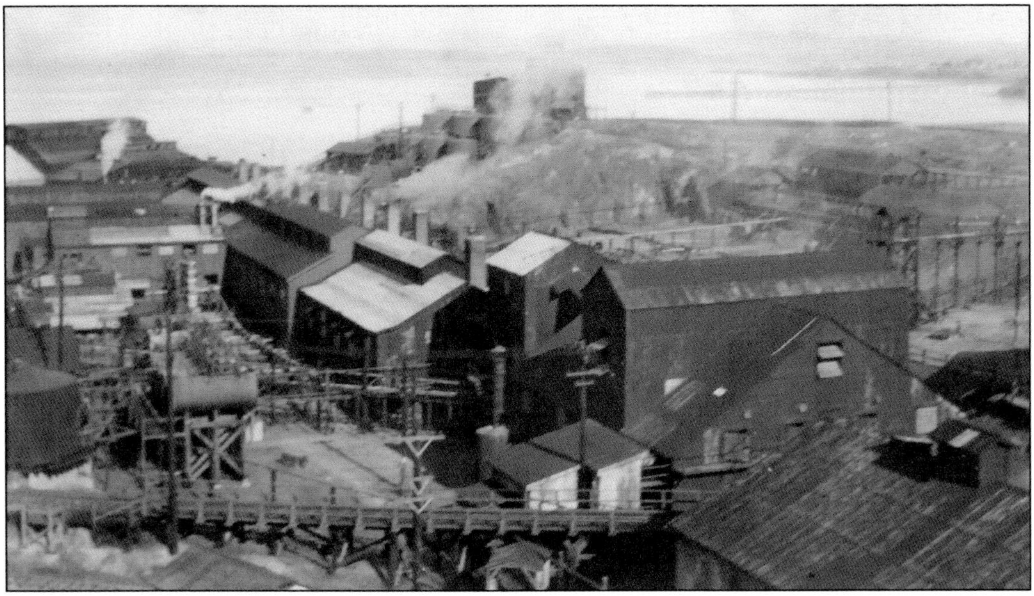

ACID AREA, 1919. An image of the acid area looking north toward San Pablo Bay appeared in the December 1919 issue of the *Hercules Mixer* that boasted, "What started as a small, West Coast powder operation, has grown to be one of the largest explosives industries in this country and has given its original name to our organization." At top right is the dynamite-loading wharf that was once located on the waterfront near the end of present-day Alfred Nobel Drive. (Courtesy Ashland Inc.)

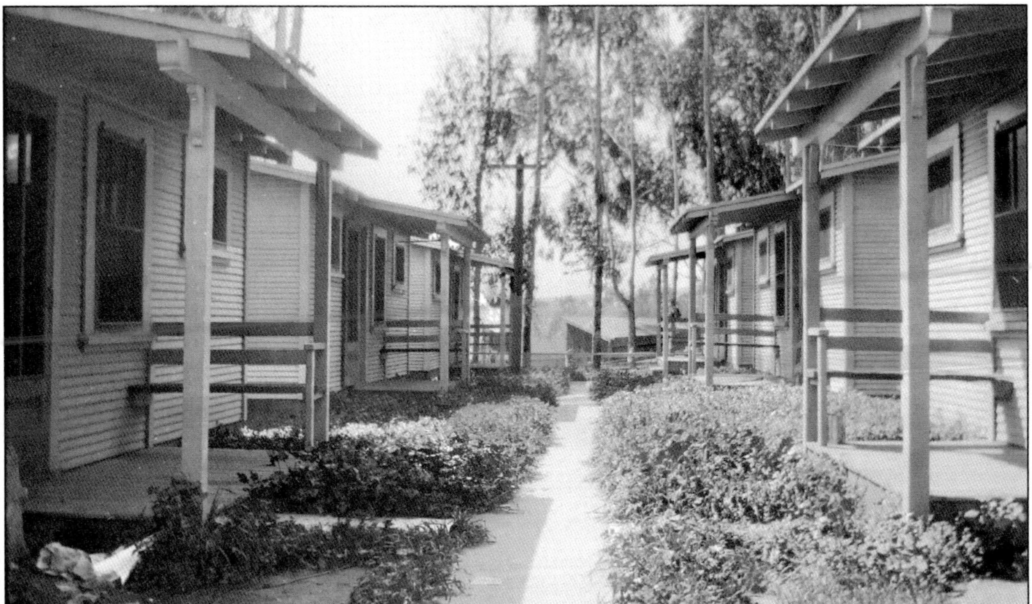

WAR-ERA HOUSING. Temporary dormitories, such as these that housed four men to a unit, were built to accommodate the influx of workers. In 1920, they were no longer needed and Symon Brothers, Oakland's leading wrecker, was hired to demolish 15 dormitories and other government-built buildings. (Courtesy Ashland Inc.)

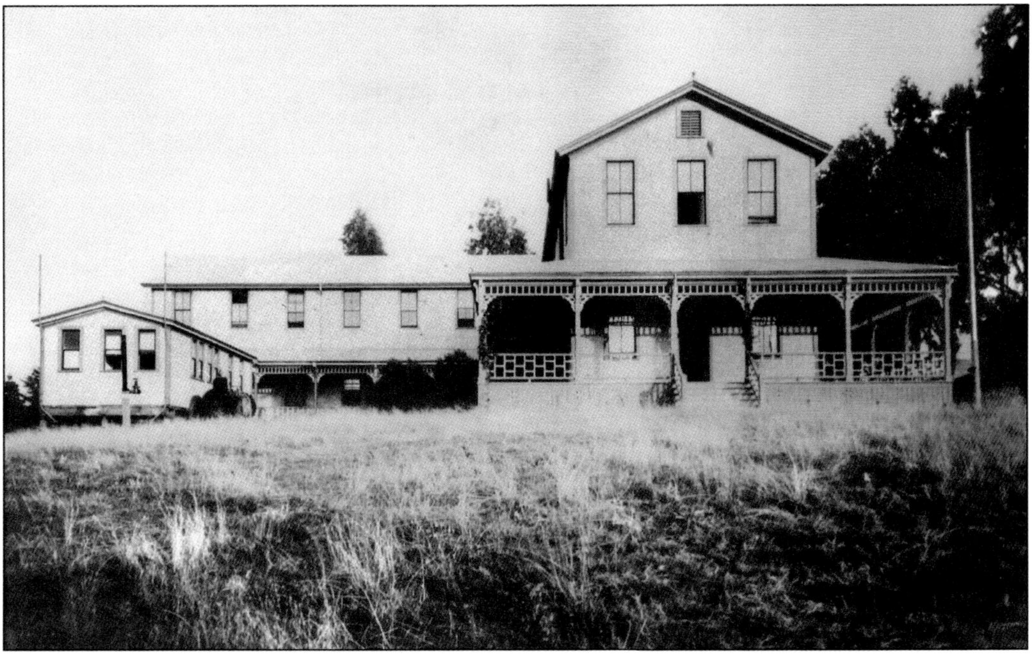

Boarding House for Single Men, c. 1912. The men's dormitory, erected in 1899, was expanded to meet the needs of the growing workforce. The second floor and a one-story wing at left were additions. A veranda wrapped around the main building at right. The clubhouse, which stood behind the dormitory in this image, is not visible. (Courtesy Contra Costa County Historical Society.)

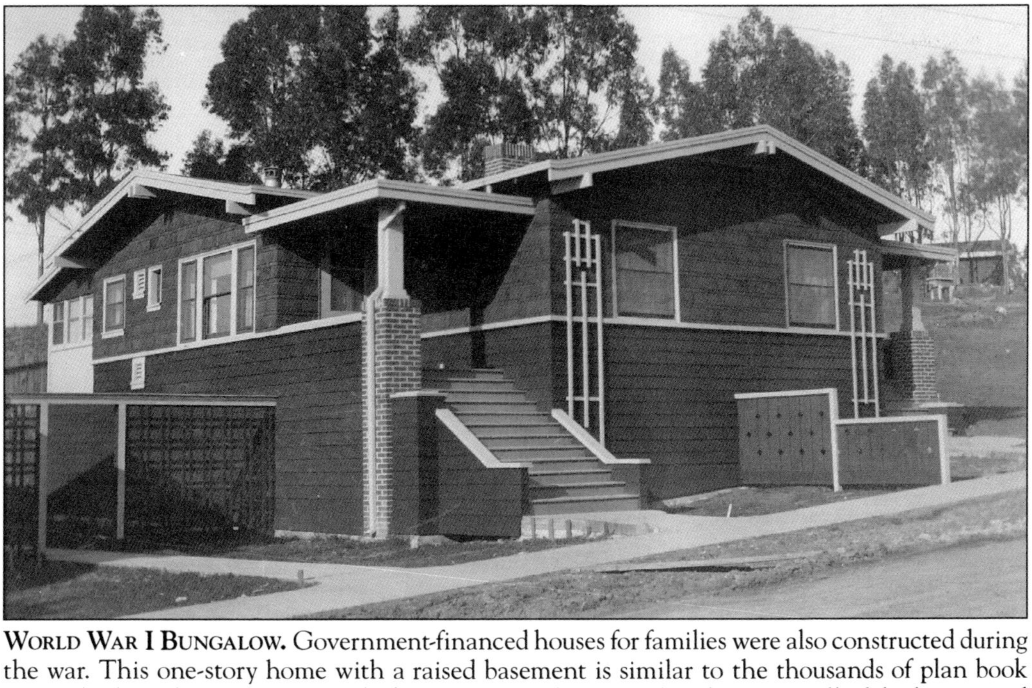

World War I Bungalow. Government-financed houses for families were also constructed during the war. This one-story home with a raised basement is similar to the thousands of plan book houses built in the Bay Area. With the exception of 1991 Railroad Avenue, all of the homes and dormitories built in this era in Hercules have been demolished or moved off their foundations to temporary locations. (Courtesy Ashland Inc.)

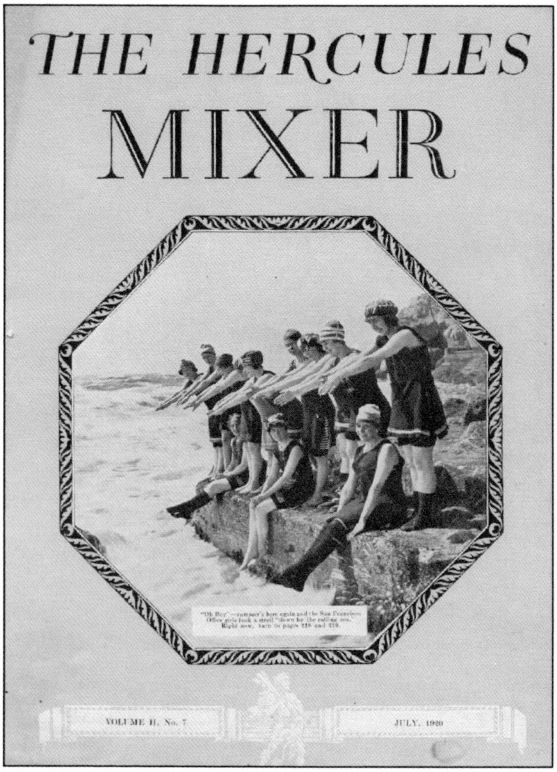

THE HERCULES MIXER. A monthly employee magazine debuted in 1919 as a publication of the Hercules advertising department in Wilmington, Delaware. The "girls" from the San Francisco office were featured on the July 1920 cover. Their bathing attire was described as "the brand that made Mack Sennett famous." (Courtesy Hercules Historical Society.)

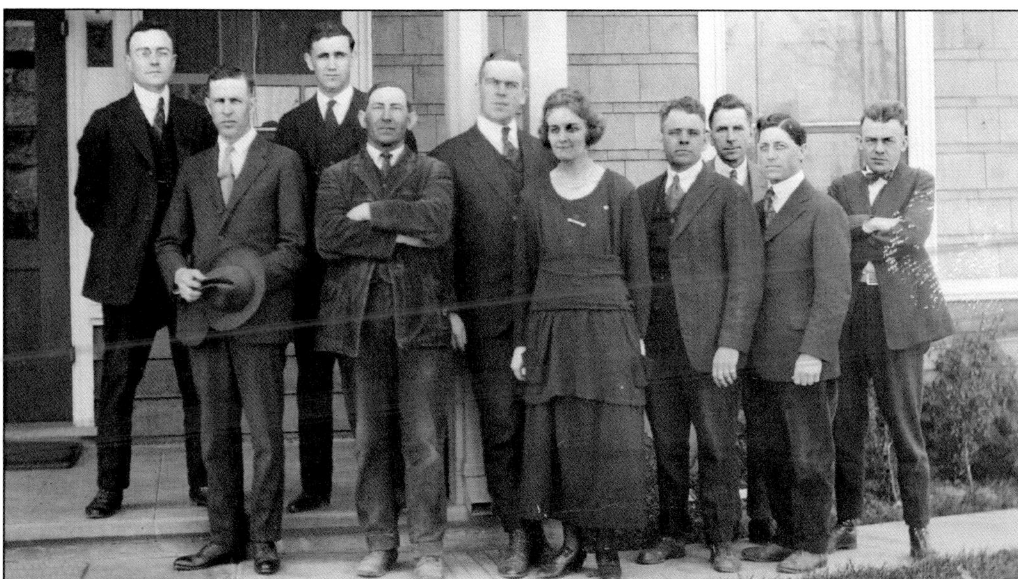

ENGINEERING DEPARTMENT, MARCH 1921. From left to right are Frank Viera, accountant; R.K. Hallett, engineer at the Joplin plant; Phil Powelson, engineer; Leander Smith, field assistant; Harold Keith, transitman; Vera Gerrish, assistant accountant; G.W. Duncan, power test engineer at the Delaware office; Harry Squire, draftsman; E.R. Weeks, engineer at the Bacchus plant; and Edmund Kuhn, draftsman. Projects included construction in 1914–1915 of the black powder line in Refugio Valley and the TNT facilities. (Courtesy Ashland Inc.)

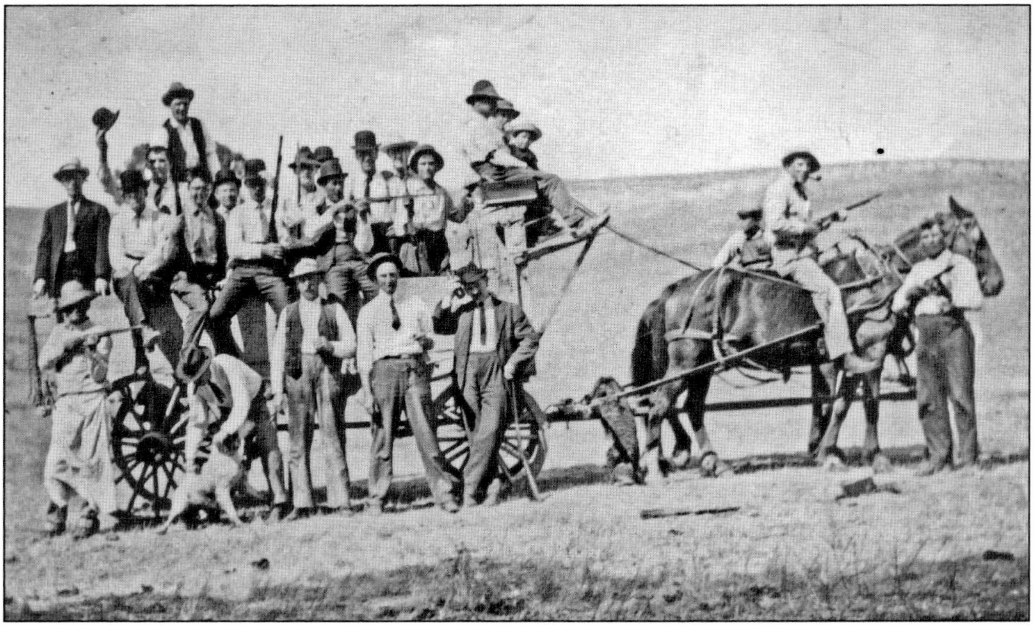

TNT CLUB, C. 1919. The club hosted employees from the San Francisco office at a weekend party that included duck hunting for the men, while the women played tennis and billiards. Among those shown here are Roy Le Febvre, Al Zehringer, and Fred Brandt. (Courtesy Contra Costa County Historical Society.)

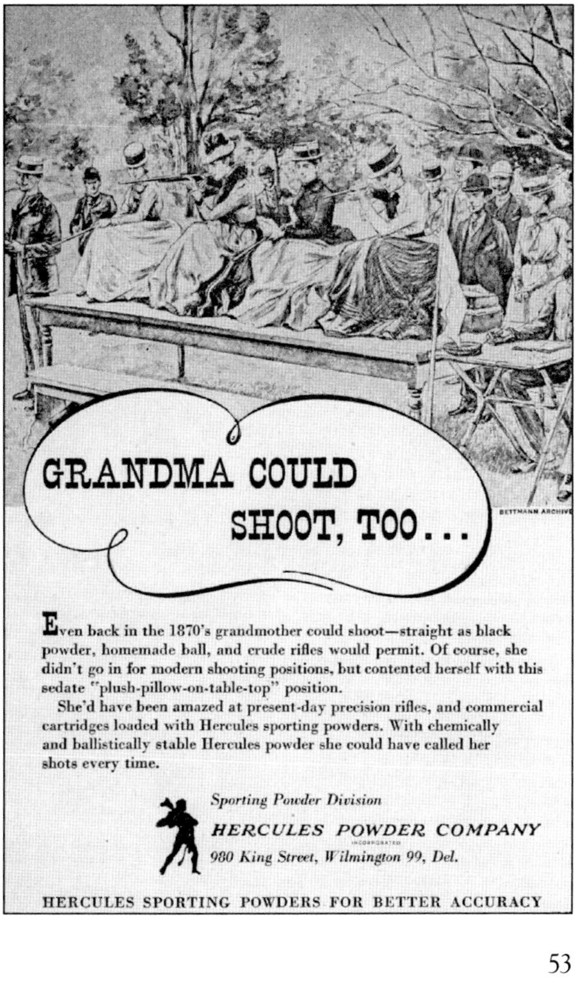

SPORTING POWDERS ADVERTISEMENT, 1946. When Hercules Powder opened for business as an independent entity in January 1913, it inherited the following brands or trademarks: Hercules, Bullseye [sic], Flag in Wreath, E.C., Lightning, New York Sporting, Orange Extra, Sharpshooter, W.A. 30 Cal., Infallible, Unique, 1908 Bear, and 1908 Stag. From 1884 to 1920, Dupont, the one-time owner of Hercules Powder, paid world renowned sharpshooter Annie Oakley to promote its sporting powders. (Courtesy Hercules Historical Society.)

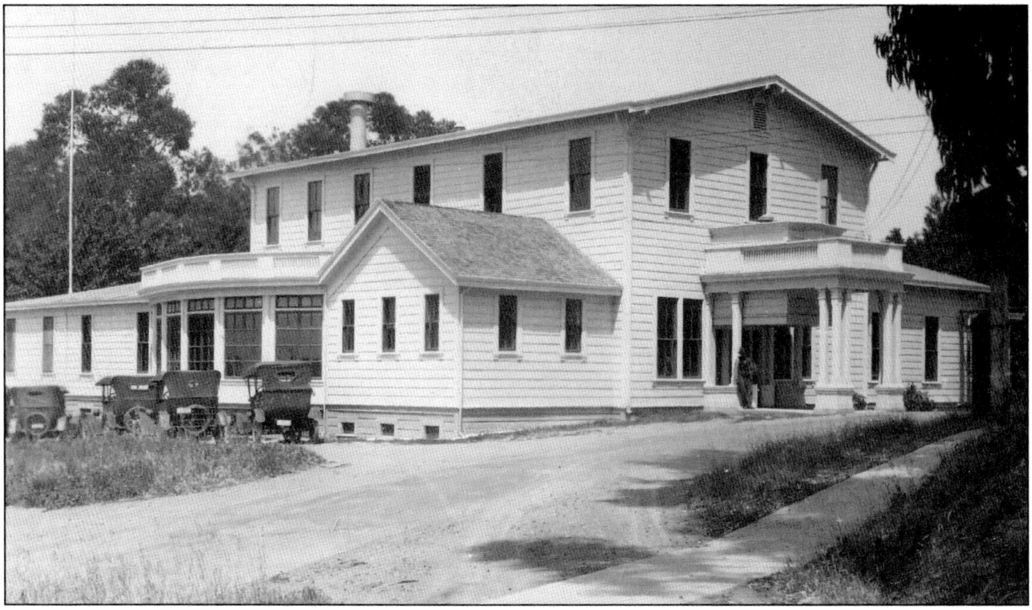

Hercules Club. The men's club featured a large meeting room with a stage and a bar. This photograph may have been taken after extensive renovations following a fire. The second floor was not original to the building. Note the ground level windows that illuminate the basement recreation area. (Courtesy Ashland Inc.)

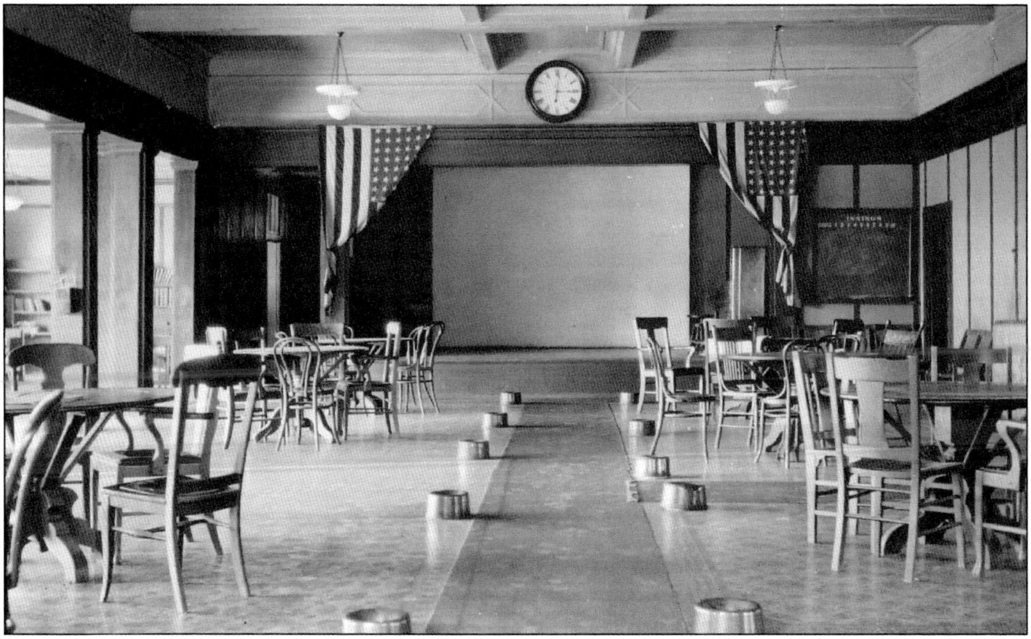

Hercules Club Stage and Screen. In 1916, the Hercules Club building was renovated and enlarged from plans by architect James T. Narbett. Born aboard a ship at Rangoon, British Burma, Narbett came to the Bay Area as a young boy. His work included several Masonic temples and the Richmond Elks' building, Richmond city hall, firehouses, and the Richmond Plunge. In addition to hosting playful high jinks, plays, and dance bands, the clubhouse was also a venue where movies were occasionally shown. (Courtesy Ashland Inc.)

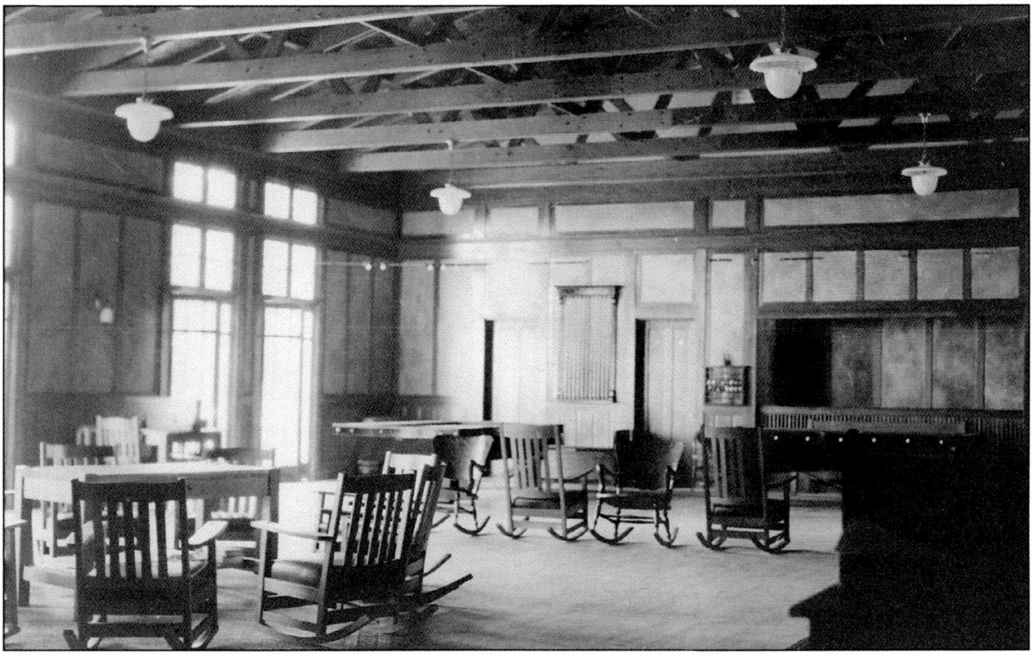

QUINAN INN BALLROOM. This building, now called the Masonic Hall, was a secondary clubhouse and lodging for unmarried men on the technical staff. The TNT Club that met here sponsored social events and dances to the accompaniment of the TNT jazz band and other live bands. A Victrola and piano also afforded musical entertainment. (Courtesy Ashland Inc.)

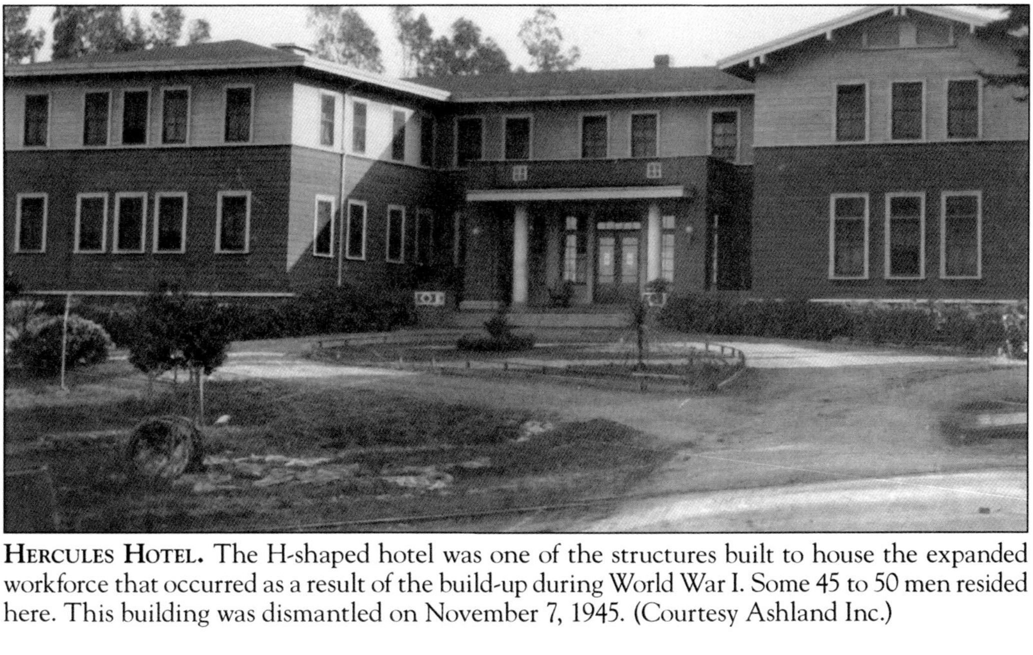

HERCULES HOTEL. The H-shaped hotel was one of the structures built to house the expanded workforce that occurred as a result of the build-up during World War I. Some 45 to 50 men resided here. This building was dismantled on November 7, 1945. (Courtesy Ashland Inc.)

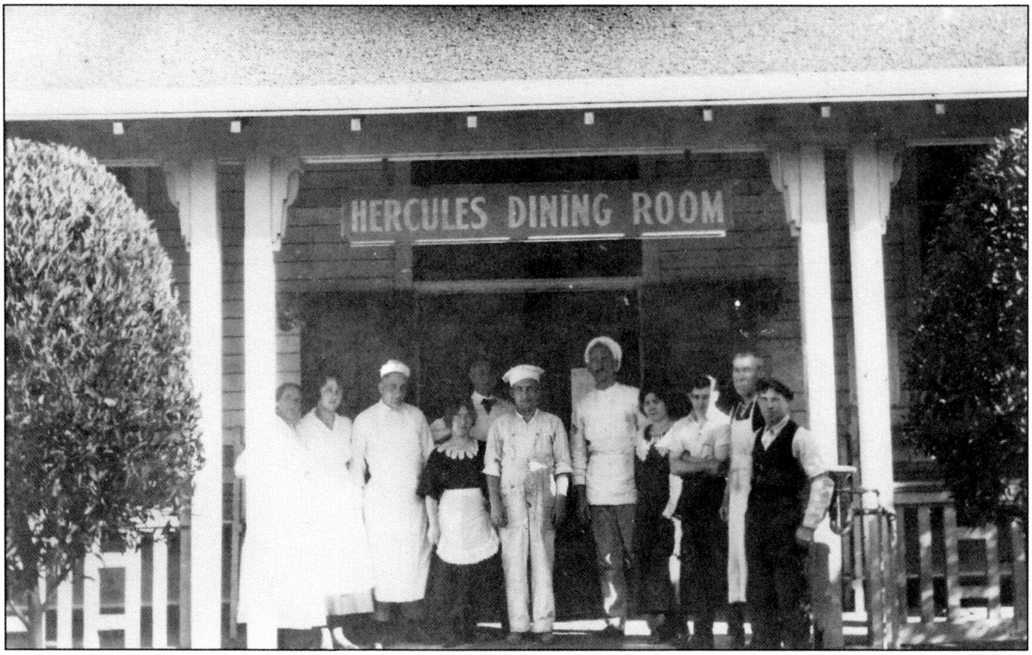

Hercules Dining Room. The staff poses at the long one-story dining room that once stood opposite the clubhouse. Three chefs prepared hundreds of meals each day during the World War I years. There were also cooks and wait staff employed in the boarding house and some of the private homes in Hercules. (Courtesy Ashland Inc.)

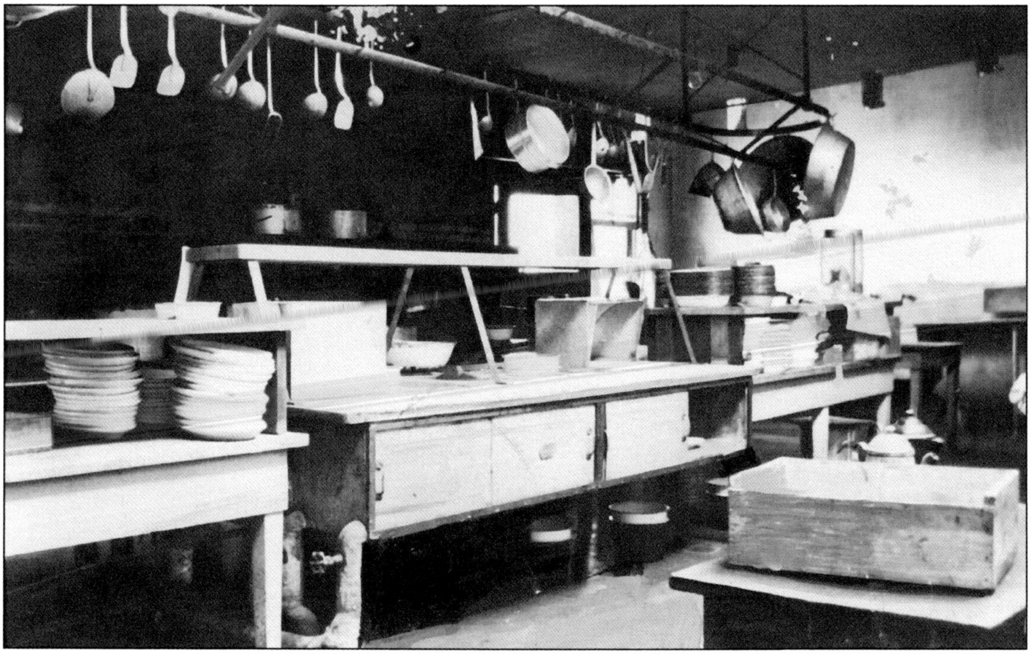

Kitchen, 1920. This large kitchen is believed to have been in the Hercules dining room, which had state-of-the-art dishwashing equipment, a refrigerating plant, and waste incinerator. Laborers working at the plant in the World War I era were offered meals at $1 per day. (Courtesy Ashland Inc.)

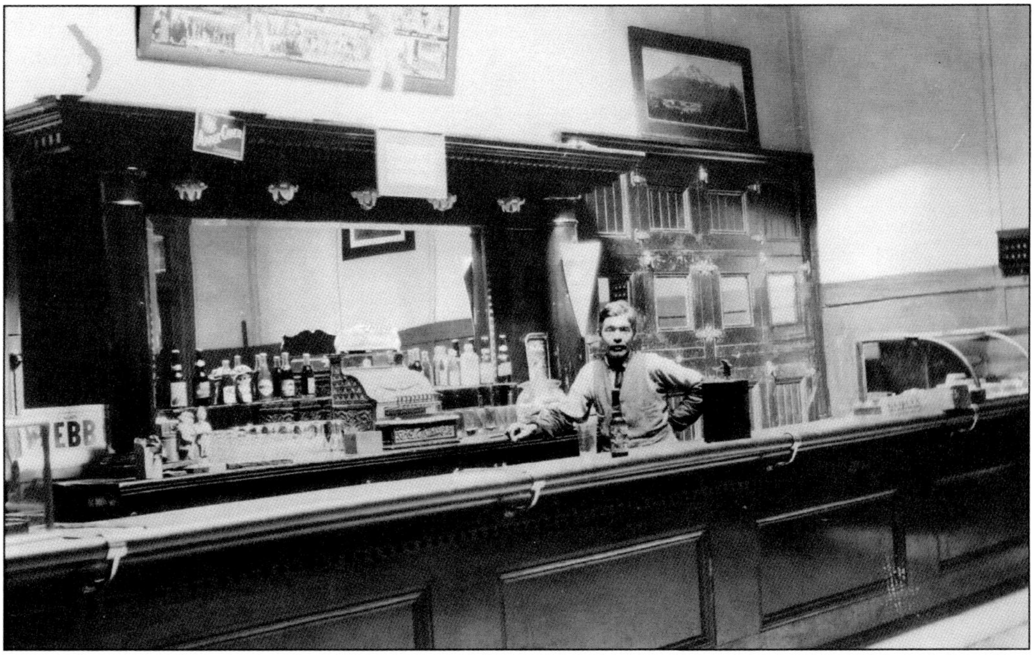

Hercules Club Bar. Club members operated the clubhouse, the social center of the town. This image was made before the Prohibition era, when sales of alcoholic beverages were outlawed. Deductions were made from wages or salary to cover bar tabs. The bar was refurbished when the clubhouse was restored in the 1980s. (Courtesy Ashland Inc.)

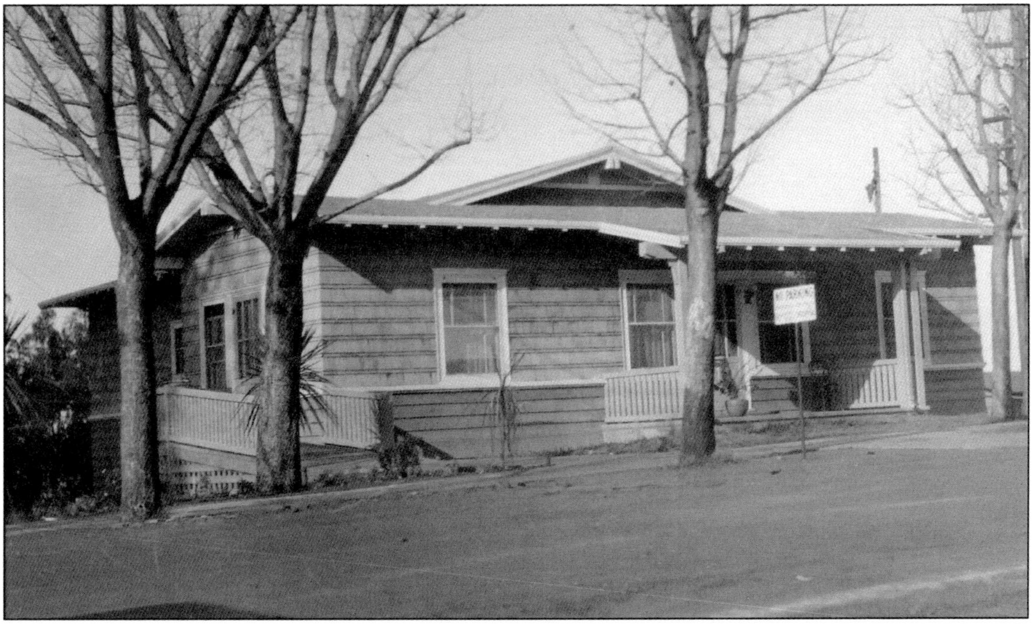

Plant Hospital. Hercules hospital was one of the first industrial hospitals in California with a resident physician and X-ray equipment. During the Great War when the plant was running at full capacity there were two physicians on duty and one nurse. Dr. Charles Wetmore was in charge. The hospital closed around 1929. In the late 1970s, the police department, with an address of 575 Railroad Avenue, was located here. (Courtesy Ashland Inc.)

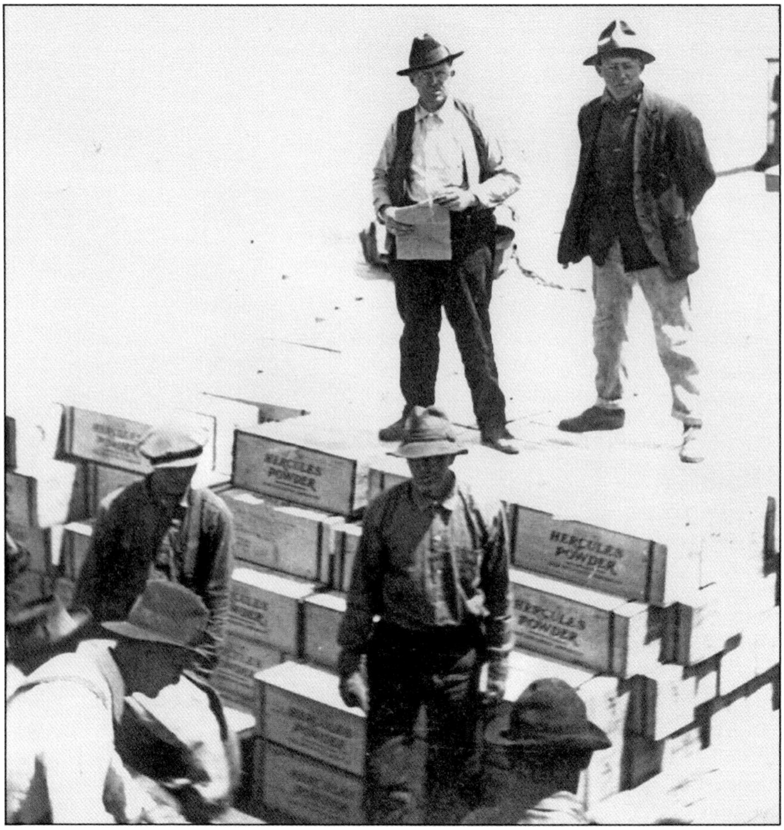

Wharf, 1930s. Hercules dynamite boxes await loading onto a powder barge. The company had a fleet of barges, including 10 built in 1916 at San Francisco's Hanlon shipyards. Barges moved black powder, gelatin, and dynamite to an area of San Francisco Bay designated for transshipment from barges to other ocean-going vessels. A second wharf was used for general freight and niter. (Courtesy Hercules Historical Society.)

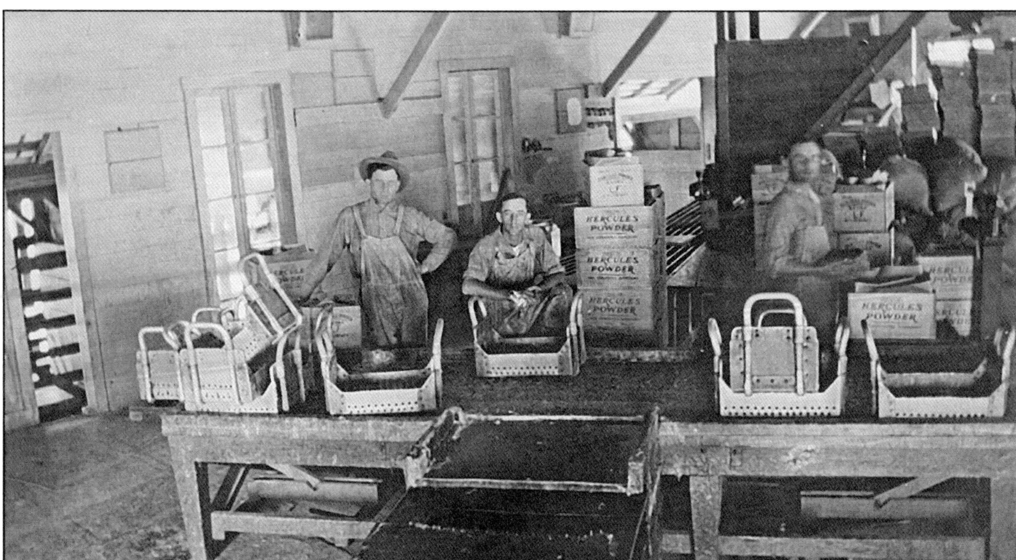

Packinghouse. Dynamite cartridges or sticks were crated in wax paper–lined cases of 25 to 50 pounds. The dynamite was packed in paper shells that were printed, rolled, cut, and treated with paraffin. The fiber or wood for boxes was purchased, cut to the proper sizes, and printed and assembled at the Hercules box factory. (Courtesy Contra Costa County Historical Society.)

RALPH ROBISON, MASTER MECHANIC. In 1898, Ralph Robison graduated from the Van der Naillen School of Electricity and Engineering in San Francisco. The next year, California Powder Works engaged him to install the first electricity at the plant. He remained as plant engineer, and in 1937, he received patent No. 2,097,080 for a shell-filling machine. He and colleague Chauncey Ingalls also operated the first moving picture show and skating pavilion in Pinole. (Courtesy Ashland Inc.)

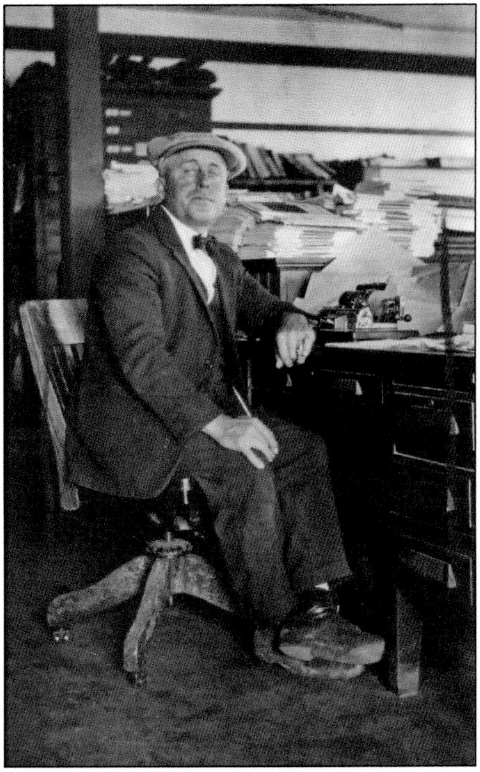

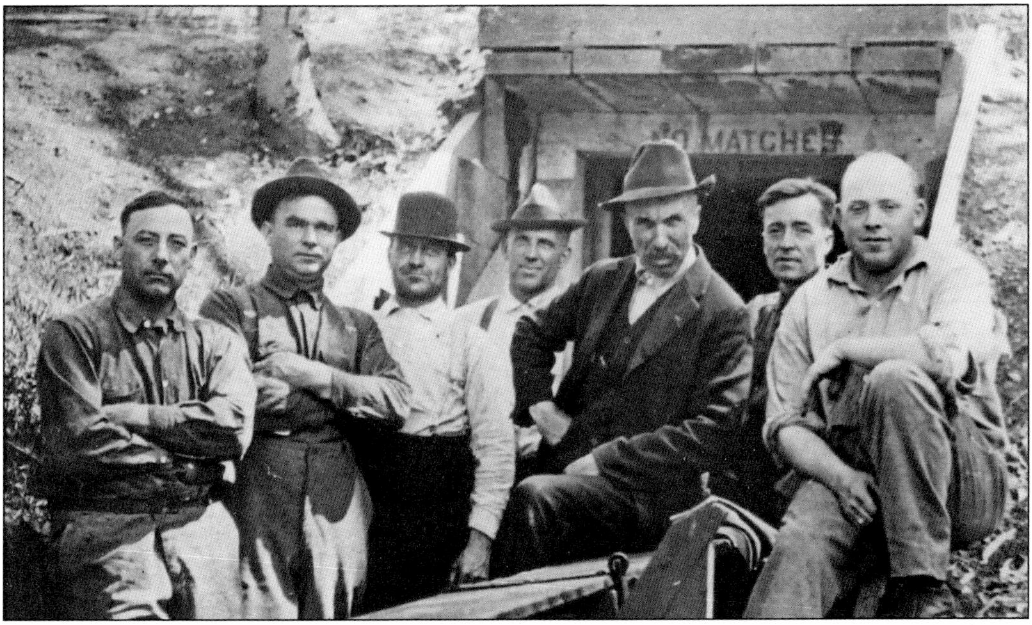

DYNAMITE CREW, C. 1919. From left to right are Tom Aspland, Fred Nunemann, Joe McAndrews, unidentified, Peter McClennan, George Blakemore, and Roy Le Febvre. Timbers and earthworks buffer the magazine in the background to limit damage to other buildings should there be an explosion. McClellan narrowly escaped death in March 1892 when 4,000 pounds of nitroglycerine exploded. (Courtesy Contra Costa County Historical Society.)

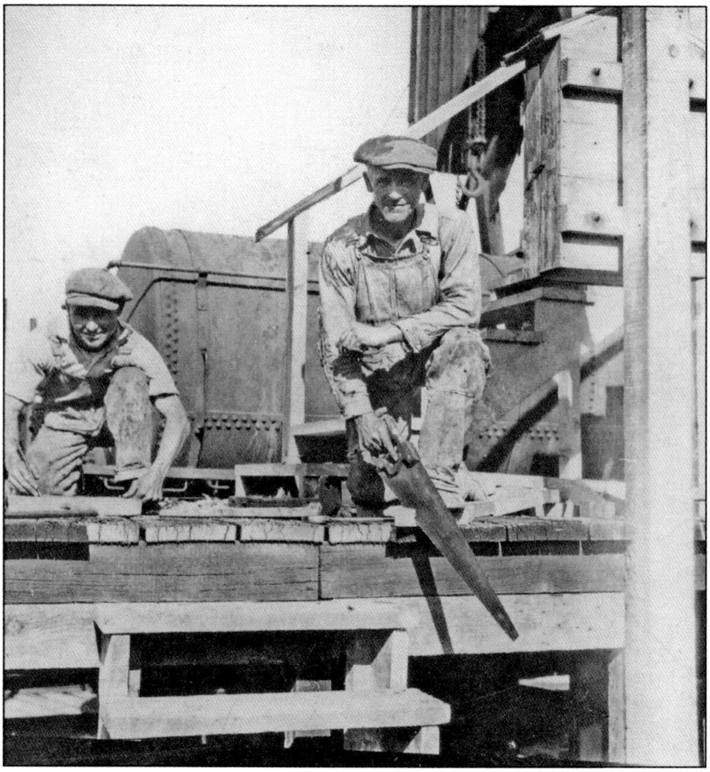

CARPENTERS, 1927. Two unidentified workmen pose for an official publicity photograph. In the age before electric tools, carpenters used handsaws. (Courtesy Ashland Inc.)

DUST HOUSE. Gasoline locomotive operators are switchman Tony Rodriguez at left and Jack Ryan in the cab. By 1924, these locomotives had replaced all of the compressed-air locomotives. The dust mill is where sulfur and charcoal are pulverized together to make "dust," one of the components of explosives. (Courtesy Ashland Inc.)

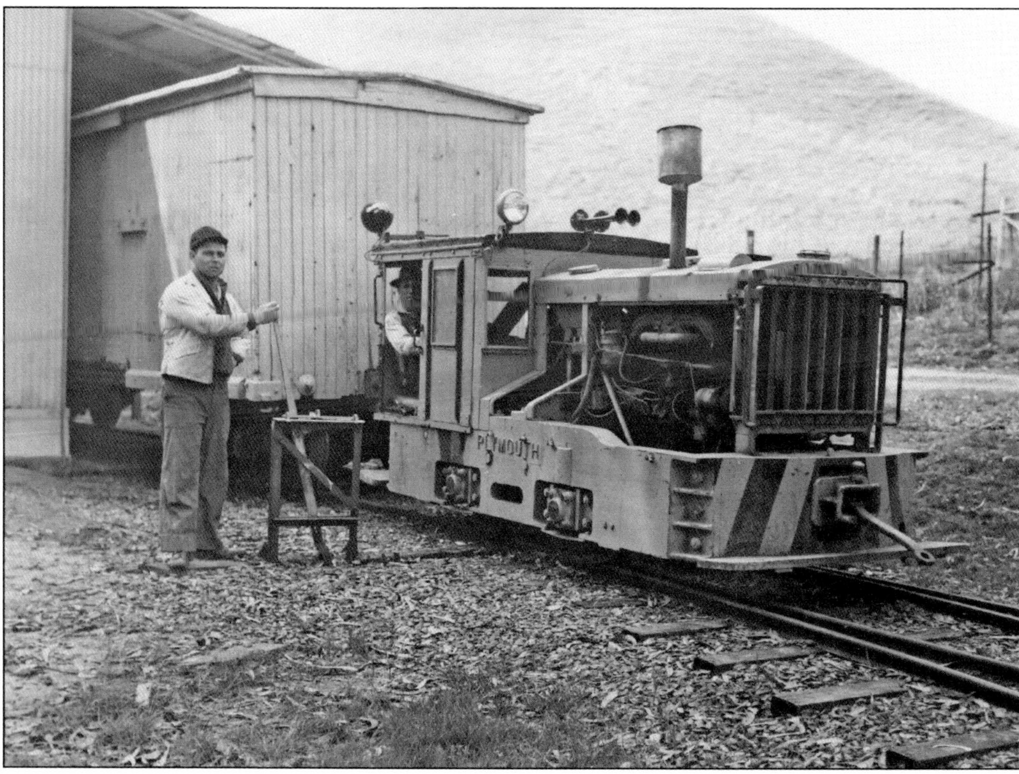

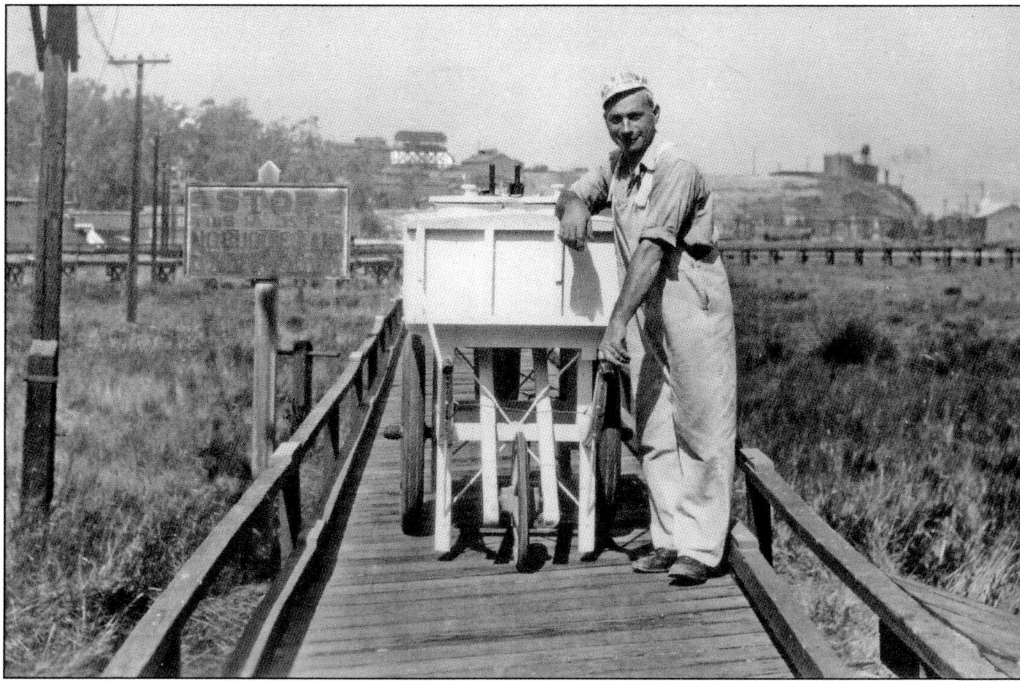

Joe Scarsella, October 1929. Highly unstable nitroglycerin was moved in a cart with two compartments in which nitroglycerin was held in suspension. One worker explained, "We called 'em angel buggies cause one sharp bump and that's what you'd be." At the mixing house, the operator poured nitroglycerin into a mixing machine by means of the rubber tube attached to the buggy. This spot is now the waterfront residential neighborhood of Hercules. (Courtesy Ashland Inc.)

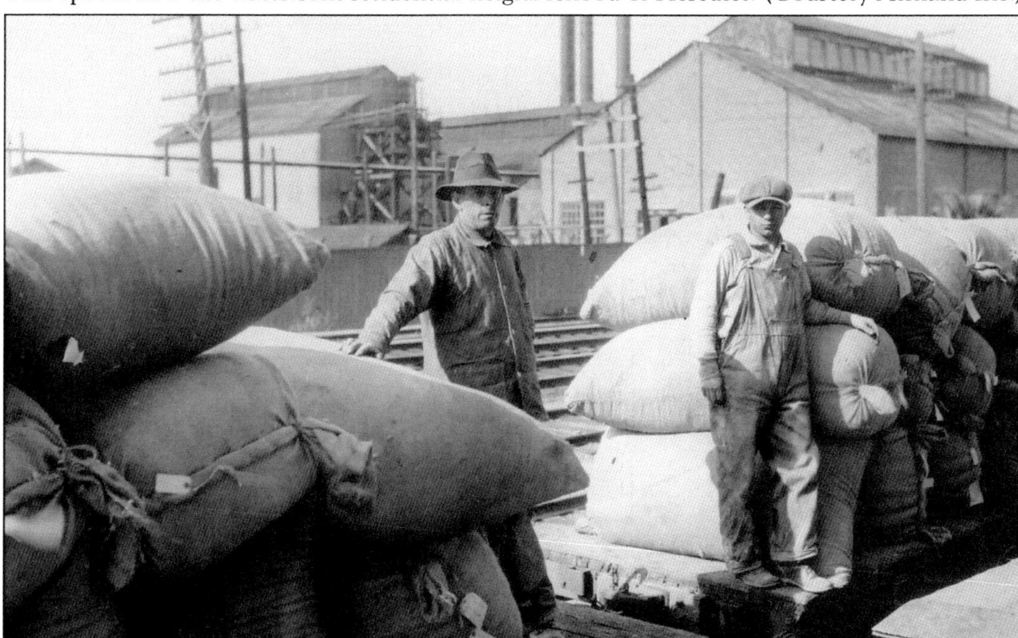

Ammonium Nitrate, 1929. Workers pose with bags each containing about 90 pounds of ammonium nitrate, colloquially known as "bag ass." (Courtesy Ashland Inc.)

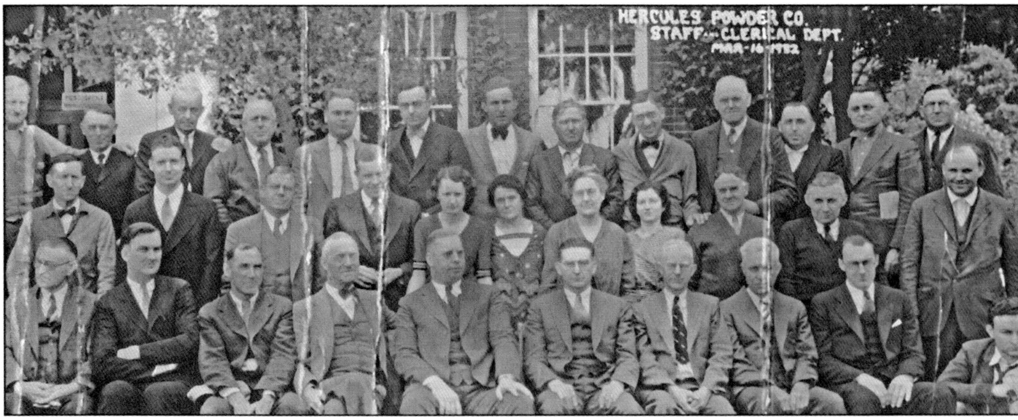

STAFF AND CLERICAL DEPARTMENT, 1932. The staff posed on March 16 outside the main office. Standing, fourth from left, is Ralph Robison. Seated in the middle row, fifth from left, is Mary Lucid. Annie Ellerhorst is seventh from left. (Courtesy Nancy M. Tooker.)

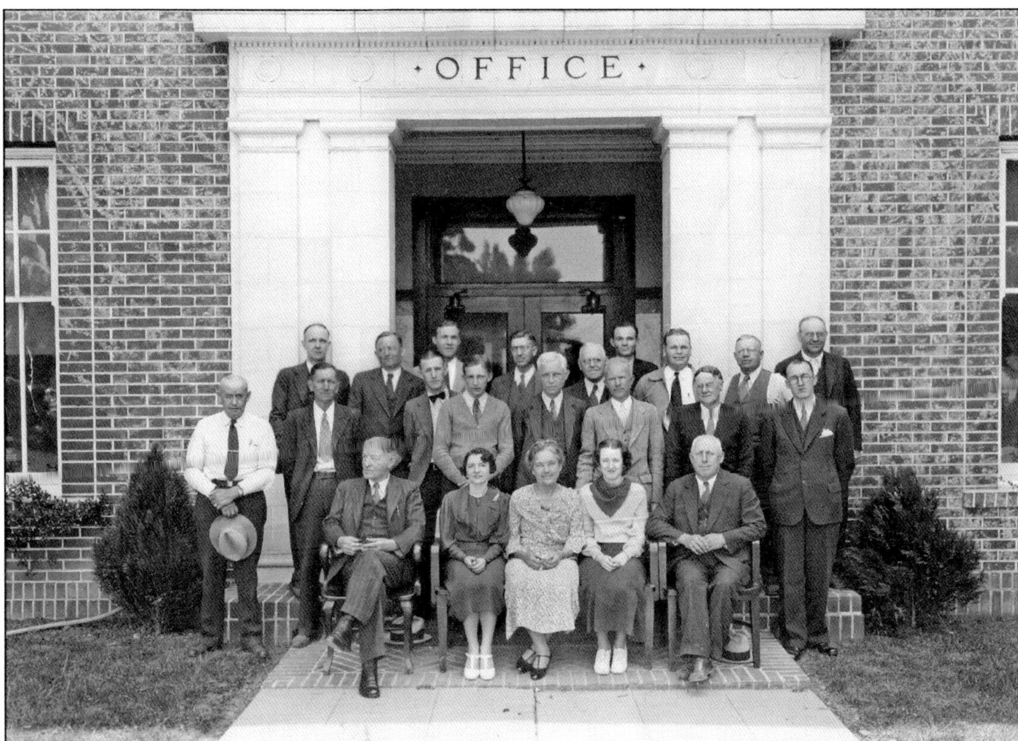

ADMINISTRATIVE OFFICE PERSONNEL, 1930S. Seated third from left is Annie Ellerhorst, fourth is Mary Lucid, and fifth is Ralph Robison, engineer. At far left is Frank Maderos, holding a hat. Ellerhorst hails from the family living on a ranch in Hercules that predates the powder company. Lucid was employed at the plant from 1929 to 1973; her father worked at Hercules for 39 years. Maderos worked at Hercules for 38 years. (Courtesy Lucid-Bender family.)

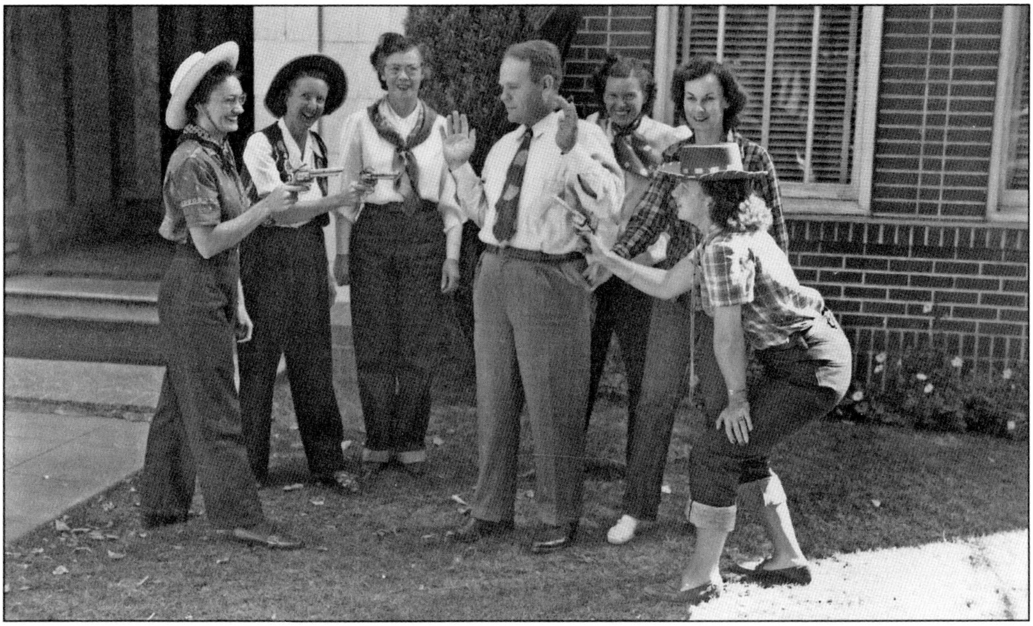

Contra Costa Day. The office staff dressed for Contra Costa Day at the Golden Gate International Exposition, held at Treasure Island in 1939 and 1940. The fair followed the opening of the San Francisco-Oakland Bay Bridge in 1936 and the Golden Gate Bridge in 1937. Pat Butler is being "held up." Lois Scarsella is at far right, and above her hat is Ruth Moses, second from right. (Courtesy of Hercules Historical Society.)

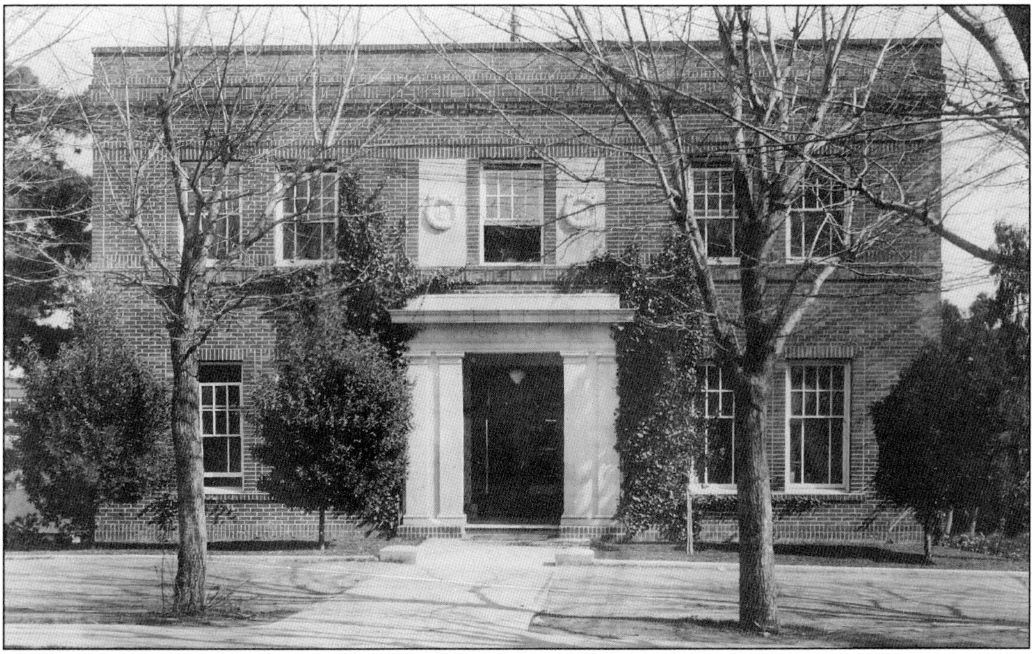

Offices, 1925. This two-story and basement building sat on a hill overlooking the northernmost plant area. At the time it was constructed in 1918, it was the largest office among the Hercules Powder Company plants. On either side above the marble-sheathed entry, two terra cotta wreaths encircle the initial "H." The building is currently in private ownership. (Courtesy Ashland Inc.)

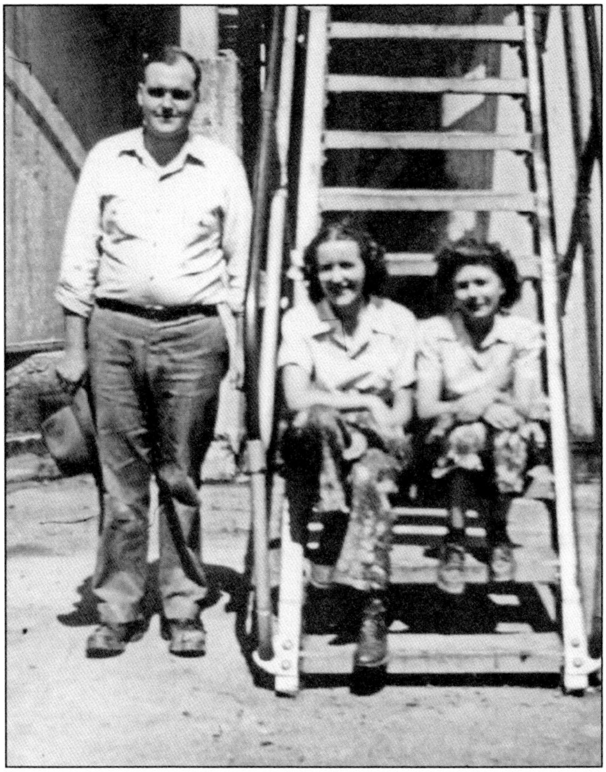

Acid Plant, 1943. Bob Bell, Marian Bullock, and Irene Silcock pose at the acid plant. Bullock's father was a supervisor at the plant, while Silcock's father was a pipefitter. After completing high school, these two joined the plant workforce. Irene Silcock worked at both the acid and oxidation plants. At that time, many men were away at war. (Courtesy Family of Irene Silcock Dias.)

Ammonia Plant Compressor. At left is Roger Reeder, at right is Charles Lenz, and at back (partially hidden) is John Classick at work on a seven-stage air compressor. Construction began in 1939 on this compressor for the commercial-scale ammonia synthesis plant. Not pictured is the photographer, Larry Ingalls, who wrote the ammonia plant maintenance manual. (Courtesy William Ingalls.)

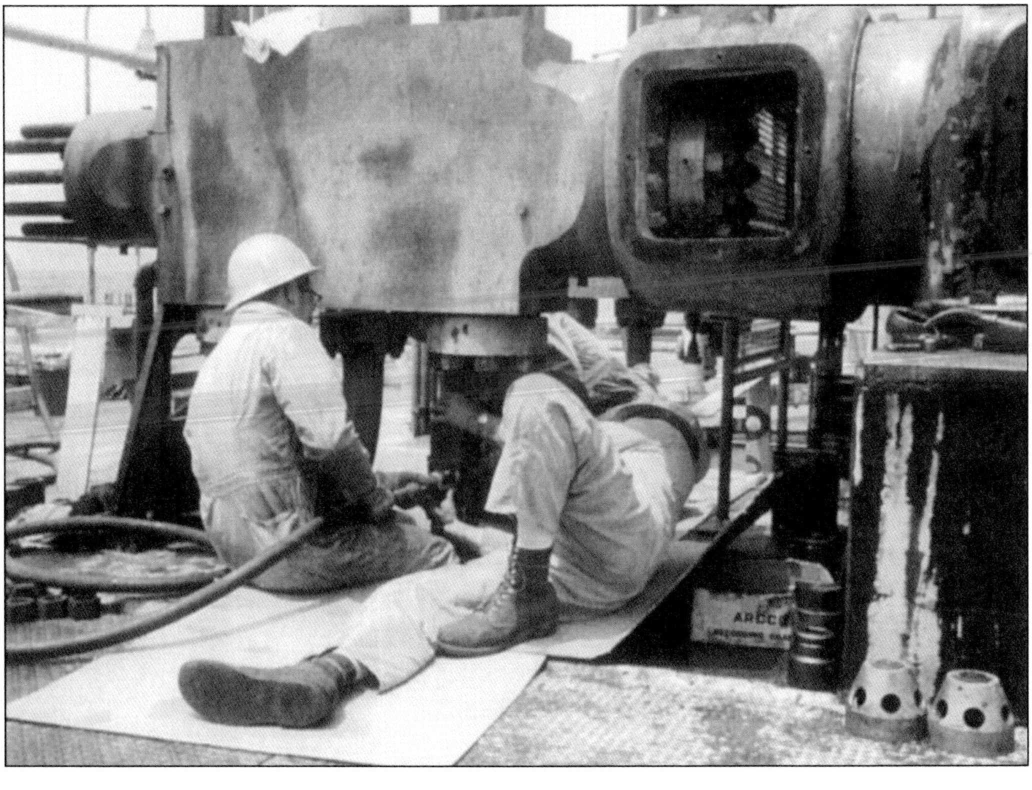

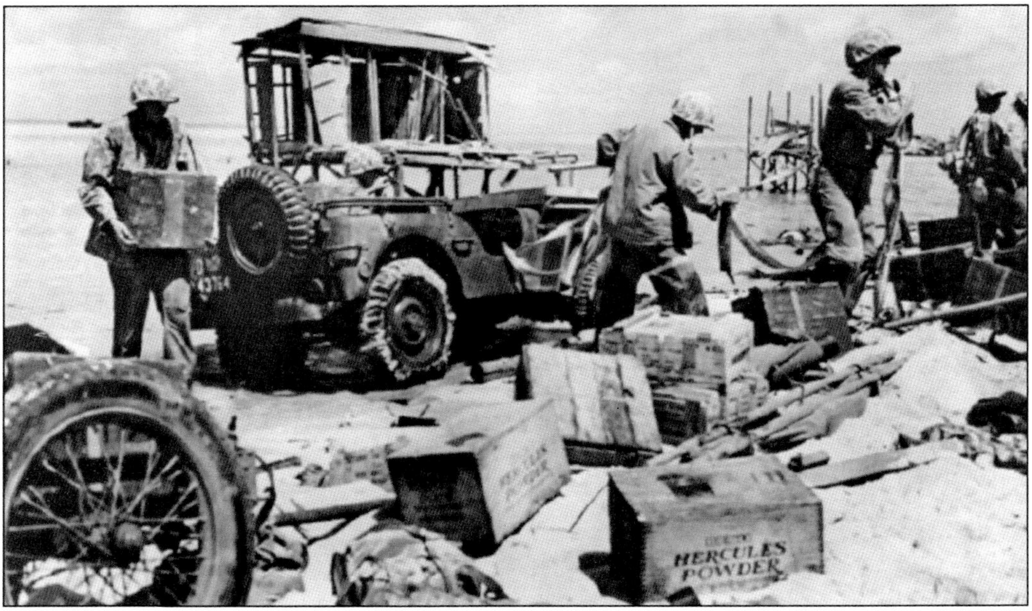

BATTLE OF TARAWA, 1943. US Navy and Marines fought a grueling 76-hour battle in November for a Japanese stronghold during which more than 5,000 soldiers died. The Allies rebuilt the airbase after the battle. This image at Tarawa Atoll accompanied an article in the *Hercules Mixer* that boasted more than 1.8 billion pounds of ordnance materials were supplied to the armed forces by Hercules owned or operated plants during World War II. (Courtesy Hercules Historical Society.)

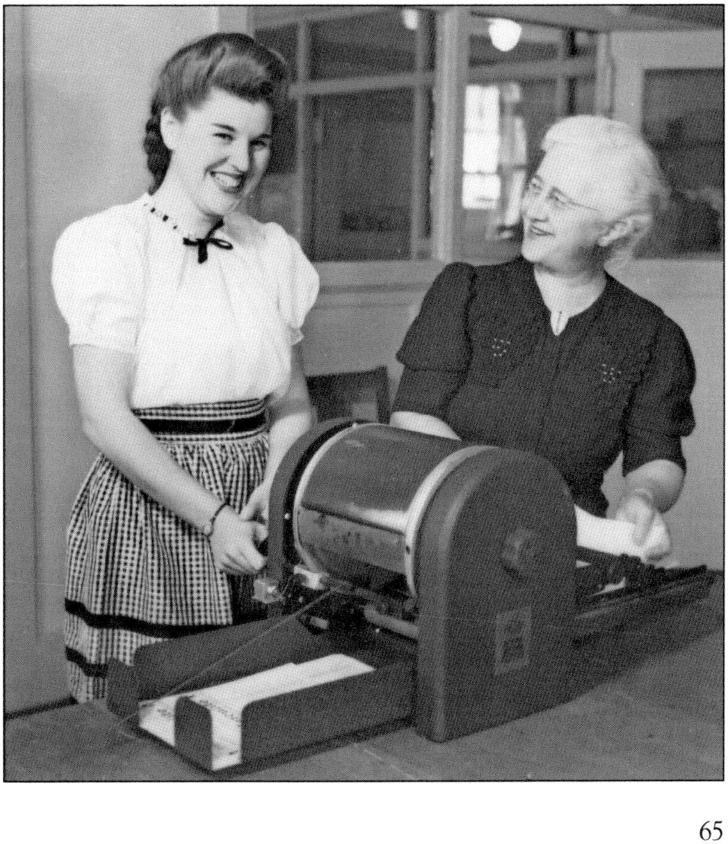

EMPLOYEE NEWSPAPER, SEPTEMBER 1944. LaVerne Lewis (left) and assistant editor Goldie Sill (right) roll out the mimeographed employee newspaper, the *Herculite*, edited by Gilbert E. Cain. It had a circulation of 350 copies, including one that was flown to China for delivery to Lt. Stewart Brown, a former plant employee. The *Herculite* was one of 14 newspapers issued at plants around the country. (Courtesy Ashland Inc.)

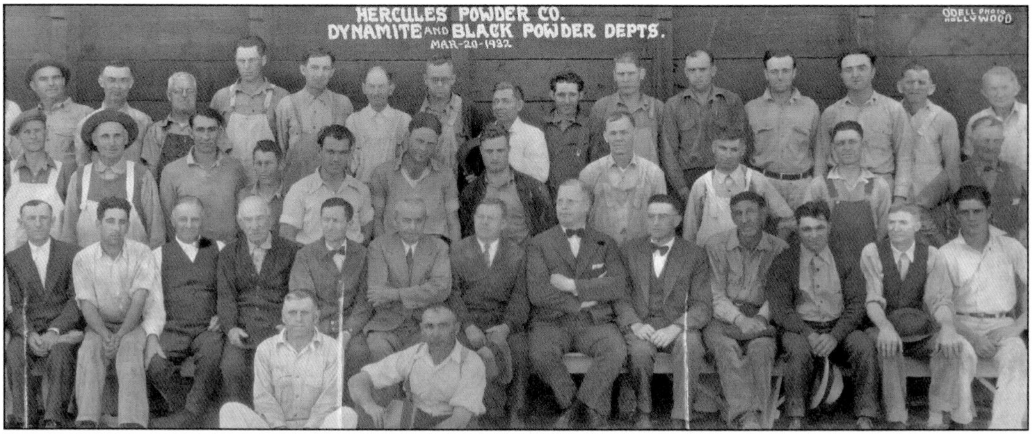

Dynamite and Black Powder Departments, 1932. Garrie Metz, wearing suspenders, sits at center with hat in hand. Frank Maderos sits behind him with his arms crossed. The names of the others were not recorded. Hercules Powder employment dipped to its lowest level and a four-day week the year this photograph was made. Dolan Lumber Company razed 50 vacant buildings at the plant in 1930 during the slowdown. (Courtesy Jennifer Posedel.)

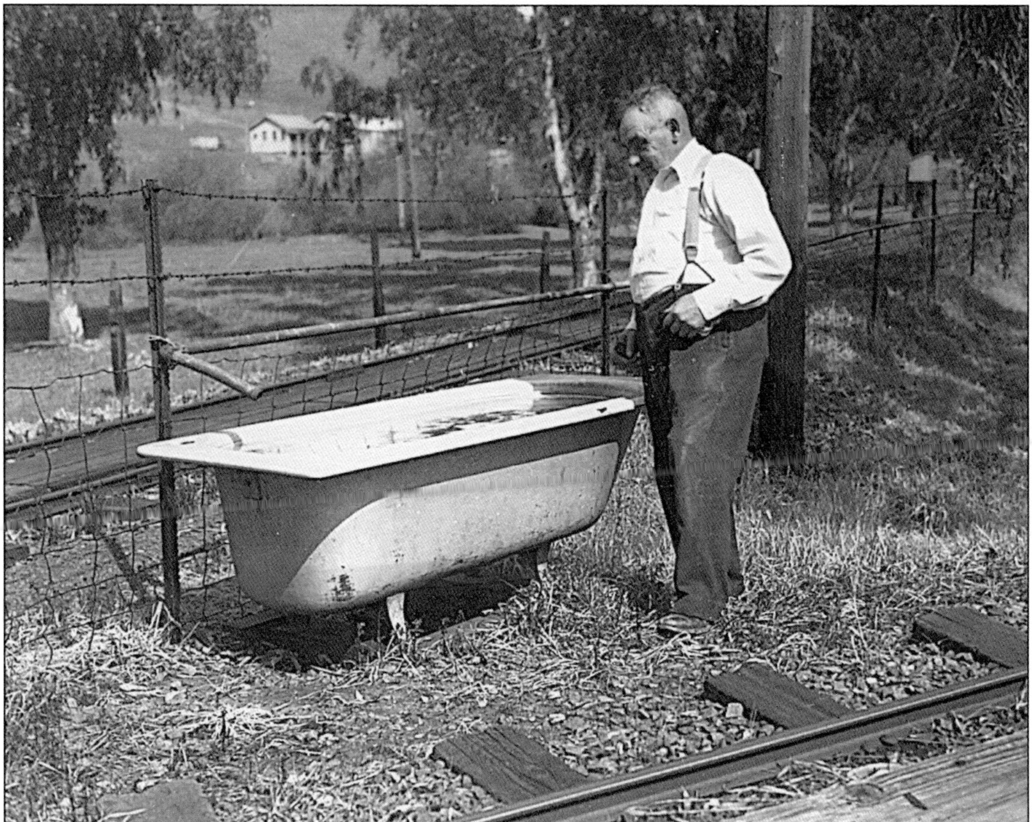

Refugio Valley, 1947. Garrie Metz inspects a bathtub for a publicity photograph. The caption in the employee magazine read, "The bathtubs, strategically located, are kept filled with water and are for use in case of fires." In the background are some of the buildings at the black powder line, also known as Plant B. (Courtesy Ashland Inc.)

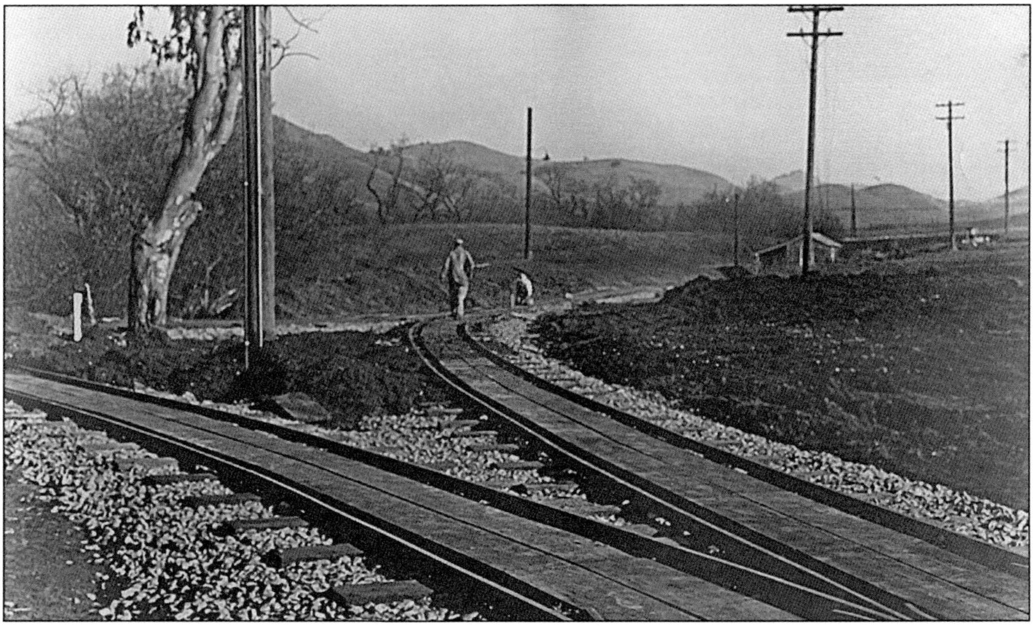

Narrow Gauge Rail, 1947. At the center of the track is a wheeling walk, which provided a smooth path along which to move handcarts. One of the men making repairs is Garrie Metz. The other is unidentified. When the extensive narrow gauge track was dismantled, some of it was sold to the Walt Disney Company. This view looks toward the hills in Rodeo Valley above Highway 4. (Courtesy Ashland Inc.)

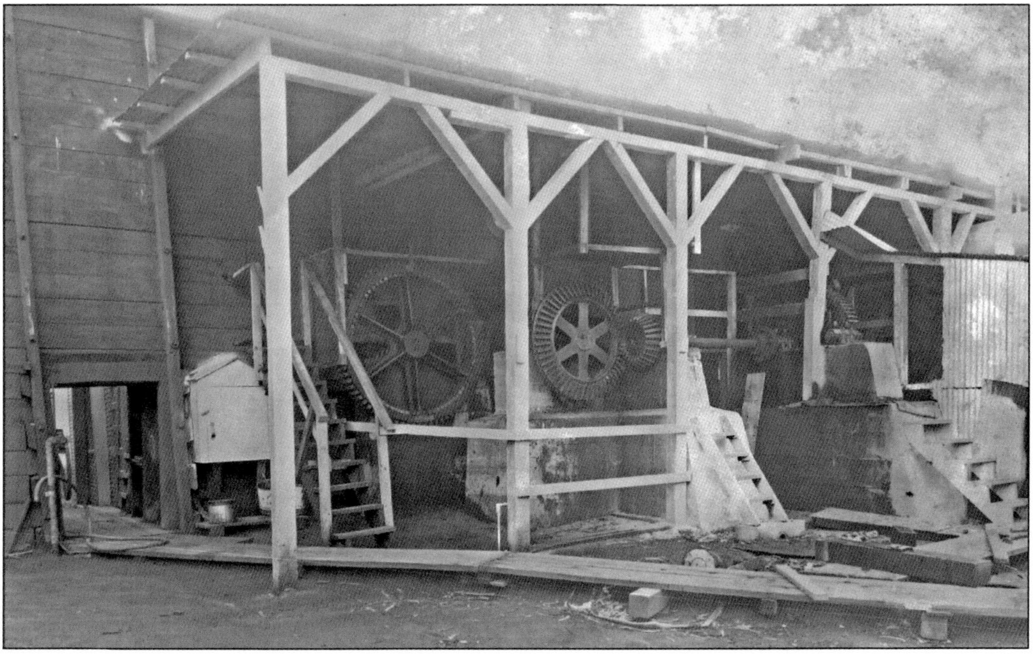

Black Powder Glaze Mill. Machine drives were located outside the building to reduce the possibility of fires. The black powder plant exploded in 1936 when it was hit by lightning and again in 1955 when it was being operated by remote control. No one was injured in either blast. (Courtesy Hercules Historical Society.)

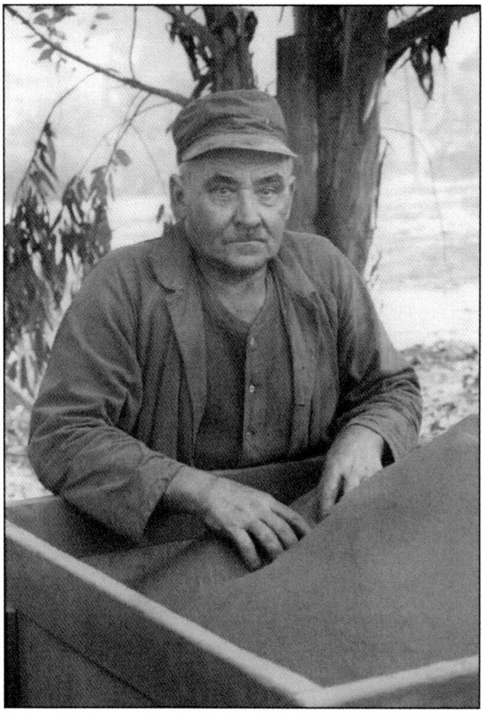

Garrie Metz, Powder Maker, 1943. In 1907, when Metz began working for the California Powder Works at Santa Cruz, black powder was said to be the leading commercial explosive. Metz was transferred to Hercules in 1914. In a 40-year career, every batch of black powder Metz made was said to be perfect. At its peak, Hercules operated nine black powder plants. (Courtesy Ashland Inc.)

Black Powder Foreman, 1947. Harold Green, who worked at the plant for 32 years, conducts a burn speed test on a batch of black powder. The powder, originally developed for use in firearms, was modified for use as a blasting powder in quarries, in construction, and as a component of fireworks. "Black," as it was known, was one of three products produced at Hercules in 1947, but it was dropped from the product line in 1955. (Courtesy Ashland Inc.)

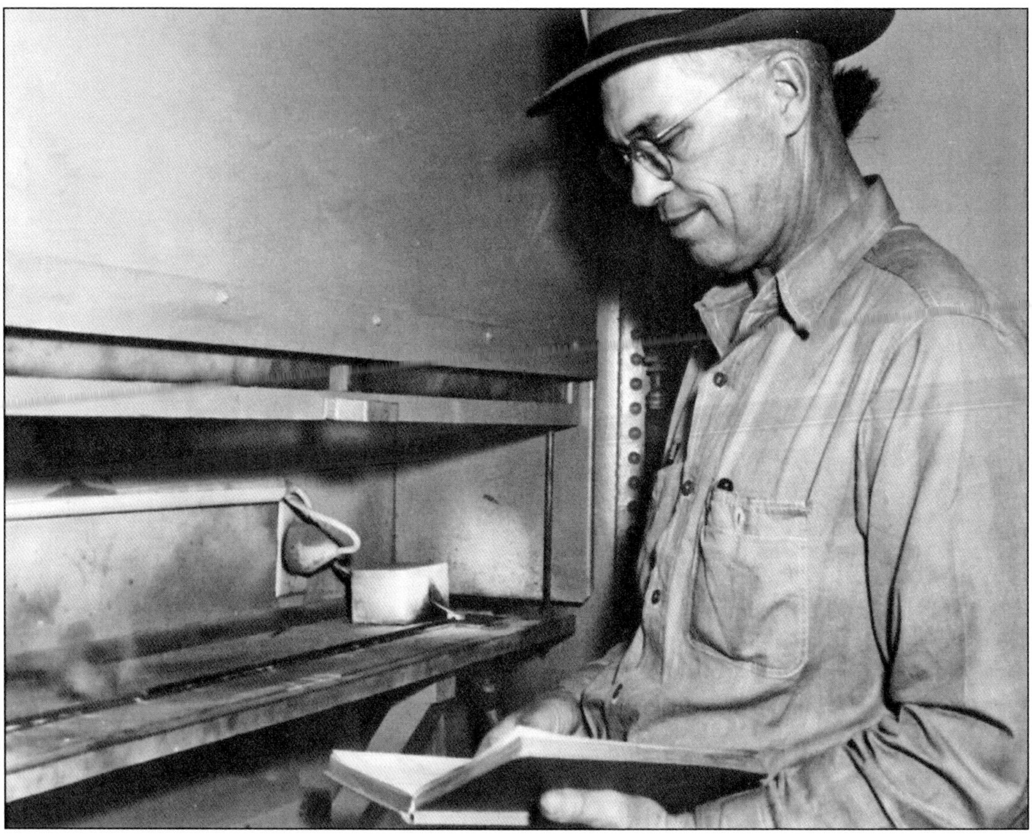

Pack House, 1947. On his last day of work following 40 years of service, Garrie Metz (at left) visits with pack house operator Manuel Nunes. (Courtesy Ashland Inc.)

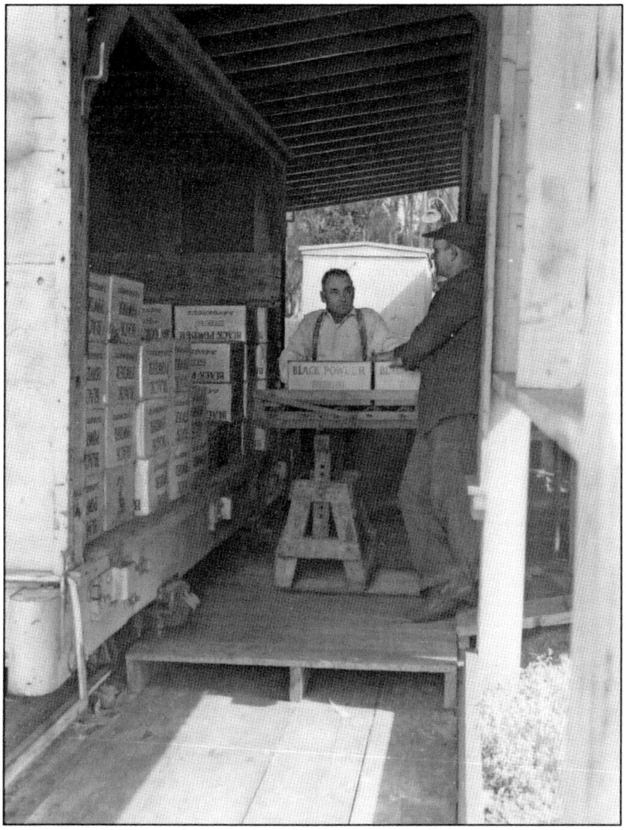

Retired Equipment. A 20-ton black powder press formerly at Refugio Valley and Falcon Way was installed at Point Pinole Regional Park, the site of the former Giant Powder Company. The press is on loan from the Hercules Historical Society. Remains of blast barriers can also be seen at the park. The Point Pinole Regional Shoreline is a California Registered Historical Landmark. (Courtesy East Bay Regional Park District Archives.)

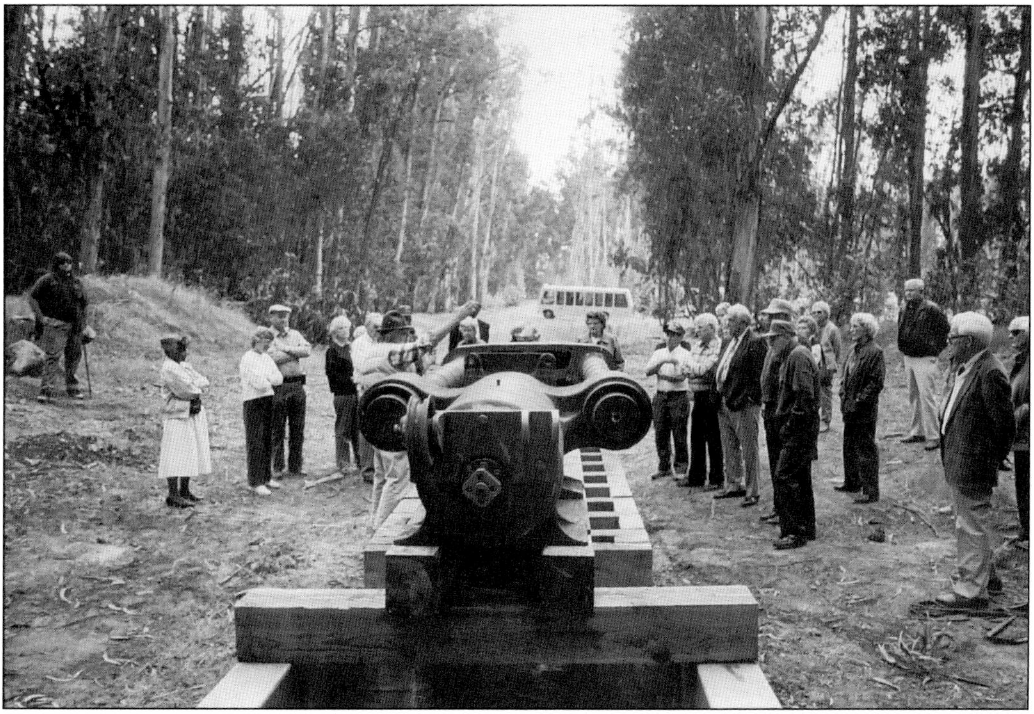

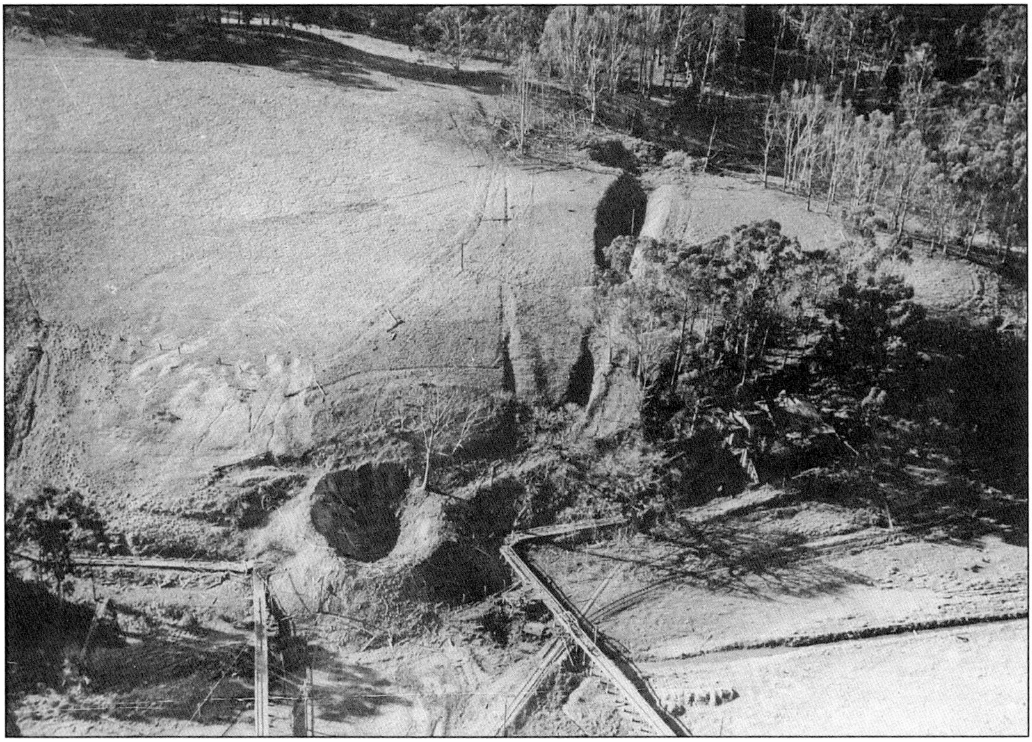

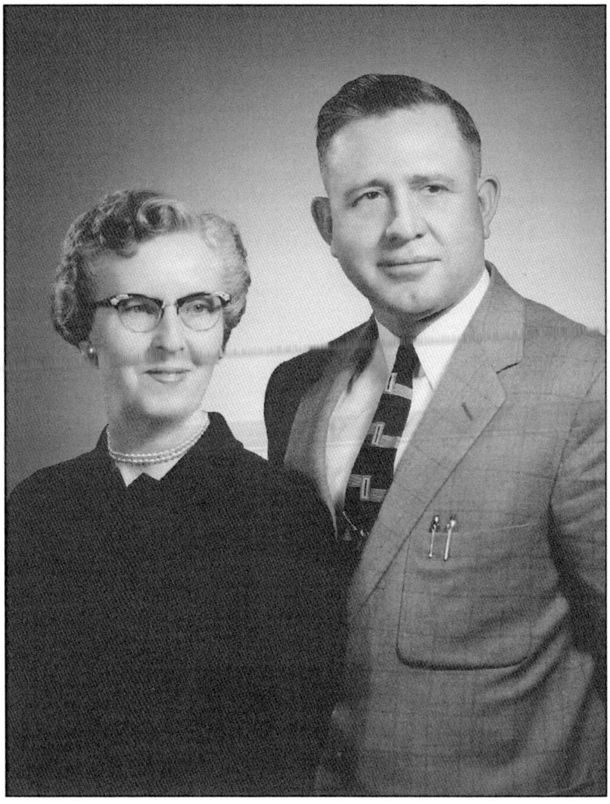

Blast Pits, 1944. The December 9, 1944 blast, felt 20 miles away, vaporized a nitroglycerine neutralizer and storage house, leaving the two deep craters shown here. The concussion stripped the trees and destroyed everything around it. The two victims who worked at this location, Louis Saph, 31, and Andrew J. Hutt, 39, were never found. A survivor said the force of the explosion "pulled the air out" of his lungs. (Courtesy William Ingalls.)

Alice and Tom Reedy. Standing 500 feet from the nitroglycerine storage building that exploded in 1944, Tom sustained serious injury. Alice was at home on Santa Fe Avenue, where the blast blew out the windows and doors. Tom received a $3,000 settlement for injuries that disabled him for two years. Years later, the Reedys wrote a book on the history of the California Powder Works at Santa Cruz. (Courtesy Robert Reedy.)

JOHN LEIGHTY, 1913–1948. Just before shift change on June 21, 1948, John Leighty, who is pictured here, and Roland "Rollie" Buckley perished in an explosion at the nitroglycerine department. The blast triggered a fire that threatened to engulf the entire plant. That same day, an explosion occurred at the Hercules plant at Kenvil, New Jersey, raising fears of sabotage. (Courtesy Darlene Leighty Hasenpflug.)

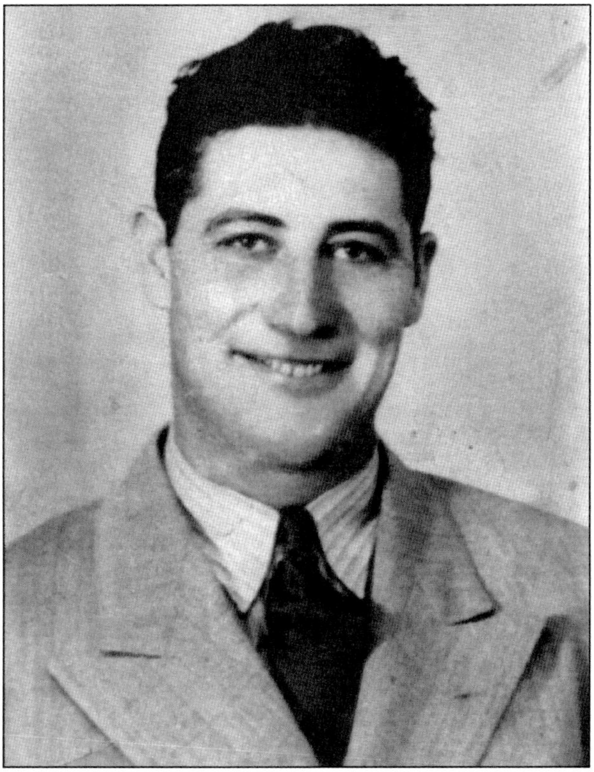

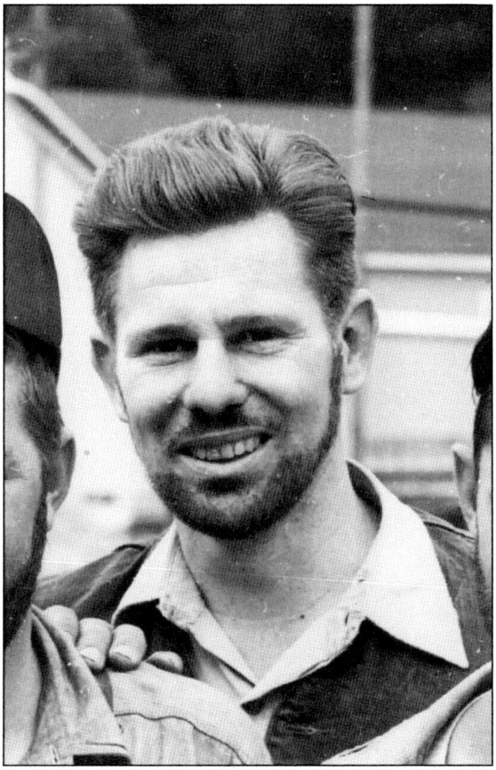

JOHN CLAIR HANSEN, 1915–1953. Hansen, a lead machinist, died as a result of the February 12, 1953, dope house explosion that killed 12 men, leaving 18 children without fathers. The 15-second shock produced a grayish-black mushroom cloud visible 20 miles away. Hansen was a life-long resident of the Pinole-Hercules area and a member of the Oil Workers' Union, CIO, Local 587. He grew the beard for the 1949 Pinole Fiesta. (Courtesy Hercules Historical Society.)

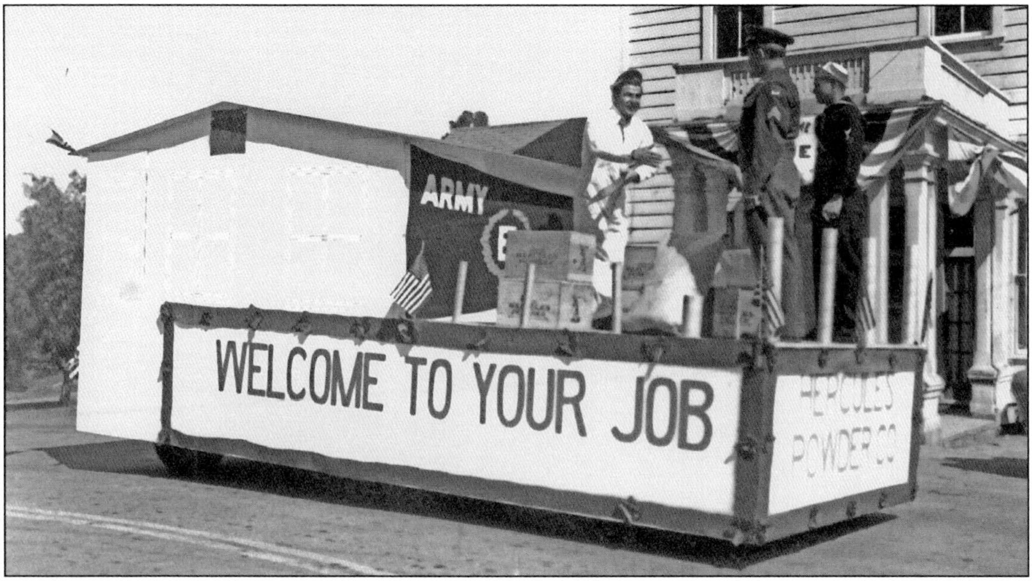

Welcome Home, August 1946. A celebration was held for soldiers and sailors returning to jobs at Hercules Powder. The honorees included the following: Zenon Allen, Leo Albertoni, John Adams Jr., Bryon Bellah, Shirley Barrett, Harry Barnes, Frank Burnham, Clifford Cunningham, Dale Clute, Clarence Chishum, Vernon Chisholm, Jesse Francis, Parley Hopkins, Clyde Mears, Pat Clark, Leo Maderia, Jimmy McCormick, William Redmond, Nestor Rard, Edwin Randall, Fred Sill Jr., Clarence Turner, Wilburn Thatcher, Alvah Westfall, Compton Gault Jr., Jean Hatfield, Jean Woodfield, Dan Bentz, John Conrady, and B.F. Chaney. (Courtesy Hercules Historical Society.)

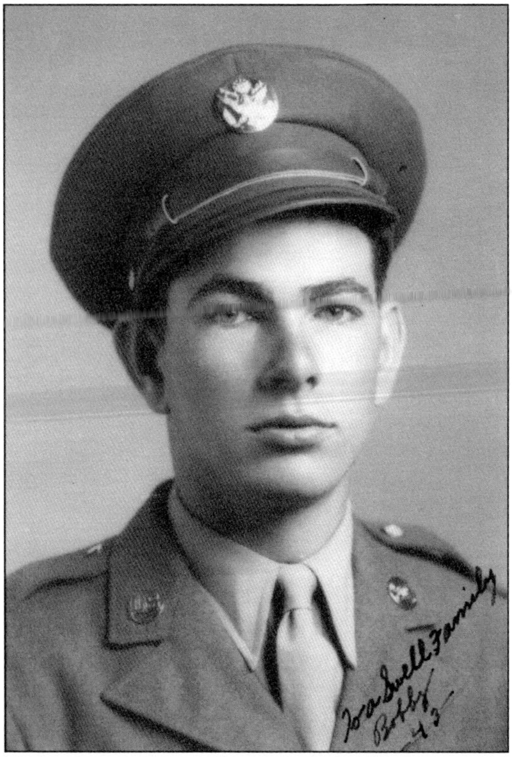

"To a Swell Family, 1943." Bobby Pearce, pictured here, was among those who joined the powder company immediately after the war. Pearce grew up in Hercules and followed his father Albert in a career in the maintenance department, where he rose to the rank of supervisor. Bobby was a D-Day survivor and much admired by the boys who worked with him in his home workshop building racing boats and drag cars. He later served on the Hercules City Council. (Courtesy Barbara Pearce.)

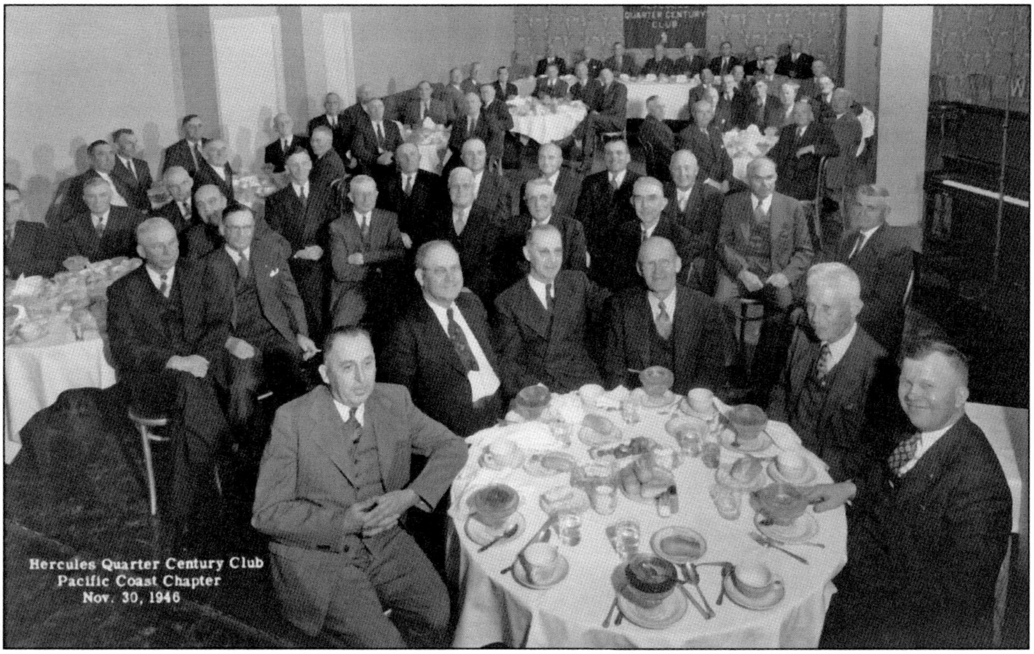

QUARTER CENTURY CLUB, 1946. Men who had worked at the plant for 25 years gathered yearly for a dinner, usually held at a hotel. The Moulin Photo studio took this photograph of the Pacific Coast Chapter on November 30. In subsequent years, the gatherings were held at Pinole's Sportsmen's Club. (Courtesy Lucid-Bender family.)

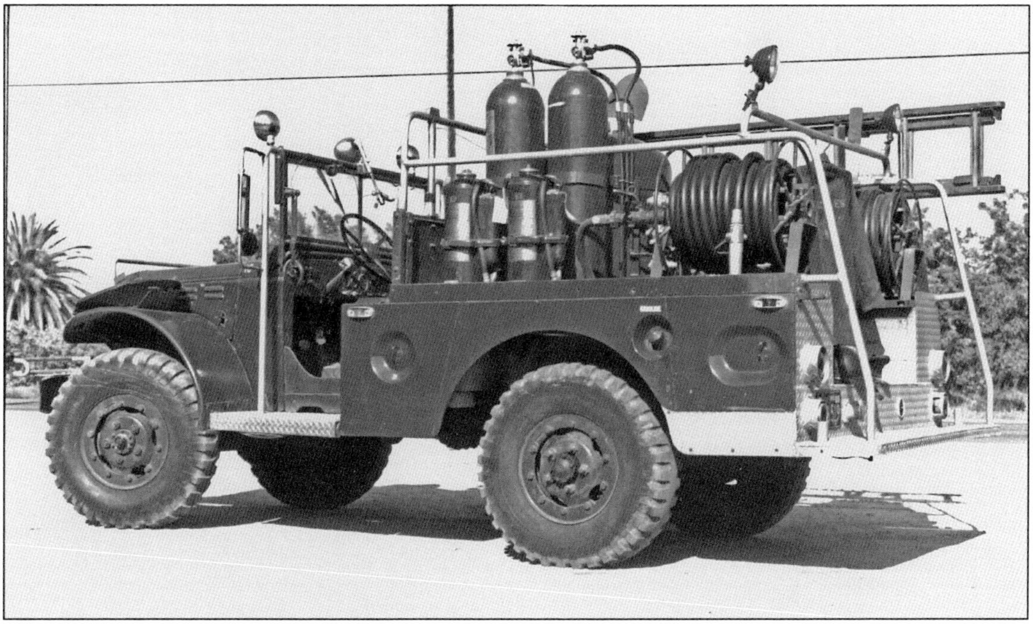

FIRE FIGHTING EQUIPMENT. This equipment was transferred to California from the Sunflower Ordnance Works, an Army Ammunition plant operated by Hercules Incorporated in Kansas during World War II. It was built on a Jeep frame and was modified as a dry chemical fire truck. Following the war, much surplus military equipment was converted to civilian use in schools and fire districts across the country. (Courtesy Ernest Fawcett.)

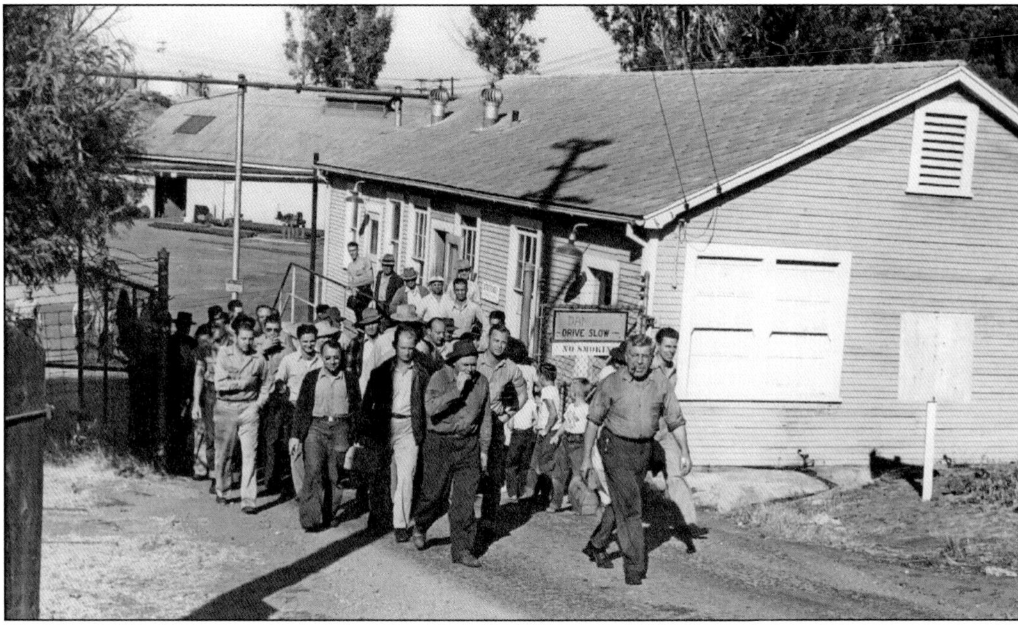

Heading Home, January 1948. Boys, wearing HP Boys Club Local 263 T-shirts, meet their dads at the gate for the walk to their homes in the nearby village. Henry Simon leads the men. Charlie Doidge is in the front with his hand to his mouth. Kenneth Dale Clute wears sunglasses; walking in front of him in a light shirt is Clyde Bartholomew; at far right is John "Jack" Hansen. Once outside the gate, the men were safely able to light their pipes and cigarettes. (Courtesy Ashland Inc.)

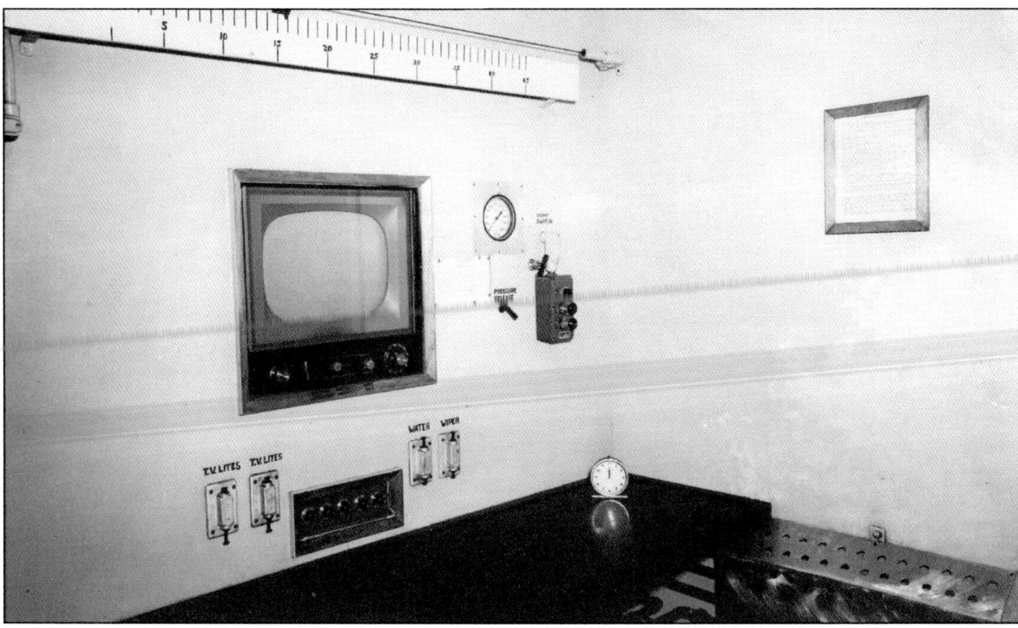

Remote Controls. A safety feature involved the use of televised images, allowing workers to operate machinery from a distance. Buildings where the actual mixing, grinding, and packing of explosives occurred were isolated and buffered to reduce the impact in the event of an explosion. Important characteristics of a powder worker included an ability to observe things that a casual observer might not notice. (Courtesy Contra Costa County Historical Society.)

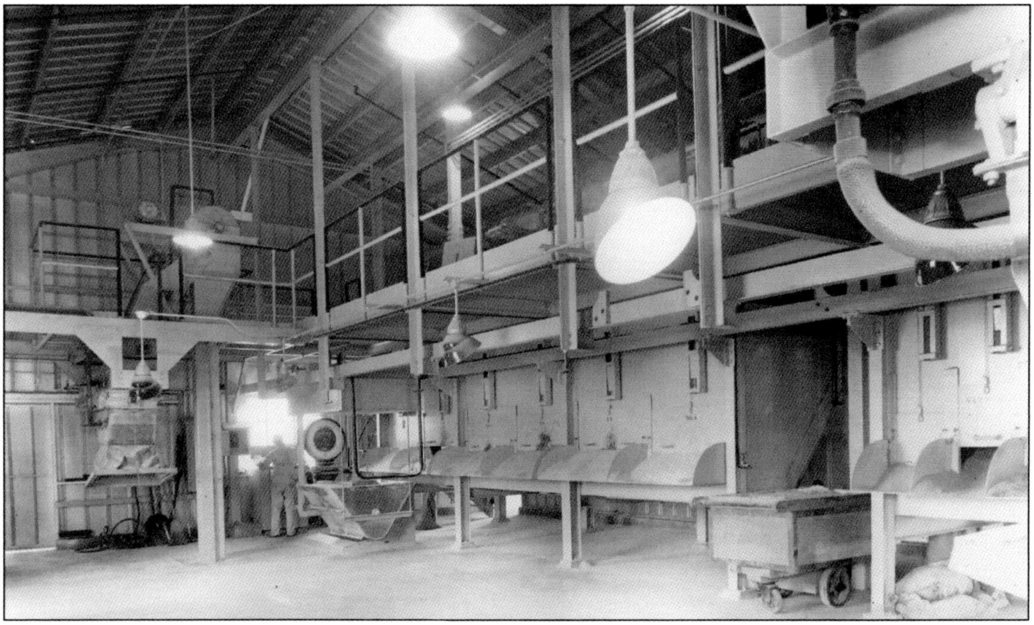

Dope House, 1954. The highly explosive nitroglycerin is mixed with an absorbent substance, called dope, in order to stabilize it. A solitary employee draws and accurately weighs it for mixing. Having no more than two men in the dope house was a safety policy aimed at reducing the number at risk. Pictured is the new building that was constructed after the devastating 1953 explosion. (Courtesy M. Wallace and W. Ryder.)

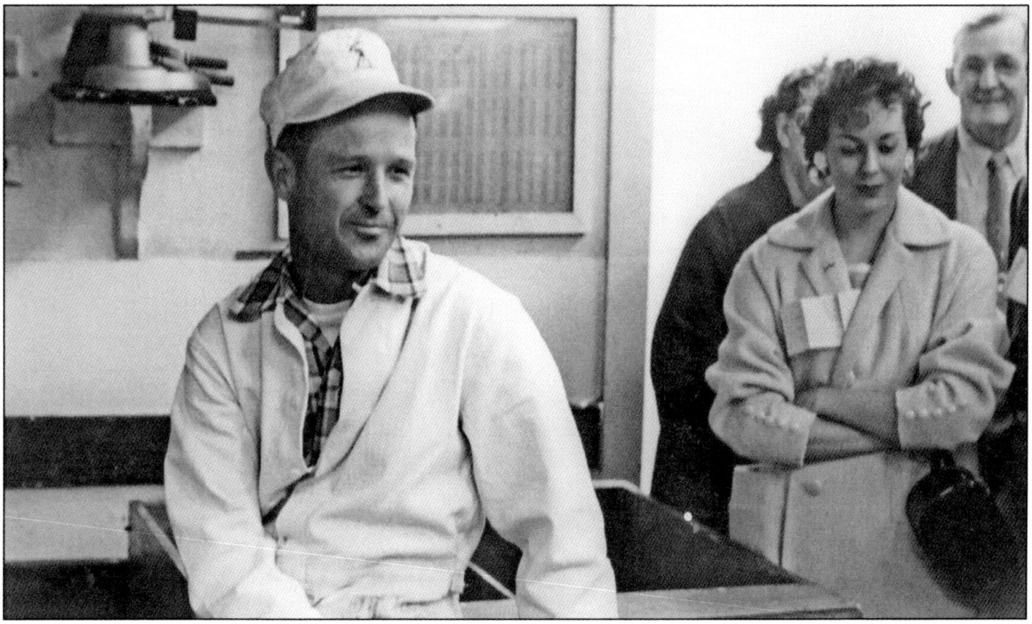

Open House, 1957. Families of the 330 Hercules employees were invited to see all aspects of plant operations during a 3.5-hour tour. Vernon Chisholm wears the specialized coveralls. They had a single pocket on the rear constructed of lattice strips of fabric, so nothing like a pack of matches could be carried without being noticed. Anything flammable was prohibited in the plant. In this photograph, Edna and Mike Taylor stand at the rear. (Courtesy Hercules Historical Society.)

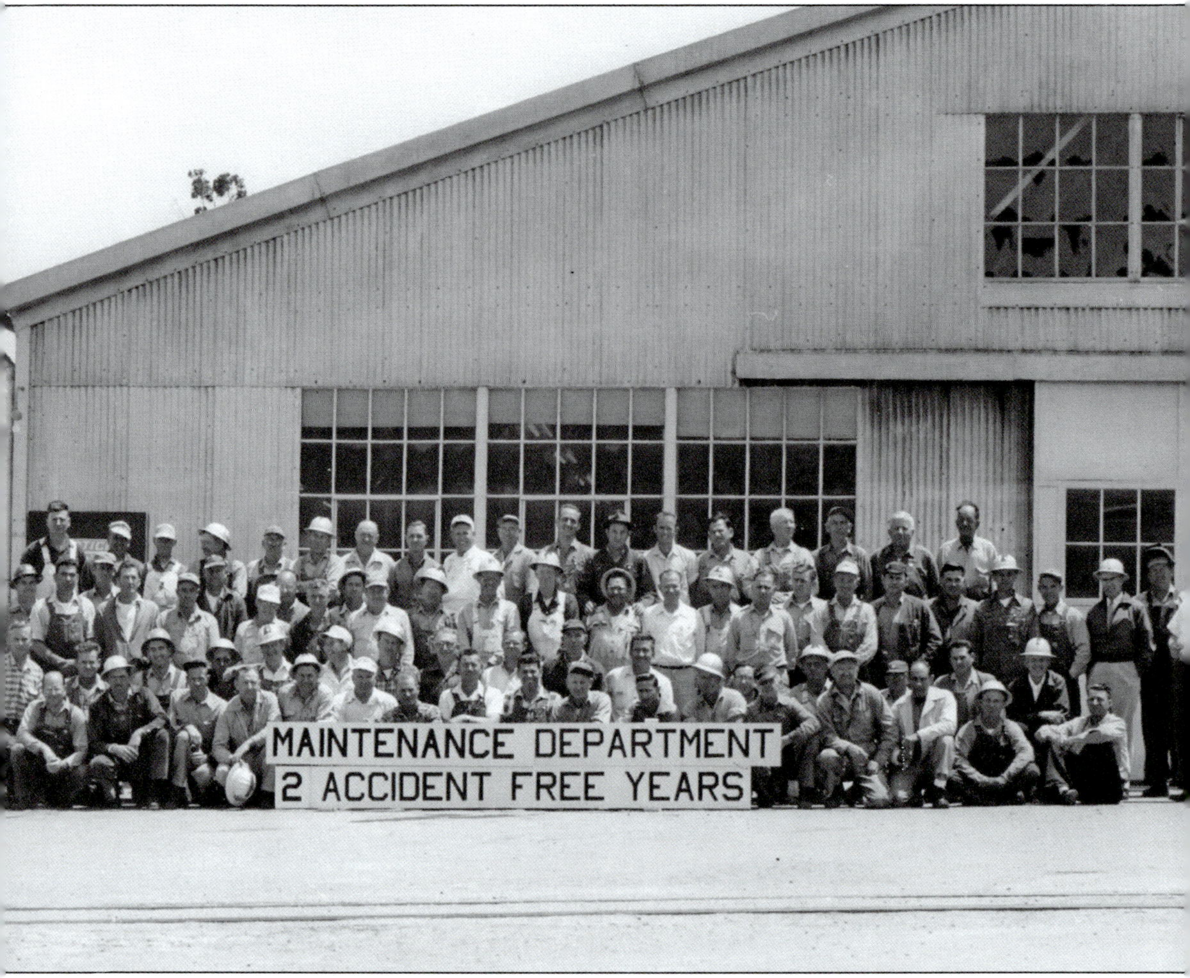

SAFETY COMMENDATION, C. 1959. Those pictured are, from left to right, (first row) Vern Hedberg, Bridger Goforth, Lee Osman, Ralph Williams, Harry Scarsella, Nestor Rard, Henry Dodson, Joe Sparks, Charlie Lenz, Norman Willis, Bill Redmond, Eldon Darrah, Vince Scanlon, Hugh Davis, Frank Maderos, Clarence Chisum, and Wade Olds; (second row) Gene Sutton, Bee Hansen, Lindow Mariuzza, Pop Johnson, John Comer, Marcus Foskitt, Al Livermore, Mel Eubanks, Gene Turner, Henry Kritzer, Bud Randall, Jimmie Hammer, Louis Gazzano, Pat Clark, Stuart Marshall, and Jack Conrady; (third row) Gene Hatfield, Bob Pearce, unidentified, Bill Nethercott, Lawrence Pereira, Russell Knight, Mike Peliot, John Classick, John Sassone, Kenny Hoover, Charlie Doidge, Al Atchison, Nigel McGillivray, Elmore Jordan, Bill Silva, Jack Fraser, George Leighty, Lars Pedersen, Paul Anderson, Dale Clute, Bryon Bellah, Tony Enos , Mike Danducci, Jimmie Ceselini, Dana Sprague (plant manager), Floyd Waford, and Don Hanrahan; (fourth row) Bob Lewis, Paul Goularte, Herman Hazen, Dan McCall, Alton Schmidt, John Payne, Herman Langford, Vern Chisholm, Tony Santaella, Lee Witman, Don Browning, Olie Wells, Vern Lasnini, John Adams, Chester Wright, Francis West, Henry Simon, and Warren Litchburger. (Courtesy Hercules Historical Society.)

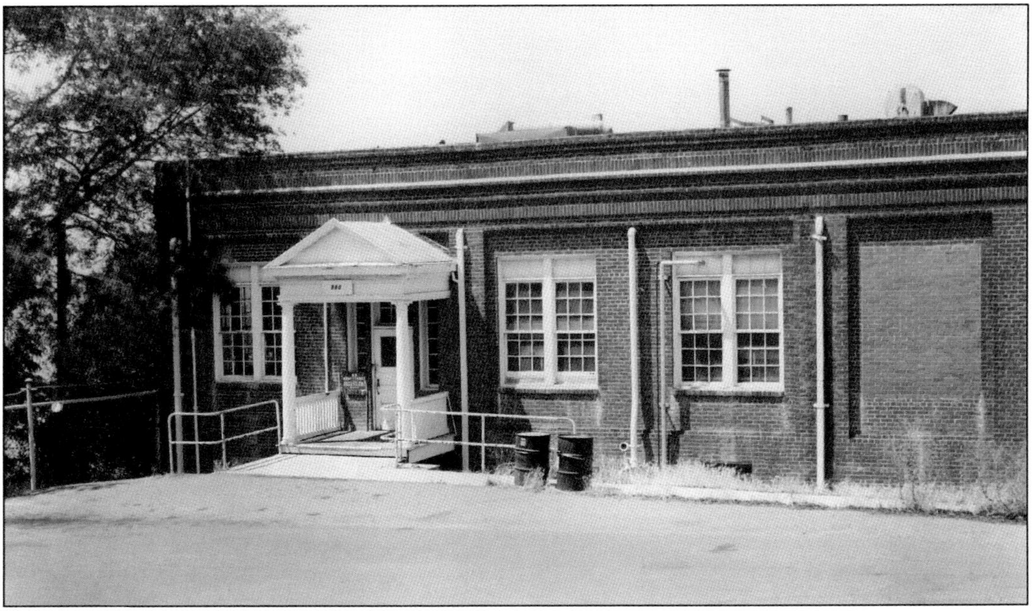

LABORATORY BUILDING. The testing and research laboratory sat at the end of Railroad Avenue, above the plant. From inception, chemists worked at Hercules. For several years after Hercules Powder was incorporated in 1912 as a result of divestiture, Dupont continued to make its Wilmington, Delaware, research services available to the former Dupont companies. This building was demolished in the late 1990s. (Courtesy Dan Russell.)

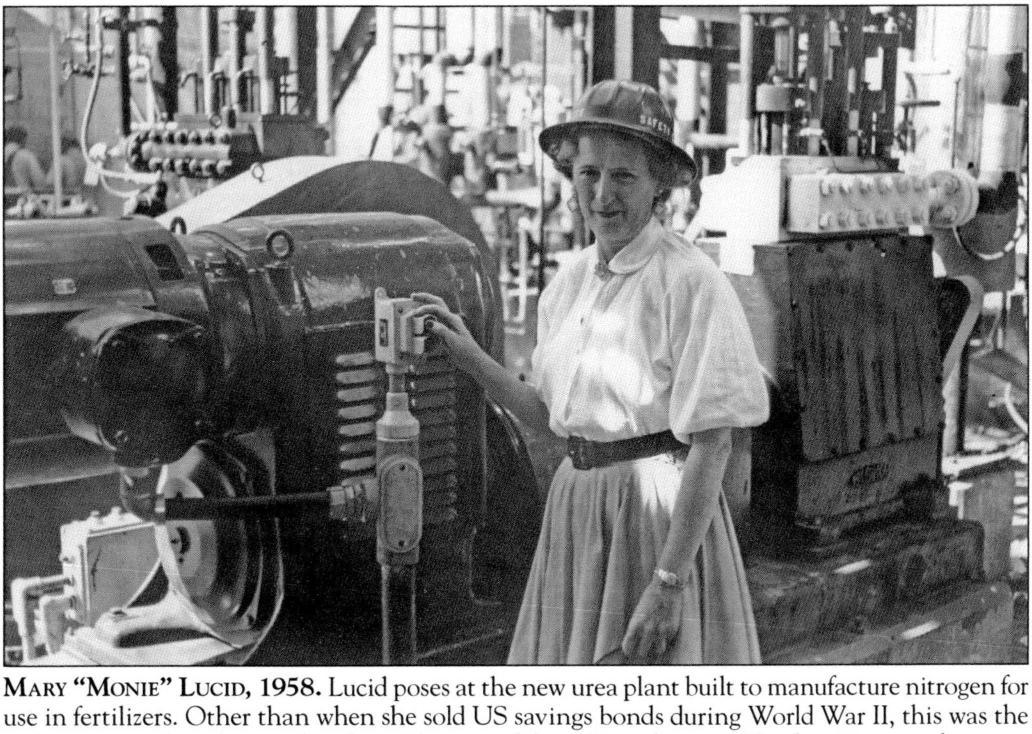

MARY "MONIE" LUCID, 1958. Lucid poses at the new urea plant built to manufacture nitrogen for use in fertilizers. Other than when she sold US savings bonds during World War II, this was the only time Lucid set foot in the plant. She retired from Hercules in 1973, after 43 years of service. Her family resided in Pinole. (Courtesy Lucid-Bender family.)

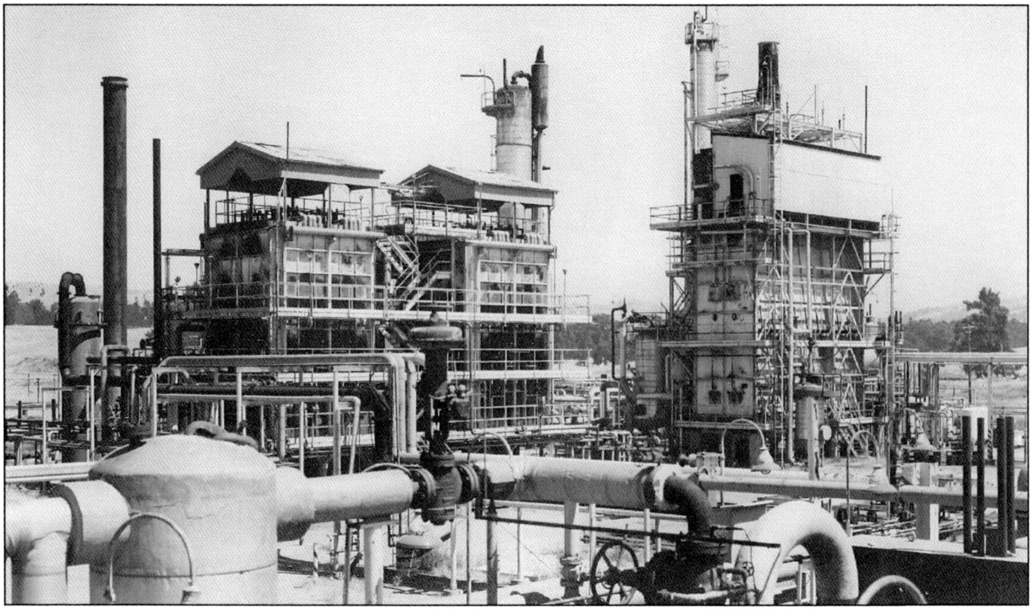

METHANOL PLANT, C. 1980. Building of the methanol plant began in 1959. Bechtel Corporation did much of the construction, working with local suppliers such as Sugar City Building Materials. During this period, the Hercules plant was a supplier of intermediate products for other Hercules Incorporated businesses. Much of this equipment continued in operation under the ownership of Valley Nitrogen Producers. (Courtesy Dan Russell.)

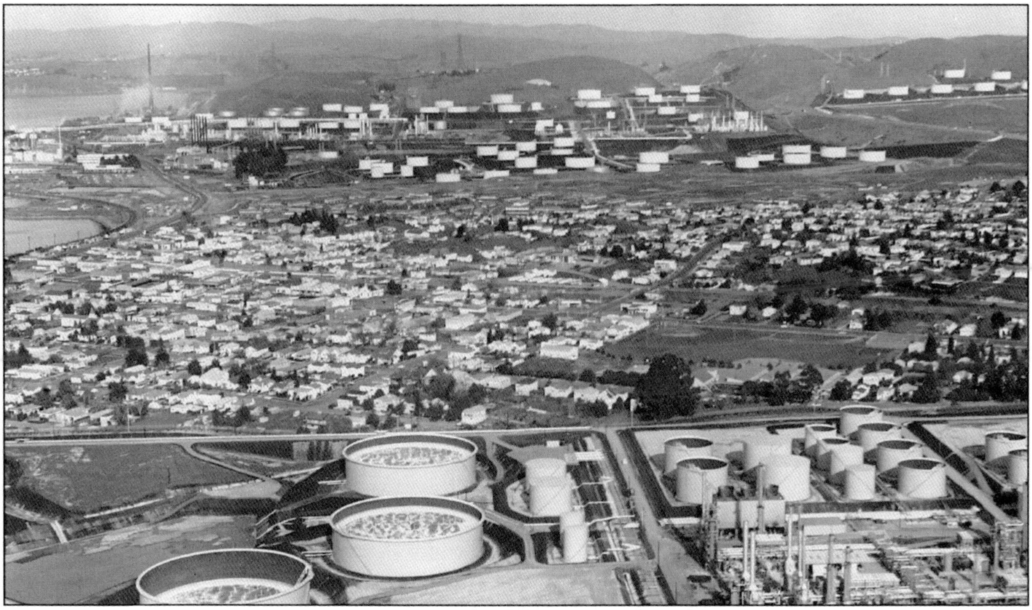

OIL REFINERY. In 1966, Sequoia Refining Corporation purchased approximately 220 acres at Hercules' northern city limit. Rodeo is in the background in this 1967 view. The 100 refinery employees produced gasoline, jet fuel, diesel fuel, heavy fuel oil, and asphalt. Christina Onassis unsuccessfully bid to acquire the facility in 1975 for $25 million. In April 1976, ownership passed to Coastal State Gas Corporation of Texas. The successor company, known as Pacific Refining, operated until September 1981. (Courtesy Jennifer Posedel.)

Four

Life in the Company Town

The company provided housing and funded institutions to stabilize the workforce. In December 1900, the territory of the plant was incorporated as the Town of Hercules, with a board of trustees composed of company officials. Around the plant's headquarters overlooking the bay, two areas grew to resemble districts of a small town. Below the ridge, shielded from blasts, stood the "Village," comprised of about a hundred company-built workers' homes. On top of the ridge were institutional buildings housing administrative, technical, and management employees; this was the "Hill."

Among the buildings on the Hill were White Columns, the superintendent's mansion; a men's clubhouse; and Quinan Hall, a bachelor quarters and social hall. The company was one of the first industrial firms in California to provide a hospital with a resident physician. Other buildings housed a post office, a dining hall, and a kindergarten. Classes in English, engineering, and chemistry were offered; lectures and dances were held.

Completed in 1899 and thereafter enlarged, the clubhouse was the social center of the community, and one of the first on the West Coast. Inside were a library, barbershop, shower baths, a bowling alley, billiard tables, card room, social hall (with boxing ring), and a bar. The Hercules Club was a social institution, funded and managed by employees with the company's support.

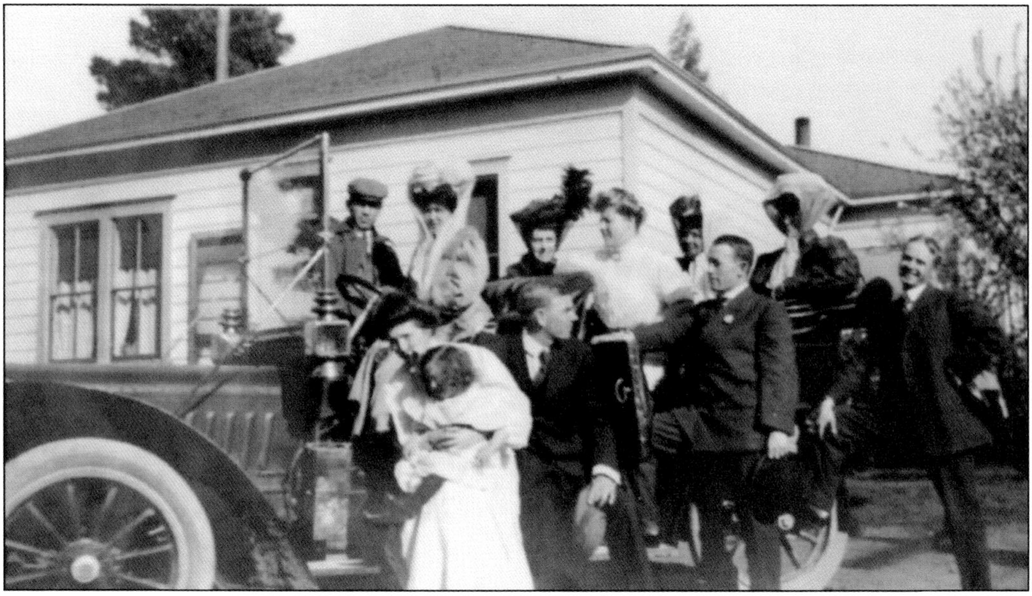

April 1908. Wearing the latest auto toggery, the ladies prepare to take a Cadillac touring car out for a spin in Hercules. Sitting on the running board looking over his shoulder is assistant superintendent Warren McBryde with his wife, Abbie, and daughter Lucile. The unidentified driver is wearing a dustcoat, specially designed for driving on the dusty, unpaved streets. (Courtesy M. Wallace and W. Ryder.)

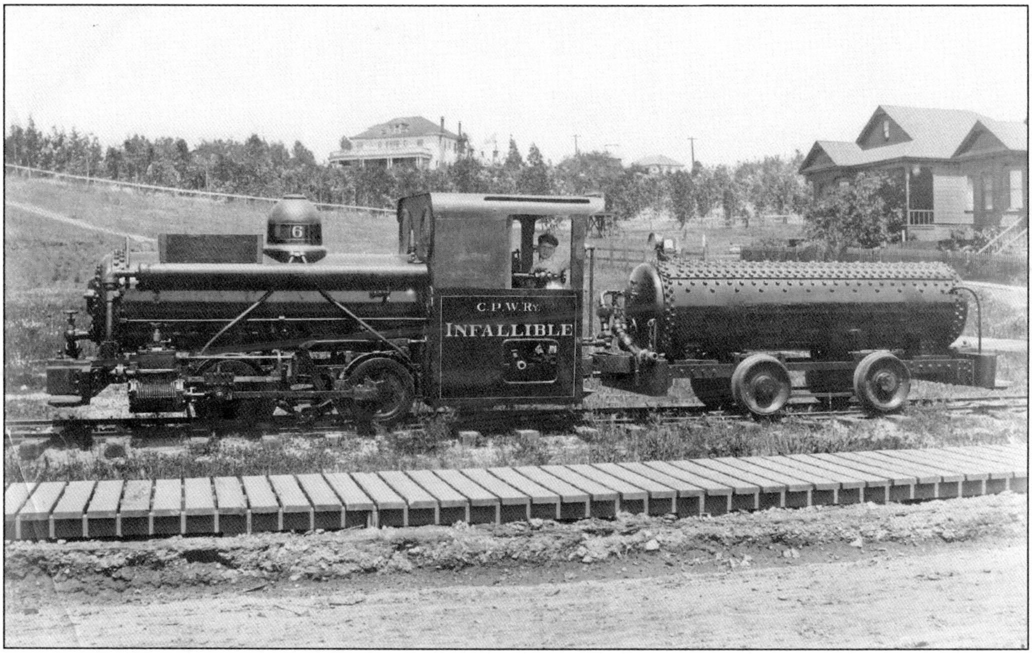

Infallible. John Bermingham III, nephew of the superintendent and son of Samuel, a plant employee, poses in the Canadian Pacific Railway fireless locomotive *Infallible*, named for a brand of smokeless shotgun powder. The wooden sidewalk in the foreground borders Santa Fe Street. In the background, from left to right, are the superintendent's home, the men's boarding house, and two company-owned cottages. (Courtesy Contra Costa County Historical Society.)

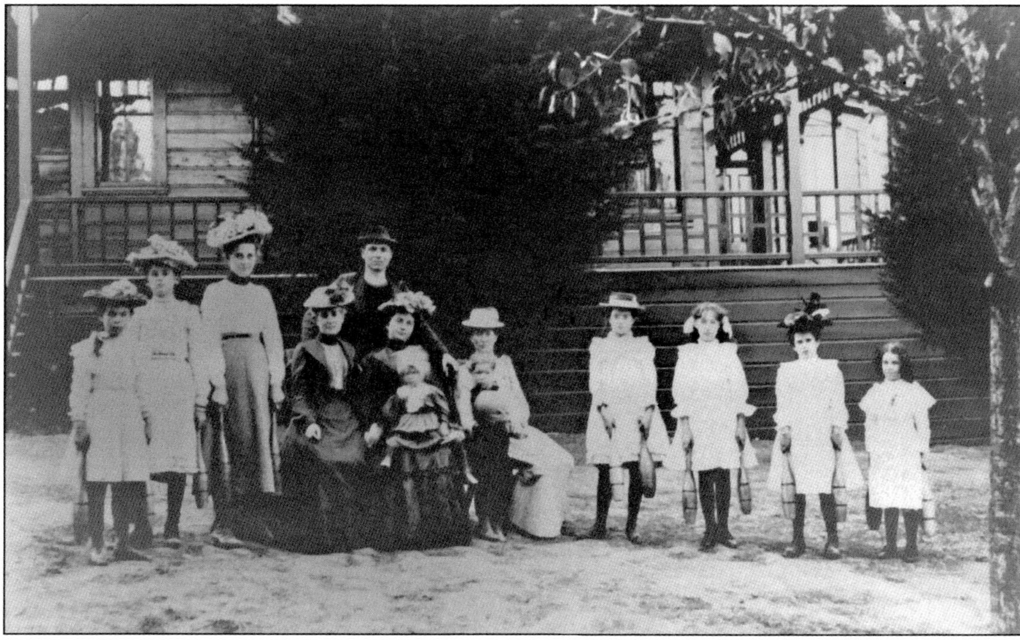

Herculites, c. 1910. This group of young women and children holding bowling pins is standing outside the men's boarding house. In this era, the clubhouse was painted in a dark color scheme. (Courtesy Contra Costa County Historical Society.)

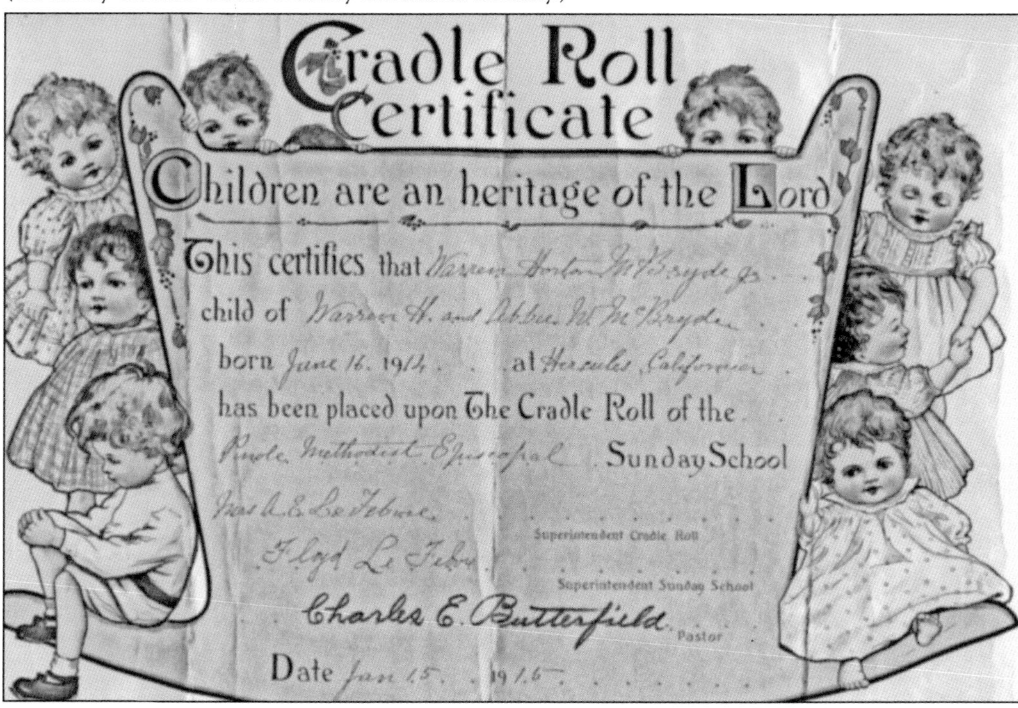

Cradle Roll Certificate

Children are an heritage of the Lord

This certifies that Warren Horton McBryde Jr.

child of Warren H. and Abbie M. McBryde

born June 16. 1914 at Hercules, California

has been placed upon The Cradle Roll of the

Pinole Methodist Episcopal Sunday School

Mrs A. E. Le Febvre Superintendent Cradle Roll

Floyd Le Febvre Superintendent Sunday School

Charles E. Butterfield Pastor

Date Jan 15. 1916

Born in Hercules, 1914. Before hospital childbirth became the norm, many children, including the assistant superintendent's son Warren Horton McBryde Jr., were born at home. The Pinole Methodist Episcopal Sunday school issued the McBryde baby's "cradle roll" certificate. Sadly, the boy's life was cut short by whooping cough. (Courtesy M. Wallace and W. Ryder.)

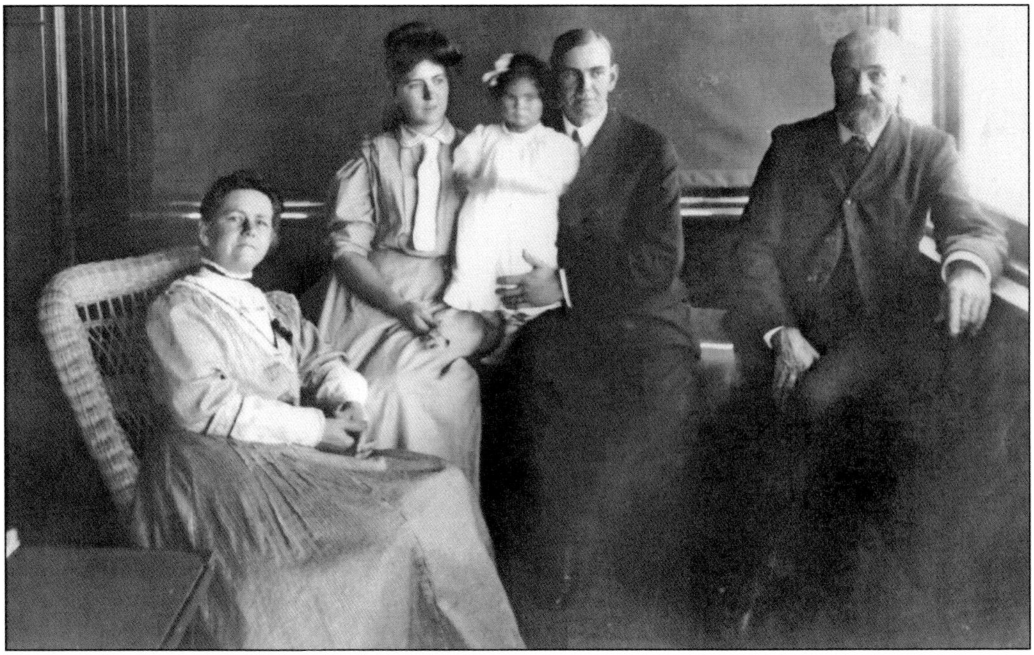

McBryde Family, c. 1907. Assistant plant superintendent Warren McBryde sits with his wife, daughter, and parents on the veranda of his Hercules home. From left to right are Julia Horton McBryde, a Vassar graduate; Abbie White McBryde; Mary Lucile McBryde; Warren; and Thomas Calvin McBryde. (Courtesy M. Wallace and W. Ryder.)

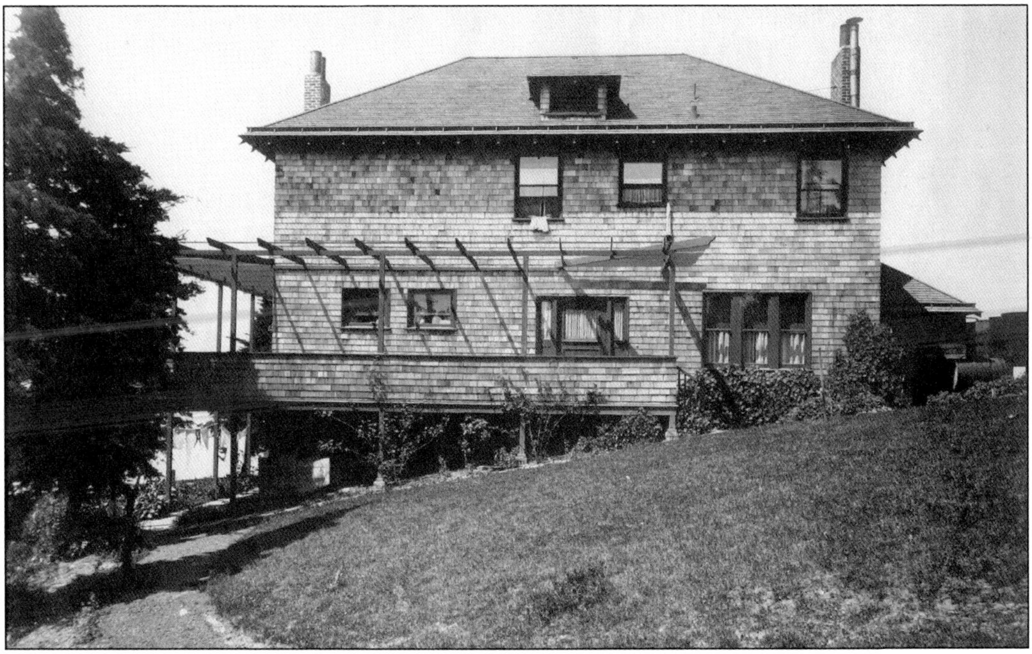

McBryde Home, Hercules. This large brown shingle home was built in 1905 on a hill overlooking San Pablo Bay for Warren McBryde and his family. The popular style is known locally as Berkeley brown shingle. Natural wood siding and an open porch were ideas borrowed from nature. The wraparound porch was later partially enclosed. (Courtesy M. Wallace and W. Ryder.)

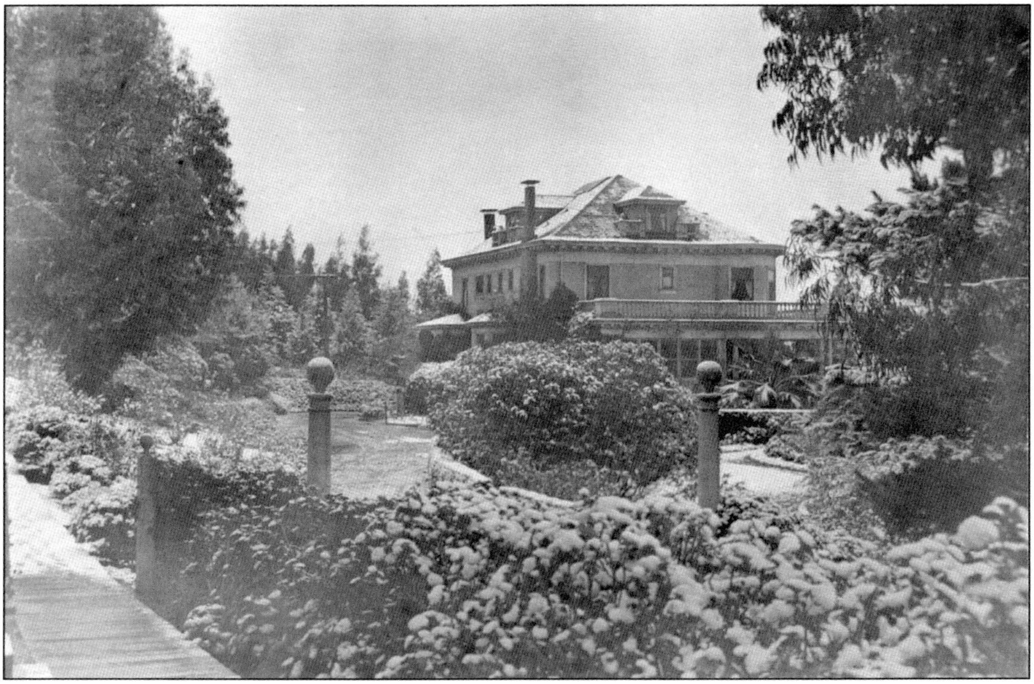

Snowfall, 1922. The first snowfall in six years, and the heaviest since 1882, occurred during a late-January storm, blanketing White Columns with three inches of snow. Steam heat supplied by gilded cast-iron radiators, installed in the 1910s, kept the house warm. The home was damaged by an explosion at the plant and was razed in 1945. (Courtesy Hercules Historical Society.)

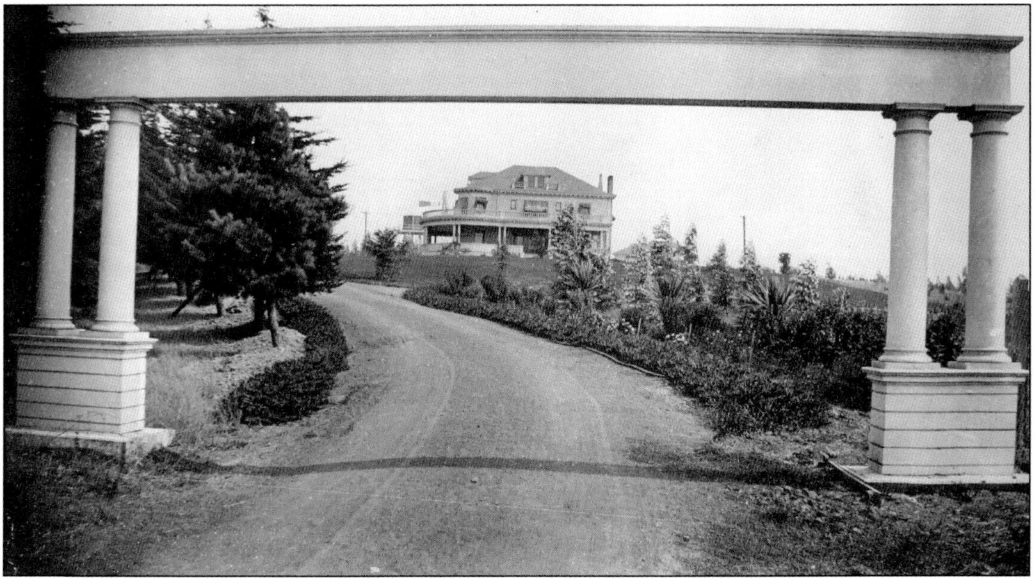

White Columns Gardens. The private garden at the superintendent's home featured greengage plum and apple trees and many varieties of palms and flowers. There was once a flowerbed that spelled out the word "Hercules." Long after White Columns was demolished, the grounds survived for many years as a park. (Courtesy Contra Costa County Historical Society.)

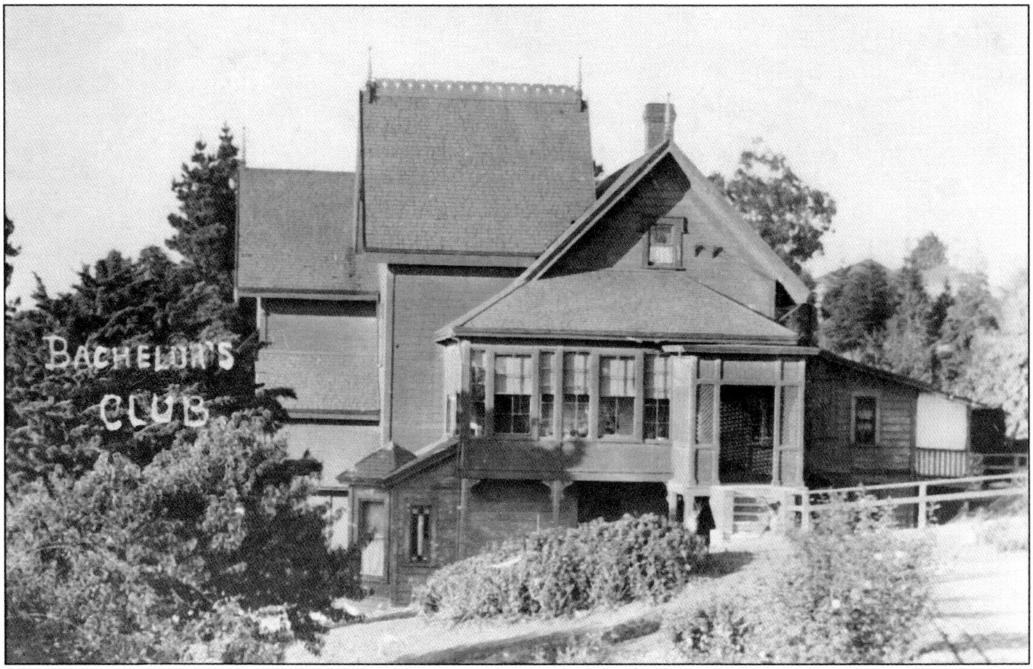

Bachelors' Club and Garden, 1908. The former management residence was later used as a guesthouse and recreation center for single men. During World War I, the ornate iron cresting likely fell victim to the scrap demands of the war. (Courtesy Contra Costa County Historical Society.)

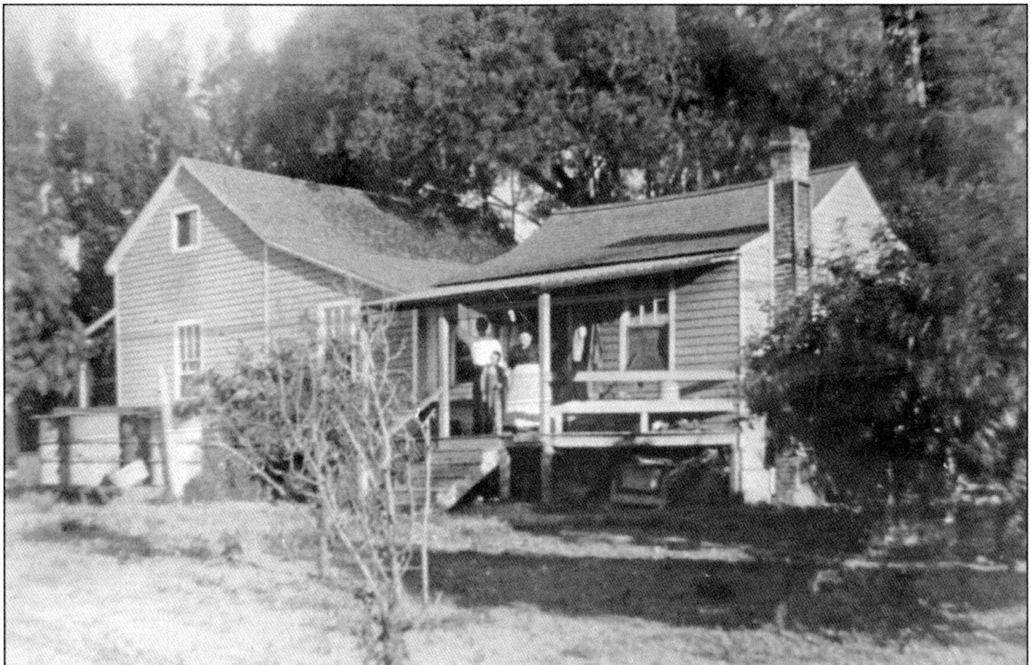

Plant B Boarding House. Situated in Refugio Valley, near the black powder line, this building was referred to as Plant B, while the area near the waterfront was called Plant A. (Courtesy Hercules Historical Society.)

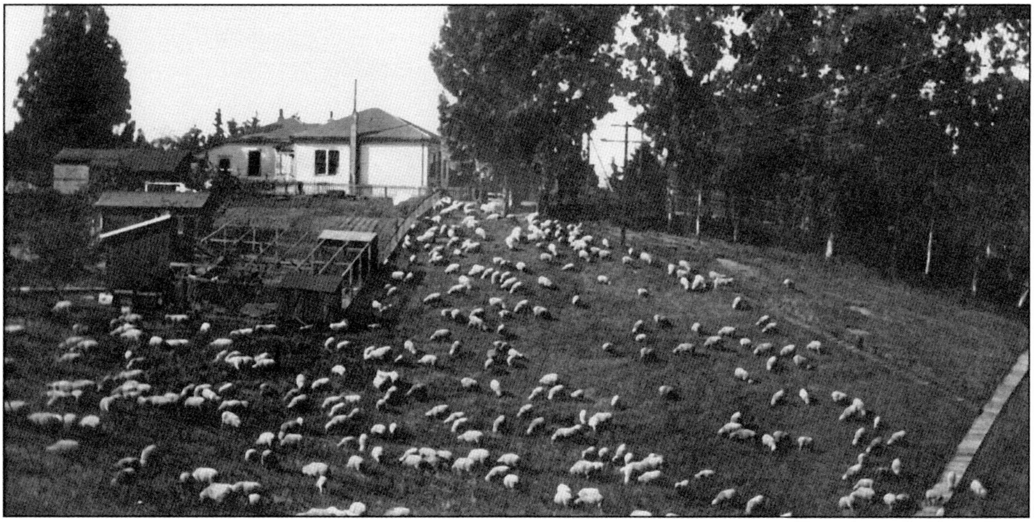

FIRE PROTECTION. To alleviate the fire hazard, some 1,500 to 3,000 company-owned sheep grazed on the hills surrounding the plant. One year, the job of selling the excess sheep fell to the plant safety supervisor (and one-time mayor of Hercules), Ralph Williams, who with his son Doug wrestled the animals onto the bed of a dilapidated truck for the drive to the Cow Palace at Daly City. (Courtesy M. Wallace and W. Ryder.)

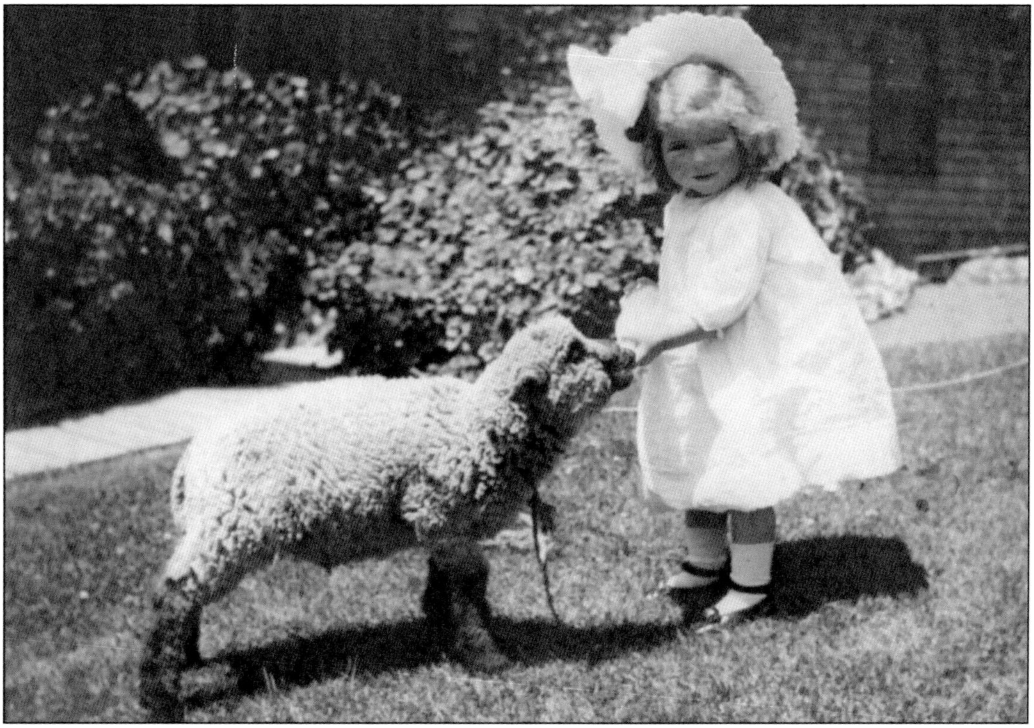

MARY LUCILE MCBRYDE. The daughter of the assistant superintendent poses with a pet lamb. A sheepherder lived on company property near the present-day telephone building on Sycamore Avenue. Another animal-husbandry enterprise was the Hercules Farm, whose stock was managed in the 1940s by David W. Clark. In the 1920s, Frank Wood ran a dairy operation in Hercules. (Courtesy M. Wallace and W. Ryder.)

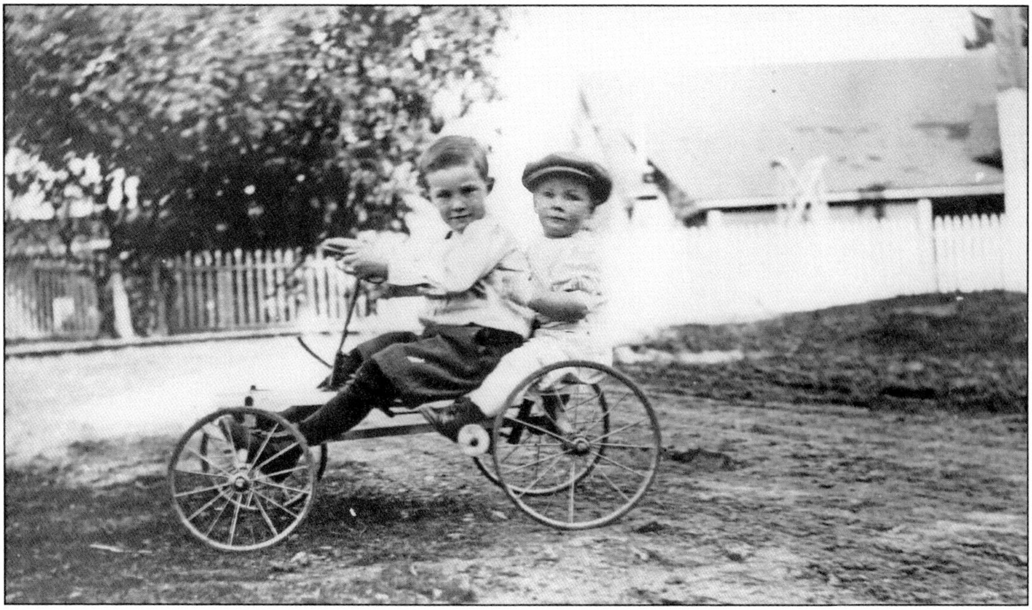

Lehmkuhl Boys, 1912. Ed and his little brother Jack pose outside "Doc" Jackson's house at 2 Kings Avenue. In 1919, Charles Lehmkuhl was the acid supervisor. Kings Avenue no longer exists as a street in Hercules. (Courtesy Contra Costa County Historical Society.)

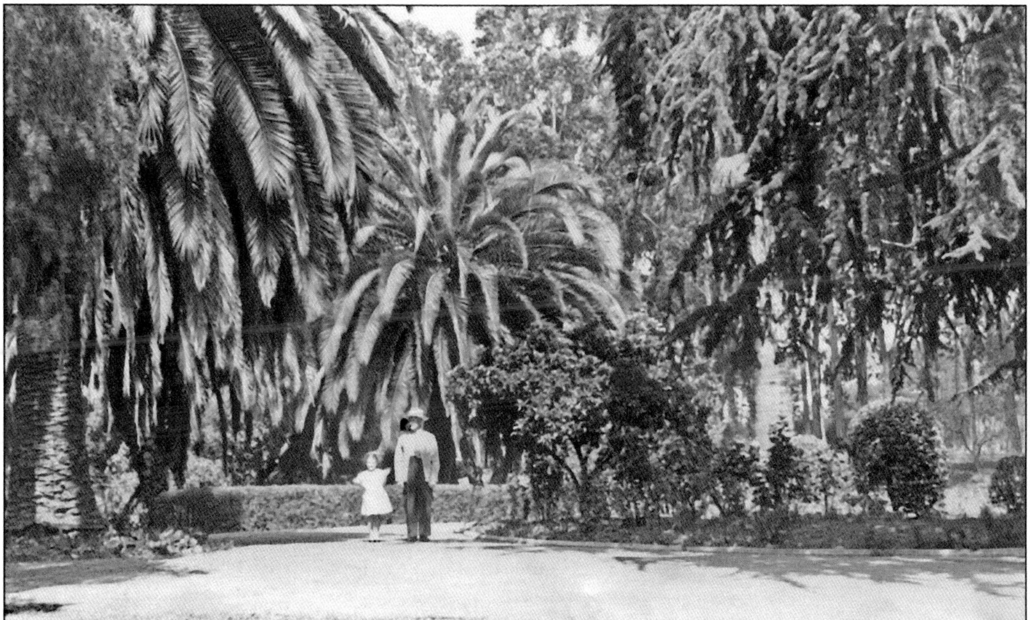

Superintendent's Home Site. Taken around 1948, this image shows Stephen Johnston and Anita McKee at the location where the great house White Columns once stood. Johnston was the plant's former safety supervisor who was no longer able to work due to illness. McKee's mother, who was a nurse, was hired to care for him. (Courtesy Anita Wennblom Broberg McKee.)

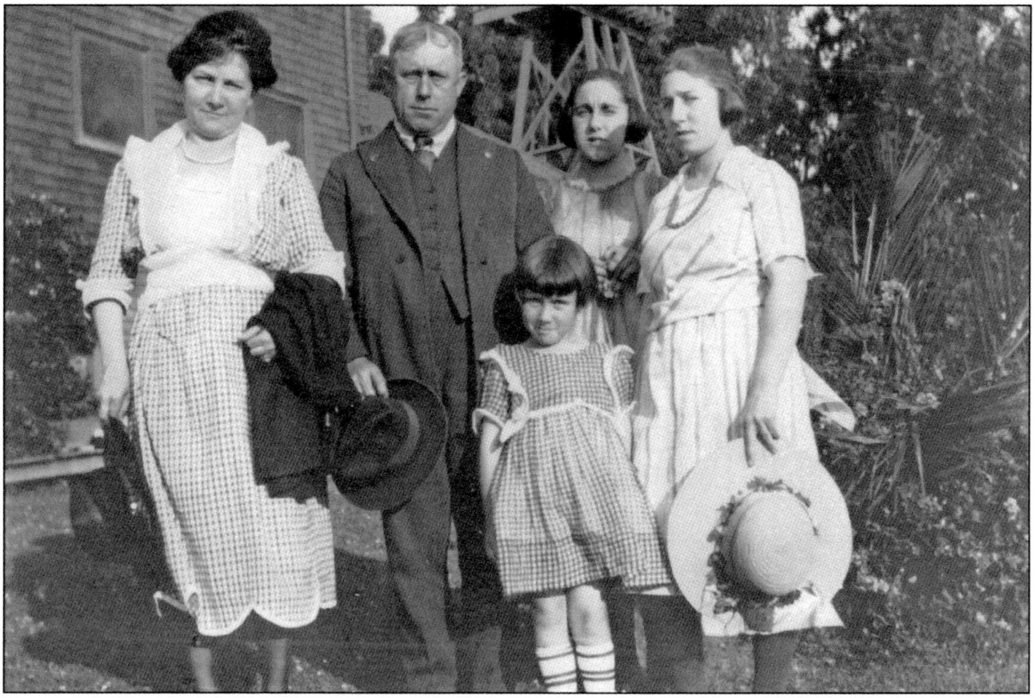

ROBISON FAMILY, 1920. From left to right are Jovita and Ralph Robison with daughters Anita (in front), Eleanor, and Ruth. All three daughters earned degrees at the University of California. Jovita is descended from the Castro family, holders of a large land grant in Contra Costa County. (Courtesy Nancy M. Tooker.)

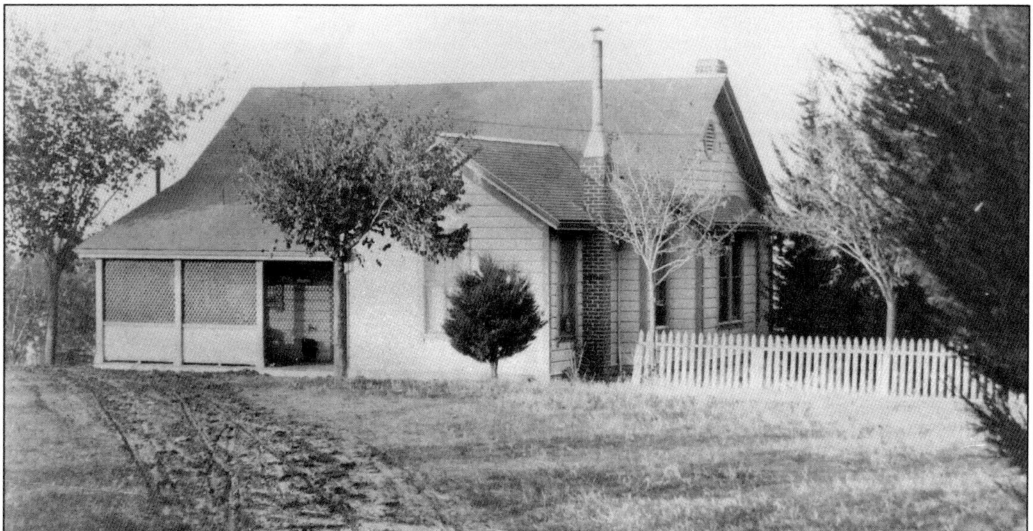

2 KINGS AVENUE. The Robisons once lived in this cottage, one of the homes on the hill for senior plant personnel. Plant engineer Eugene Woodfield and his family later occupied the home. A park and street in Hercules are now named for Woodfield, who served as Hercules mayor from 1962 to 1975. The home's final occupant was William Thatcher, a former Hercules employee and watchman for Valley Nitrogen Producers, which operated the plant as successor to Hercules Incorporated. (Courtesy Contra Costa County Historical Society.)

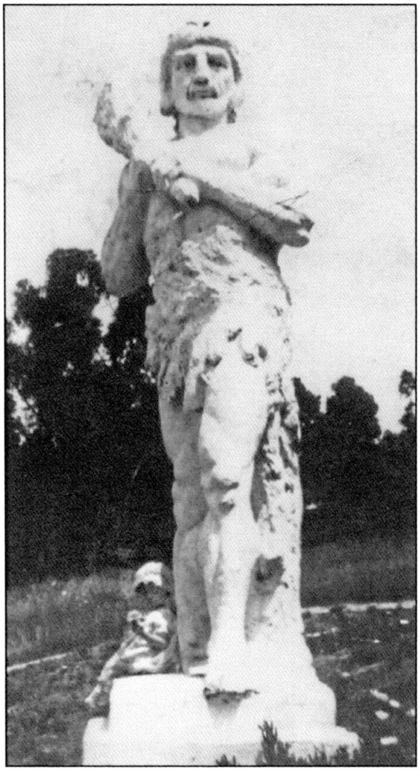

Irene Silcock, c. 1924. The toddler posing here has a connection to the powder works that goes back two generations. Her grandfather was Capt. John McLean (see page 17), who went to work for the powder company in the 1870s, which was when it was located in San Francisco. (Courtesy Family of Irene Silcock Dias.)

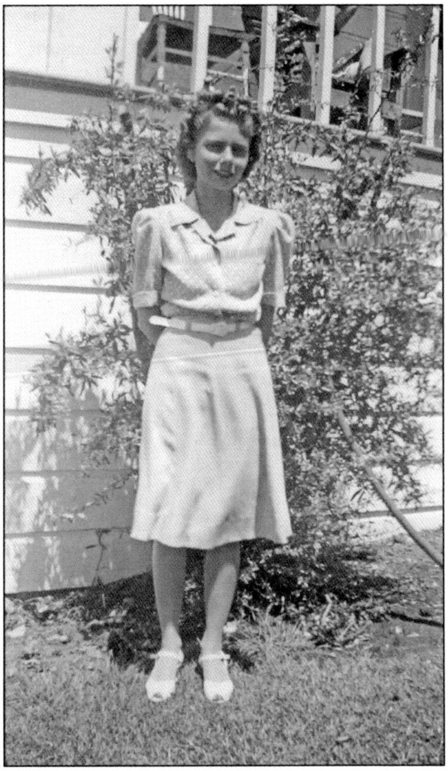

Irene Silcock, 1940. A grown-up Silcock poses at home. Three years later, when the country was at war, she traded the stylish dress for work togs. The family lived at 1 Pinole Street. (Courtesy Family of Irene Silcock Dias.)

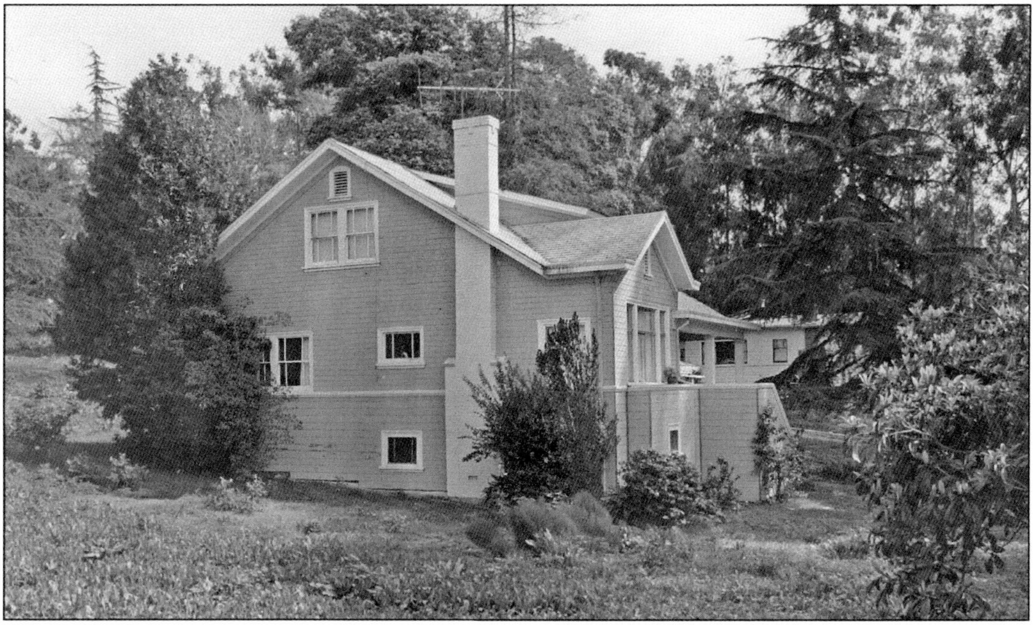

1 Talley Way. Frederick G. Huxster and his family once lived in this home. Huxster worked his way up from dynamite line supervisor to plant supervisor between 1931 and 1940. He was mayor of Hercules, school board trustee of the Pinole-Hercules School, and president of Hercules Water Company. The household's animals included a flock of chickens and a horse. (Courtesy Dr. Joseph Mariotti.)

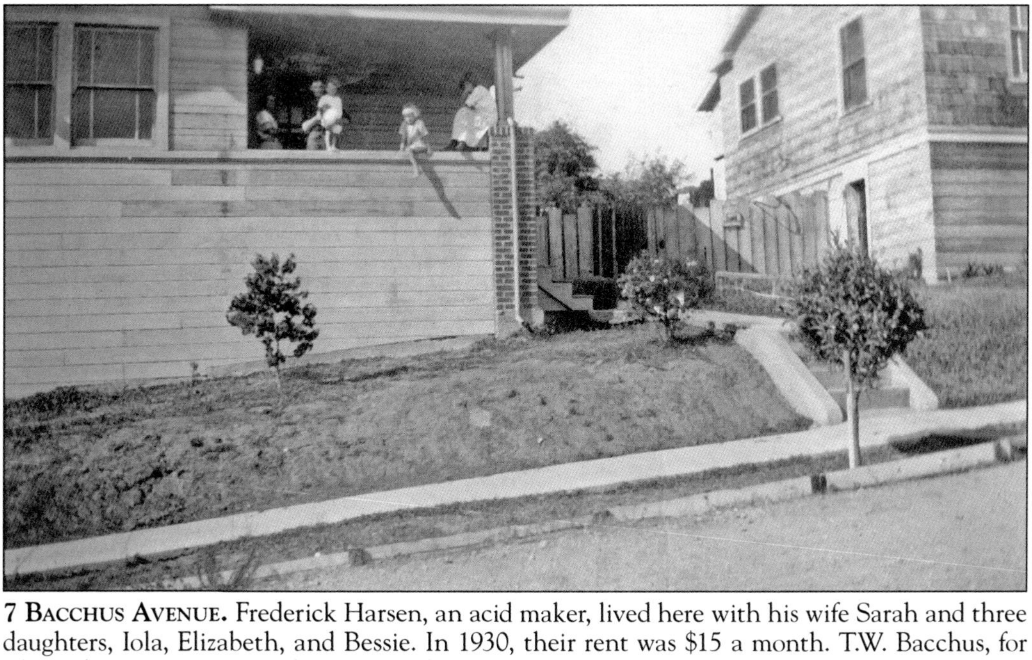

7 Bacchus Avenue. Frederick Harsen, an acid maker, lived here with his wife Sarah and three daughters, Iola, Elizabeth, and Bessie. In 1930, their rent was $15 a month. T.W. Bacchus, for whom the street was named, was a member of the first management team of the Hercules Powder Company. (Courtesy Family of Irene Silcock Dias.)

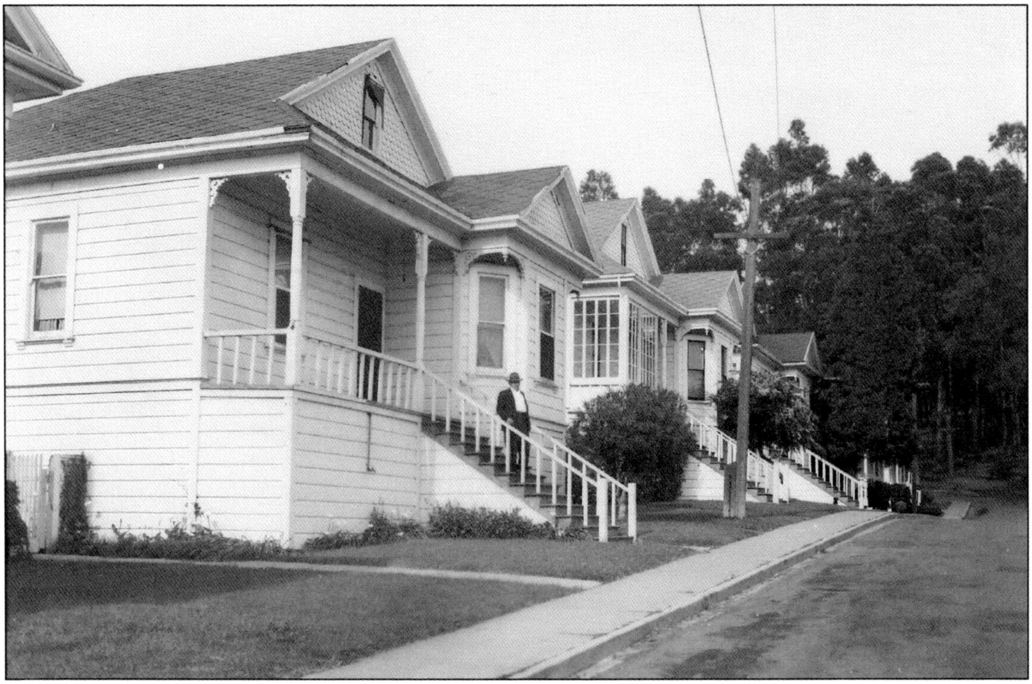

PINOLE STREET RESIDENCE, 1947. For an article on his last day at the plant for the employee magazine, the *Hercules Mixer*, Garrie Metz was photographed departing his residence at 3 Pinole Street. (Courtesy Ashland Inc.)

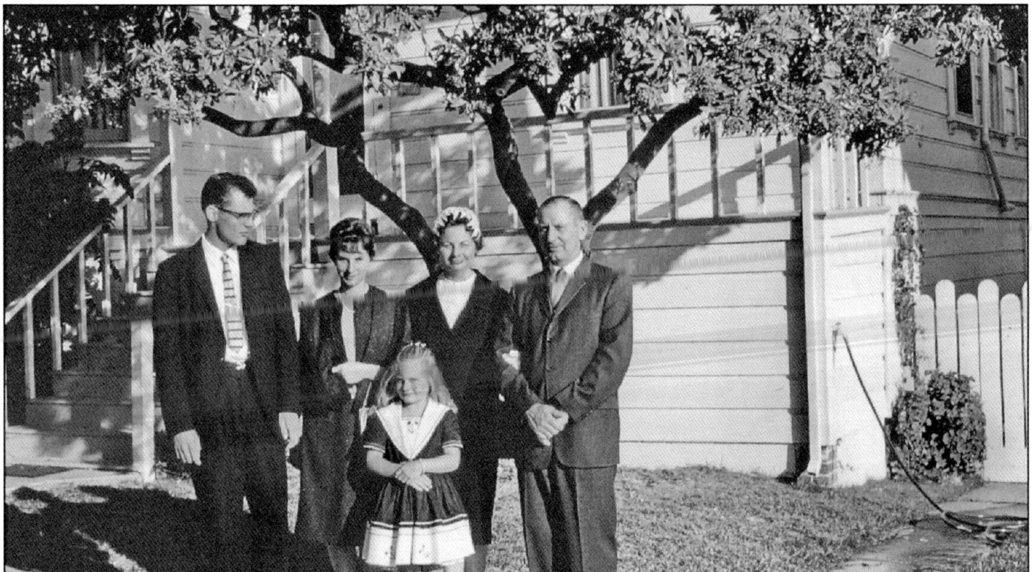

WILLIAMS FAMILY ON PINOLE STREET. The Williams family next occupied the Metz house. They were photographed across the street at the Hopper residence. Susann Williams is in front, and at rear, from left to right, are Douglas, Nancy, Edna, and Ralph Williams. Ralph Williams was the plant fire chief and also served as city mayor. When he retired in 1974, Edna was appointed postmistress of Hercules, and they were allowed to remain in their village house. (Courtesy Douglas Williams.)

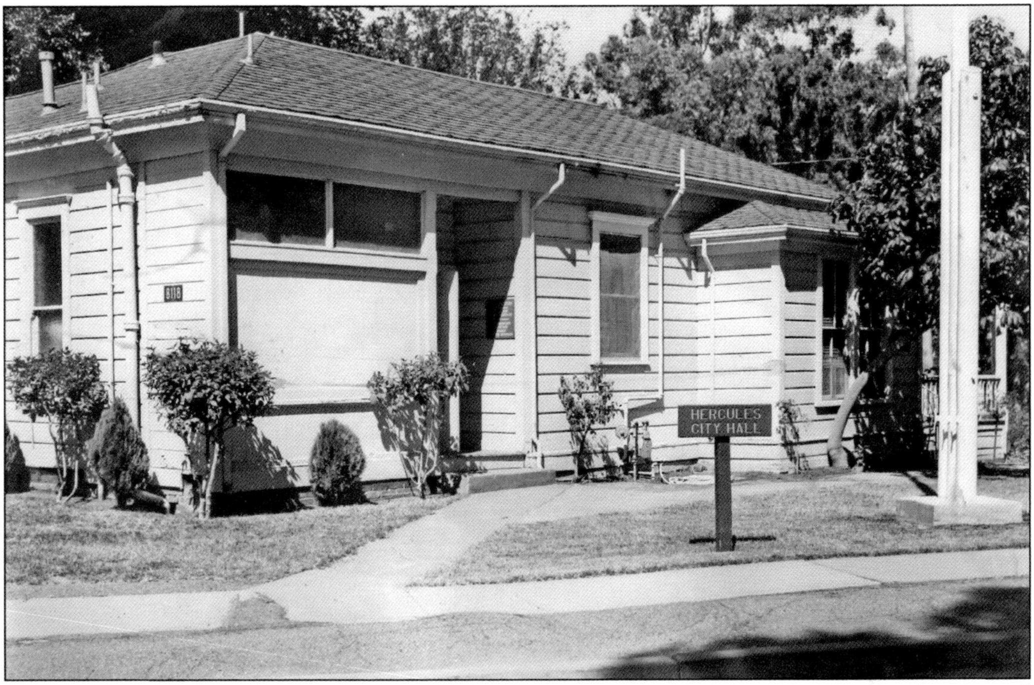

CITY HALL. After 1 Kings Avenue was converted from a residence for managers and technical personnel, it became the Hercules City Hall, housing a variety of city services. At that time, the address was changed to 555 Railroad Avenue. (Courtesy Dan Russell.)

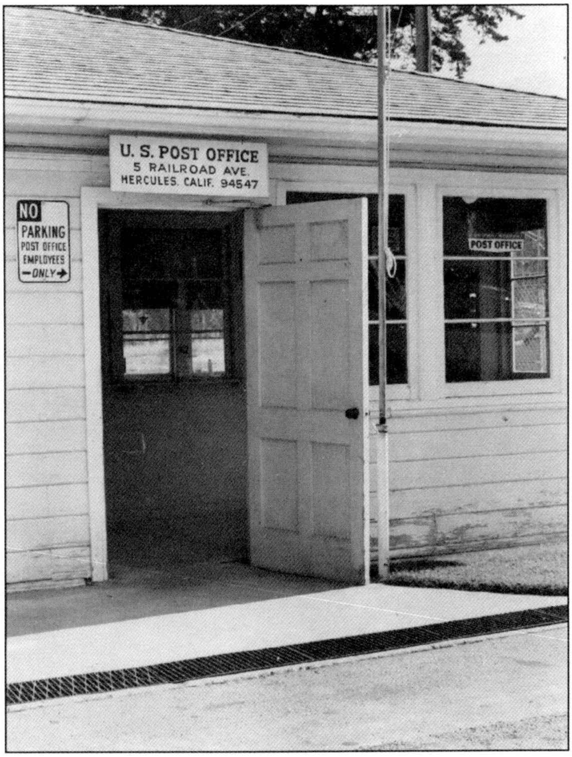

HERCULES POST OFFICE, 1968. The Hercules Post Office was established on March 19, 1914, as a branch of Pinole Post Office. It was previously located inside the company office building. It then moved to this location at 5 Railroad Avenue in a small building that also housed a guard station. The first postmaster, Andrew M. Ashenfelter, was also an employee of the powder company, as were many of the early postmasters. (Courtesy Contra Costa County Historical Society.)

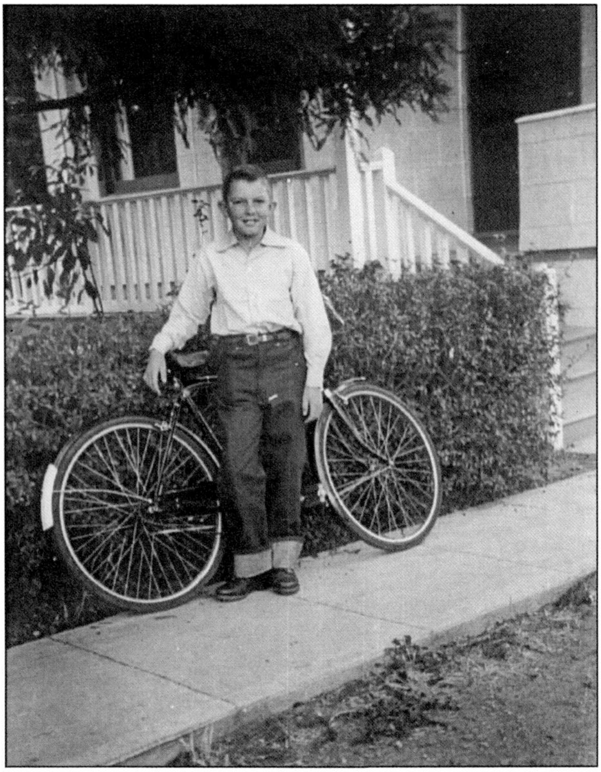

William Ingalls, 1954. Ingalls poses with his new English bicycle at 9 Park Street. He remembers the December 1944 explosion that blew out the windows in their former house on Dunham Avenue. A falling pipe in the kitchen burned his arm. Shattered glass ended up inside the kitchen's closed cabinets and drawers that had been forced open and slammed shut by the power of the blast. (Courtesy William Ingalls.)

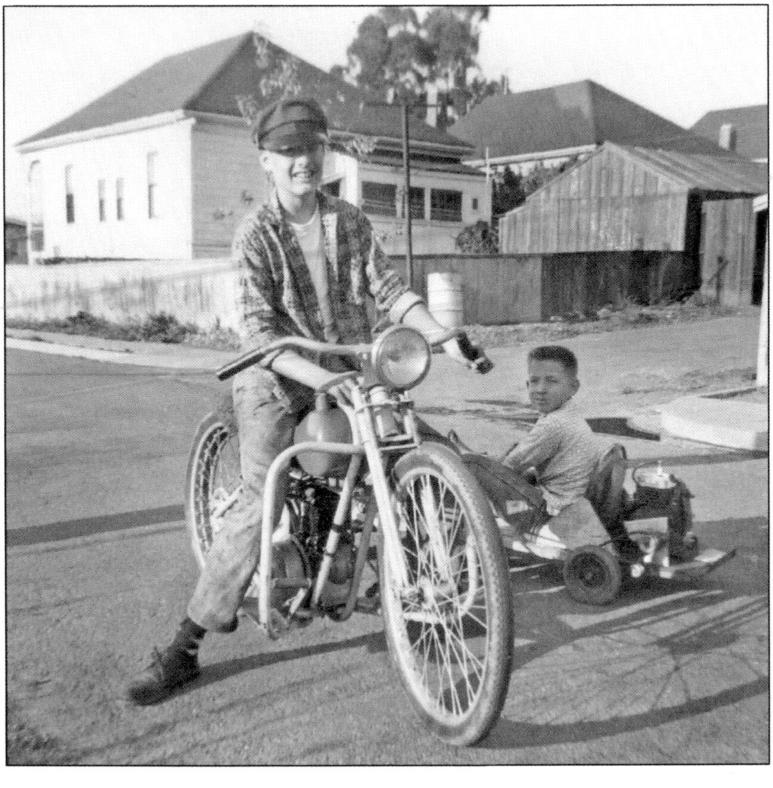

November 1956. Douglas Williams sits on a Servi-Cycle he purchased from a friend for $15. Georgie Fraser is on a go-cart made by his father. The boys are stopped on Santa Fe Avenue at the foot of Pinole Street. The backyards at left belong to houses on Bay Street, which is now part of the re-configured historic district. (Courtesy Douglas Williams.)

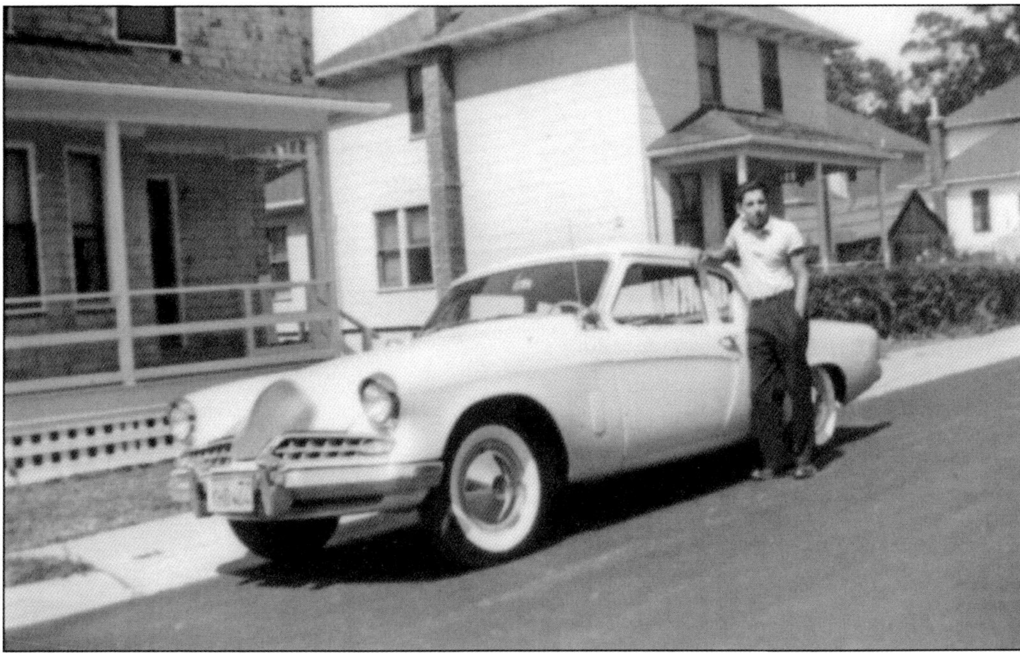

Park Street, 1957. John Darke stands beside his 1954 Studebaker. Darke belonged to the Pinole Gear-Grinder car club and is a 1955 graduate of Richmond High School. His father William hired on at Hercules in 1939. (Courtesy John Darke.)

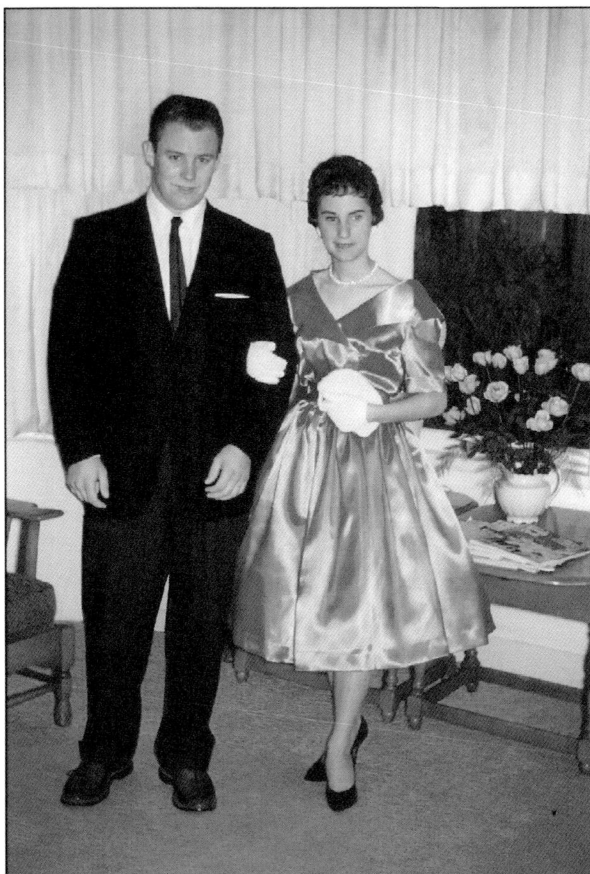

Prom Night. Nancy Williams and Jim Bender pose at 3 Pinole Street. Both of their fathers worked at the plant. Williams was a student at Richmond High School and lived in the Hercules village. She is wearing an outfit made by her mother, Edna. Bender, who lived at that time in Pinole, went to De Anza High School. His father, grandfather, and aunt worked at Hercules. (Courtesy Estate of Edna and Ralph Williams.)

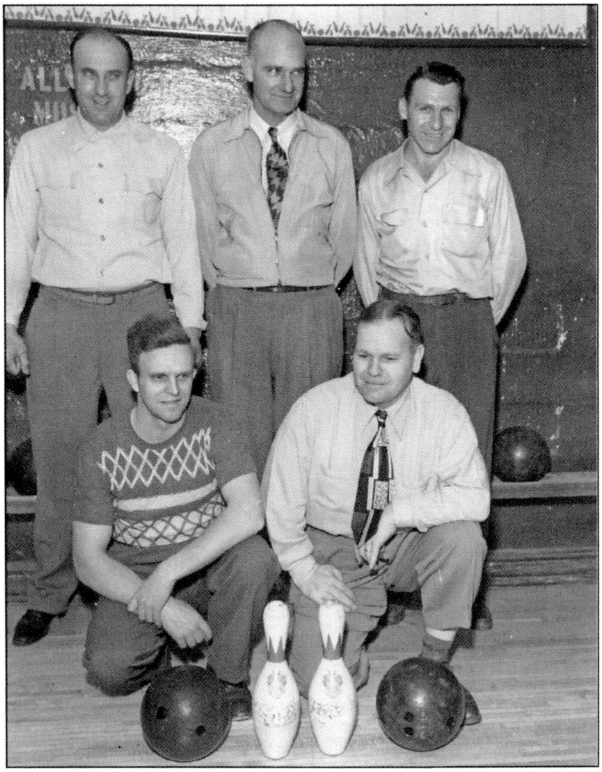

Telegraphic Team One, 1949. At front is Fred Bartholomew (left) with Pat Butler. Standing behind them are, from left to right, Louie Leverone, Lou Thielan, and Harry Scarsella. These photographs were taken in the clubhouse bowling alley. In later years, company leagues also played at Golden Gate Lanes in El Cerrito. (Courtesy Gig Reloj.)

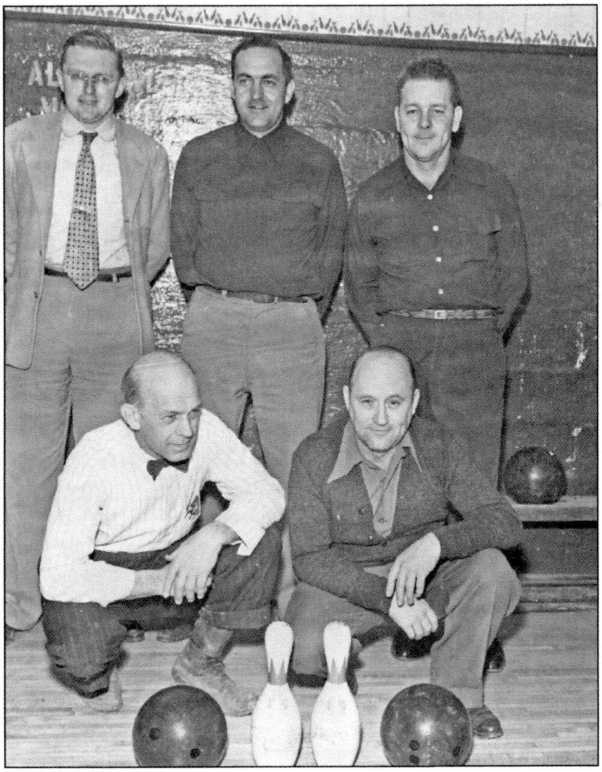

Telegraphic Team Two, 1949. Kneeling are Lawrence Hileman (left) and Herman Langford. Behind them are, from left to right, C. "Pete" Weiss, George Zuells, and O.B. Wells. These teams participated in the 30th annual Telegraphic Tournament. (Courtesy Gigi Reloj.)

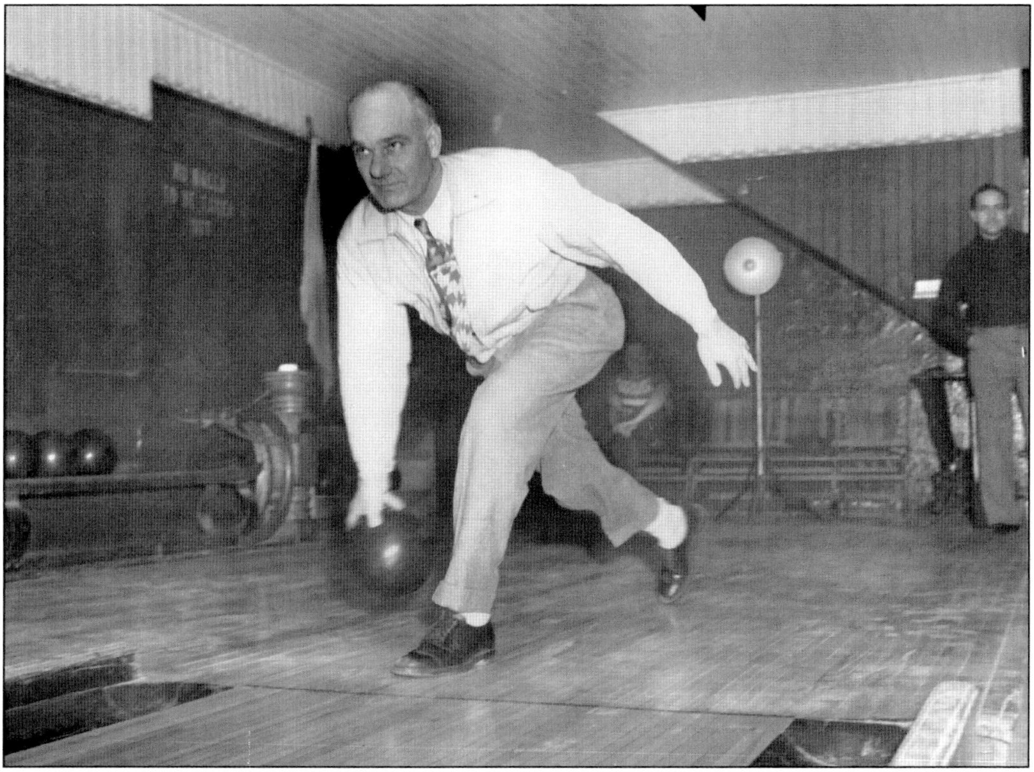

PERFECT SCORE. The ammonia department area supervisor Lou Thielan (above), bowls 300 in the Hercules club alley. The job of hand setting the pins provided income for some of the boys in the village. Note the fan behind him that provided the only air conditioning in the basement. The bowling alley remains intact, although not currently in use. (Courtesy Gigi Reloj.)

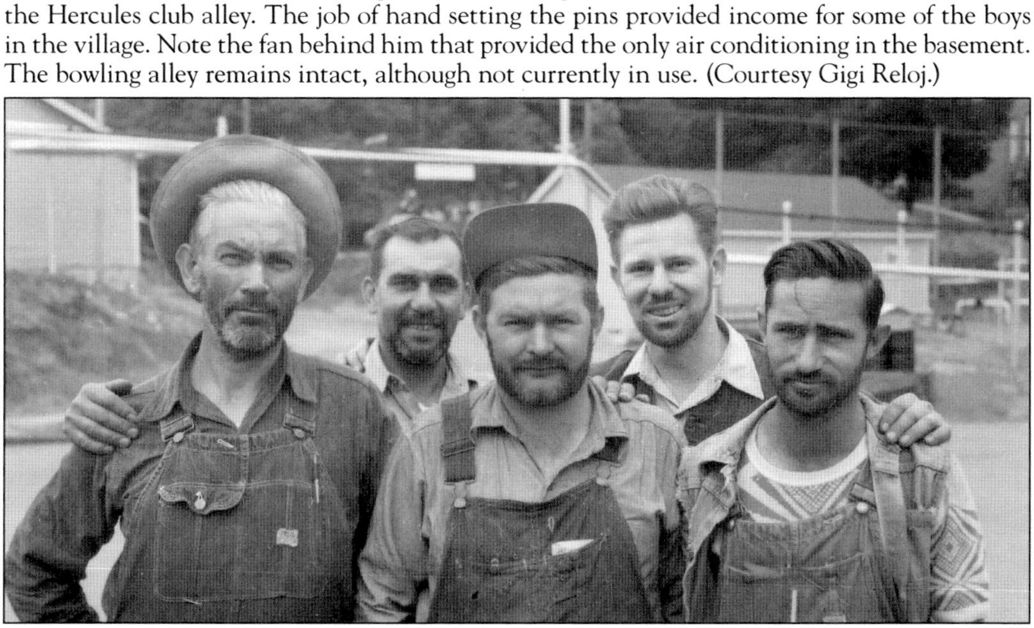

WHISKERINO, SEPTEMBER 1949. Men known as "the gang" grew beards rather than be "jailed" by the Pinole Lions Club during the Pinole Fiesta, which also celebrated the centennial of the Gold Rush. In front, from left to right, are Francis West, Charlie Doidge, and Bill Redmond. At rear, from left to right, are Bill Silva and Jack Hansen. (Courtesy Hercules Historical Society.)

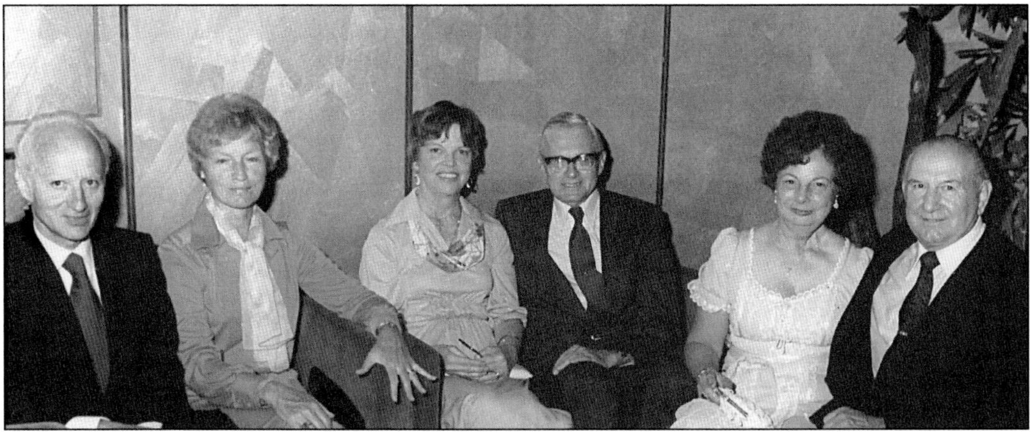

THREE COUPLES. Plant supervisors with their wives are, from left to right, Chester and Helen Sausaman, Anna and Christian Weiss, and Edna and Ralph Williams. Sausaman, a chemist, was the assistant technical manager. Weiss was a purchasing agent, and Williams was the fire chief. Two streets in Hercules now bear the family names Weiss and Williams. (Courtesy Estate of Ralph and Edna Williams.)

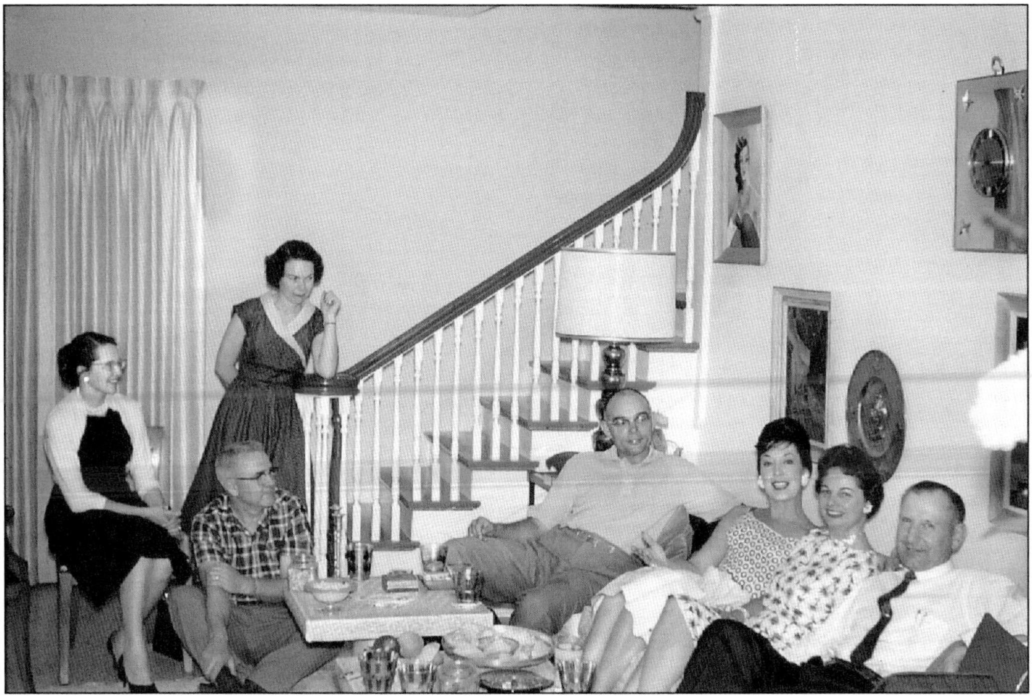

Village Party. The village is remembered for having frequent social gatherings in the 1950s and 1960s. The partygoers who have been identified in this photograph are the three at far right, Sherry Sayler and Edna and Ralph Williams. Sayler was an actress with the Contra Costa Civic Theater. Her husband, Richard, was the dynamite department supervisor. (Courtesy Estate of Ralph and Edna Williams.)

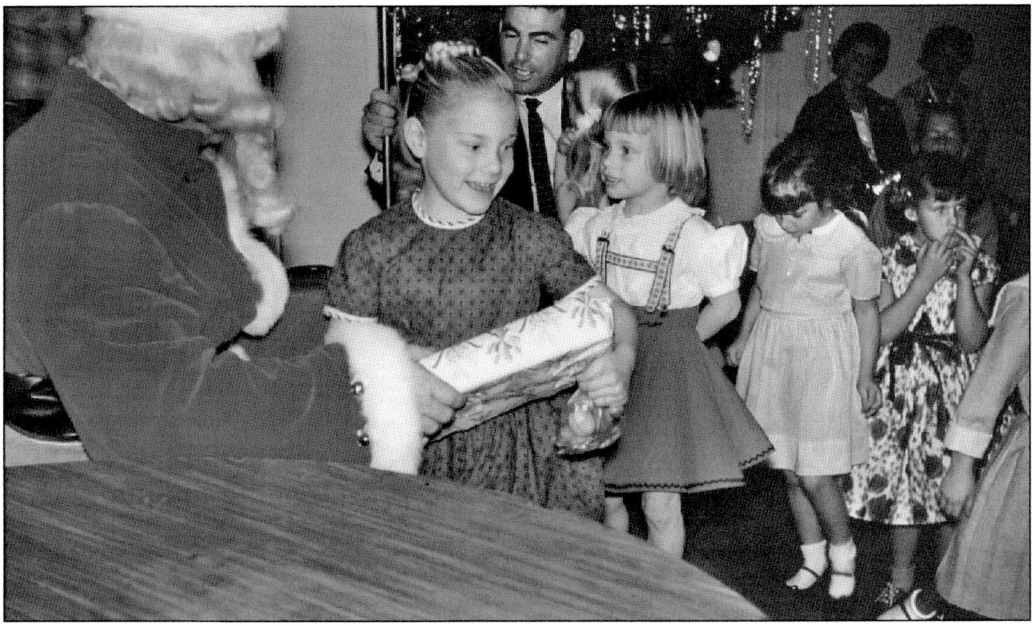

Visit from Santa, c. 1960. For years, an annual Christmas party was held at the Hercules Clubhouse with a gift provided for each child. Receiving a present is Susie Williams, while Marcia Ludwig waits directly behind her. Santa is not identified. Bobby Pearce is shown in the background. (Courtesy Estate of Ralph and Edna Williams.)

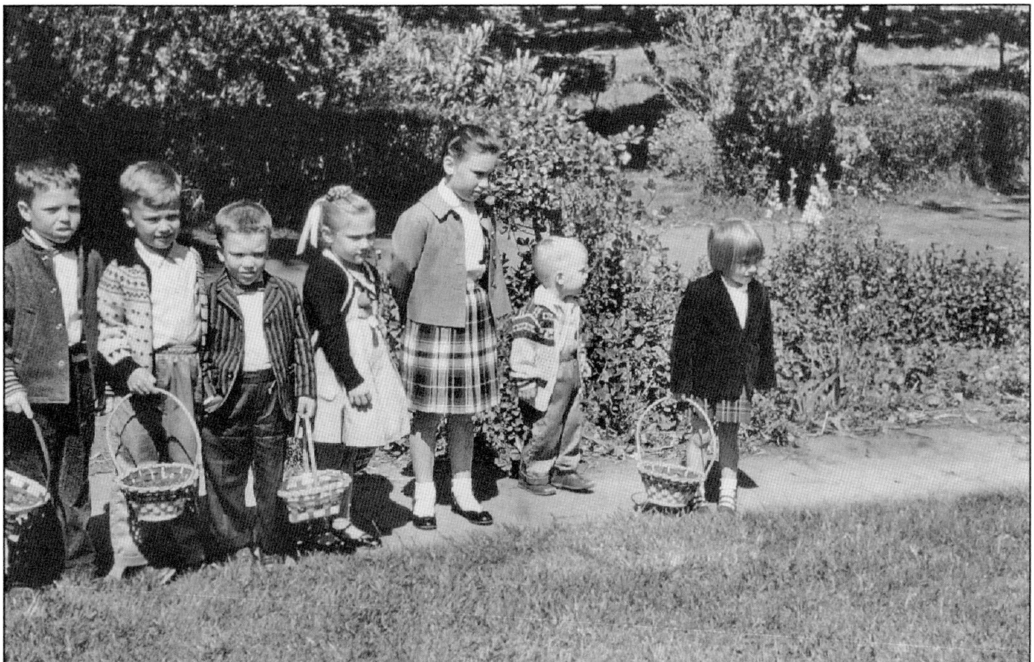

Egg Hunt, c. 1959. An Easter egg hunt was held for Hercules children on the grounds where the superintendent's house once stood. From left to right are Jimmy Weiss, Charles Ludwig, Richie Weiss, Susie Williams, Debbie Ludwig, John Ludwig, and Marcia Ludwig. (Courtesy Estate of Ralph and Edna Williams.)

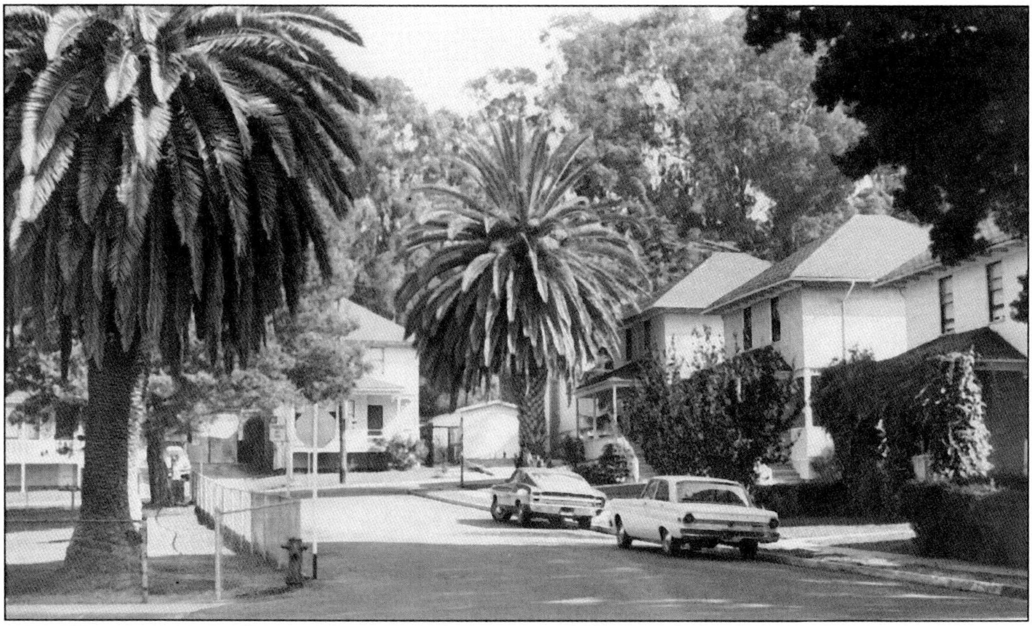

Park Street, 1968. This picture was taken at the corner of Hercules Avenue looking toward Park Street. At one time, the Hatfields, Turners, and Atchisons occupied the residences on the right. The house at the top center was home to the Pavones. Working at Hercules became something of a tradition for five Pavone family members who were all employed at the plant. (Courtesy Contra Costa County Historical Society.)

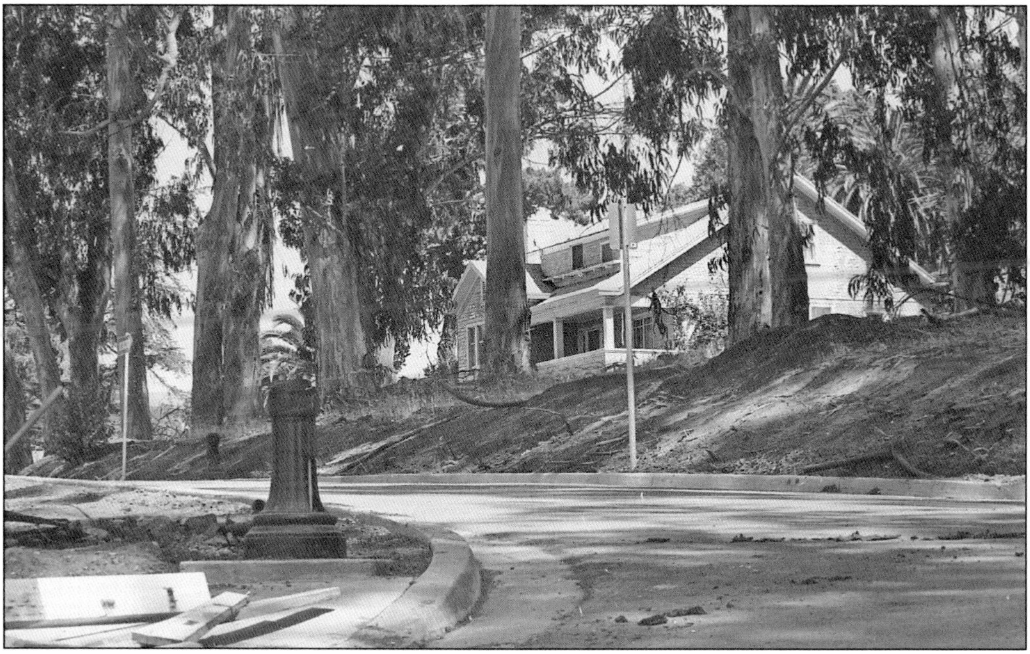

1 Talley Way, 1984. New homes now occupy the site where this home once stood in a eucalyptus grove at Talley Way and Bay Street. To the right (not visible) is the detached garage shared with 4 Talley Way, the house shown at the bottom of the next page. (Courtesy Aegis Corporation/ Drake Property Group.)

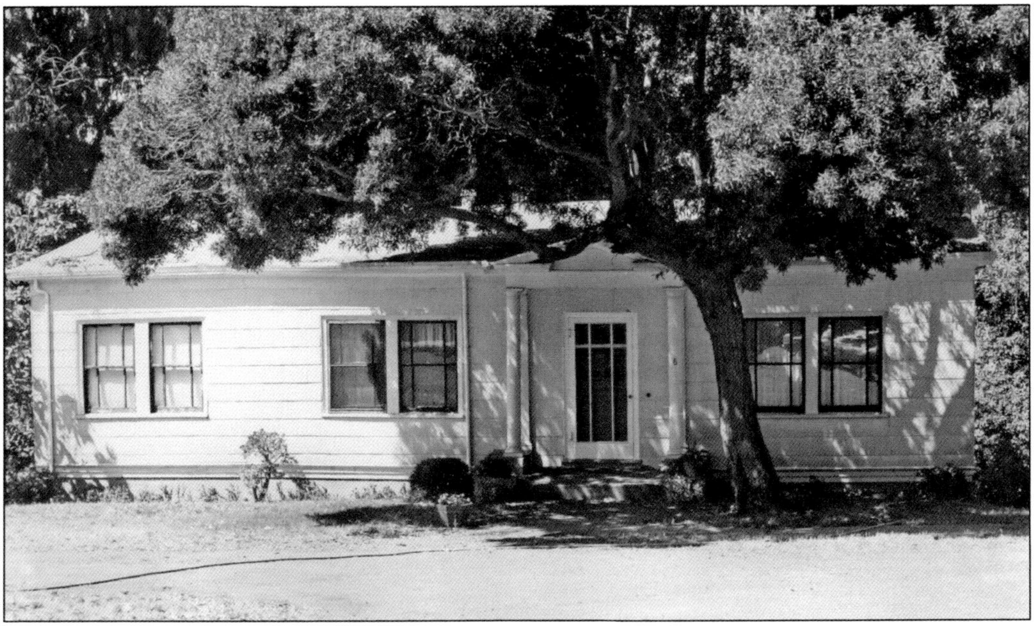

6 Kings Avenue. The house at Kings Avenue was the residence of senior plant personnel. Ernest Fawcett, a Hercules employee and one-time mayor, continued as plant manager for Valley Nitrogen Producers, occupying this home until about 1977. Fawcett liked being able to walk to work. The area around the house was open, making it a great place for his children to play. (Courtesy Dan Russell.)

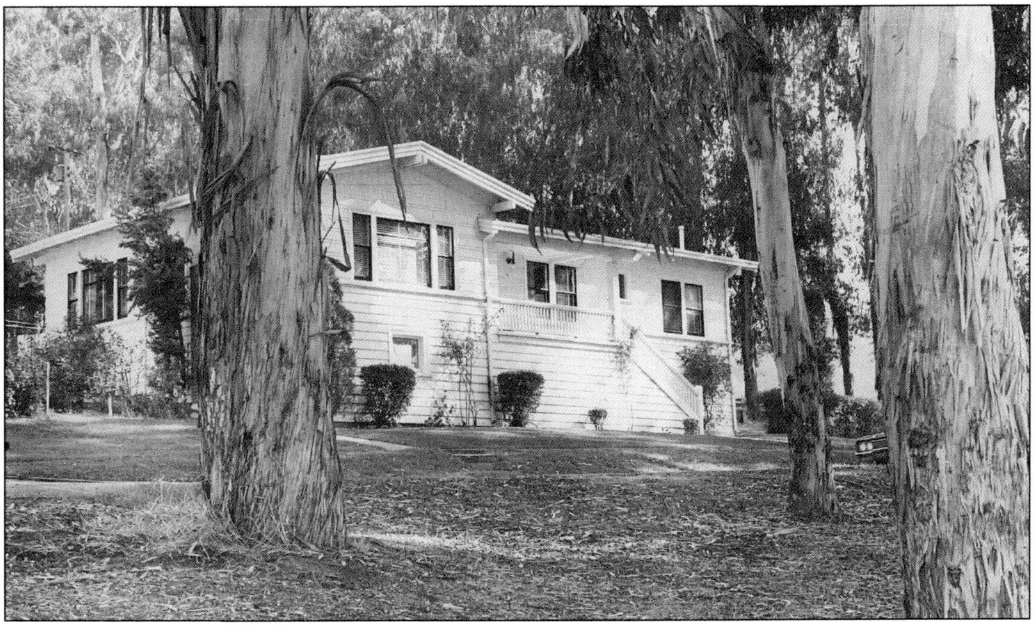

4 Talley Way, 1968. Purvis Nettleton, an engineer and one-time mayor of Hercules, resided here. Nettleton took credit for getting a paved street in front of the house. The Gordon Hoffman family lived here when Hoffman was assistant plant manager. Larry Deeg, technical superintendent, and his family were next, and then Don and Pat Browning made it their home. (Contra Costa County Historical Society)

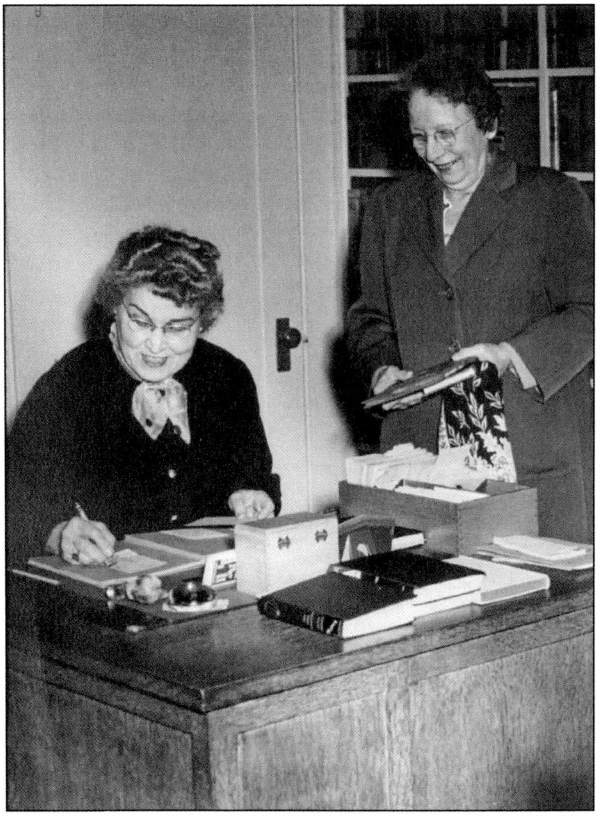

CLUBHOUSE LIBRARY. Librarian and teacher Edna Jackson checks out a book to an unidentified patron. Edna's husband, Walter, was a master mechanic at the powder company. The Hercules Club Branch of the Contra Costa Free Library was established on November 13, 1913. At its beginning, it held only 57 volumes for the use of the men of Hercules Powder Works. The image below, dating from 1980, shows a small library sign attached to the southeast corner of the club building (to the right above the hand rail). (Left, courtesy Walt Seidl; below, Hercules Historical Society.)

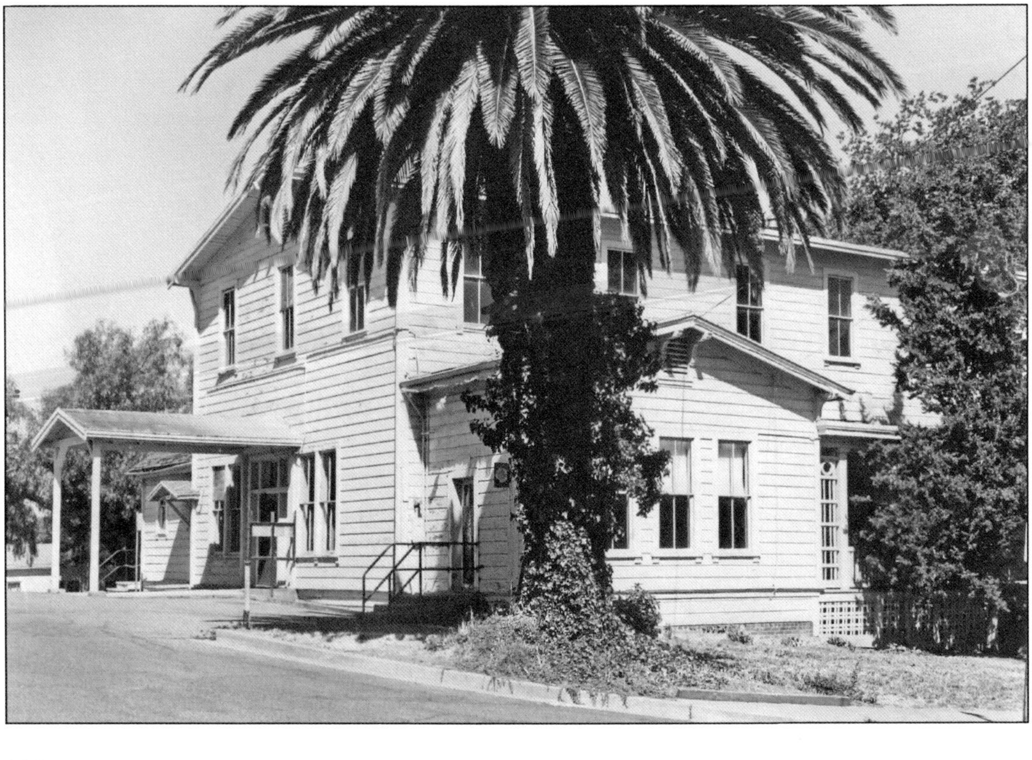

Five

The Pinole-Hercules Community

The towns of Pinole and Hercules were united by their economies and social life. Many of the workforce lived either in the company town of Hercules, or in Pinole, a 20-minute walk away. There were no stores in the Town of Hercules, but Pinole had merchants, churches, saloons, a movie theater, and a bank; thus, the payrolls of Hercules Powder supported Pinole's merchants and institutions.

Children attended the Pinole-Hercules School up to grade eight. Hercules officials served on its board. It was noted for strict discipline and high academic standards. After school, children roamed the fields, fished from the company wharves, played on the baseball field, and enjoyed the lighted tennis courts. Older children and the adults supported many social and fraternal organizations, whose traditions and annual events are fondly remembered.

Pinole, with two passenger railroad stations, was also the gateway for travel to the larger cities of the Bay Area. San Pablo Avenue, the 1865 stage road connecting the two towns, followed the hills south to Oakland and east towards Sacramento. It was designated in 1927 as a segment of US Route 40, the Lincoln Highway, the first transcontinental improved road. In 1959, Interstate 80 was constructed through the hills on a route parallel to US 40, bisecting the Hercules Works property.

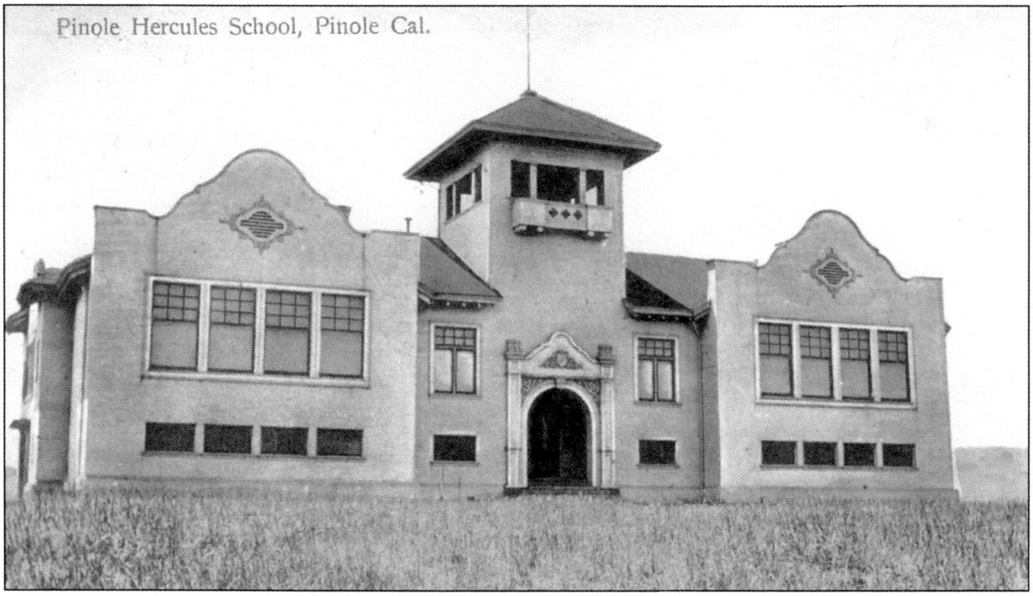

PINOLE HERCULES SCHOOL. This postcard featuring a view of the school has a postmark date of 1909. Hercules Powder participated in its construction in 1905–1906. The sender wrote to his friend, "Come down to Hercules Saturday so we can go hunting, trapping, and swimming." This building was demolished in 1968. (Courtesy Jennifer Posedel.)

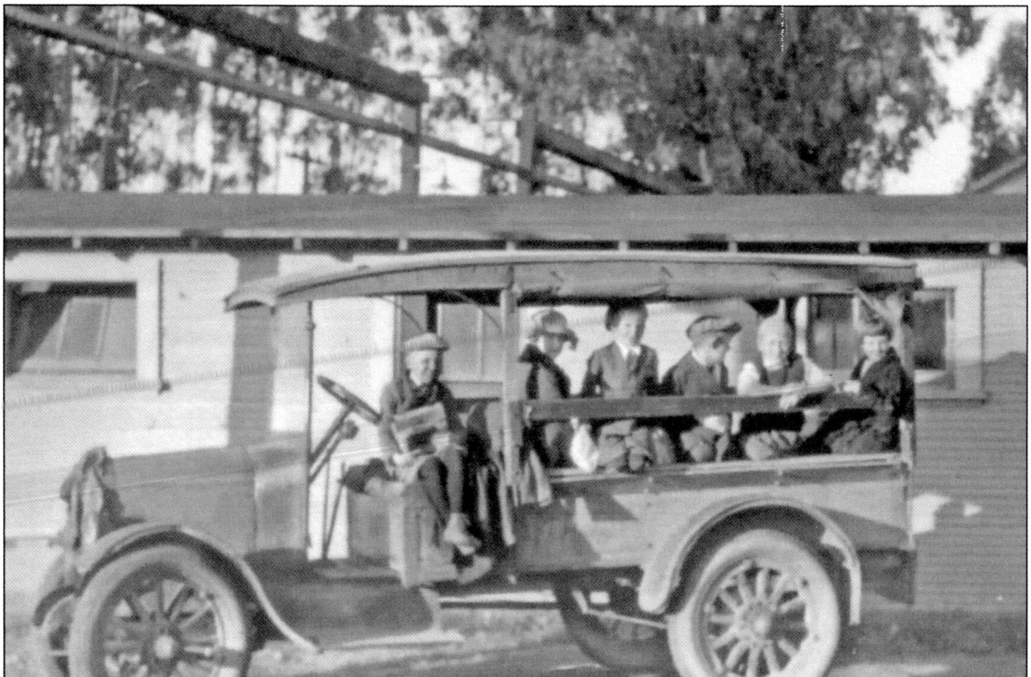

SCHOOL JITNEY. A teacher and the children of management personnel were driven to school in this omnibus. Everyone else had to walk, crossing a wooden trestle that spanned the Santa Fe tracks and climbing the steep hill to reach the school on John Street in Pinole. (Courtesy Hercules Historical Society.)

FRANCES L. ELLERHORST. Ellerhorst and her six siblings, none of whom married, lived at the family's ranch in Hercules. Ellerhorst taught locally from 1895 until 1947, retiring as principal of the Pinole-Hercules School No. 1. Her final salary was $250 a month. Sisters Emma and Dora kept house, Alice taught, Annie worked at the powder company, and brother Henry farmed. (Courtesy City of Pinole and Pinole Historical Society.)

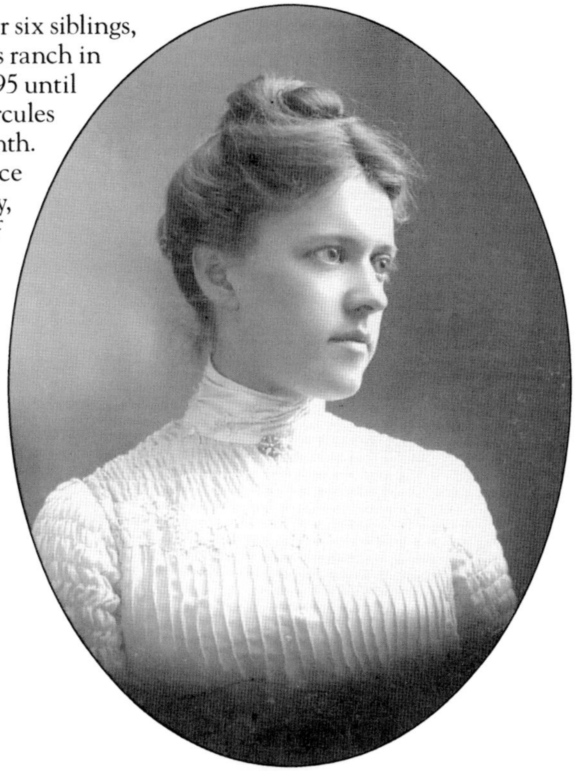

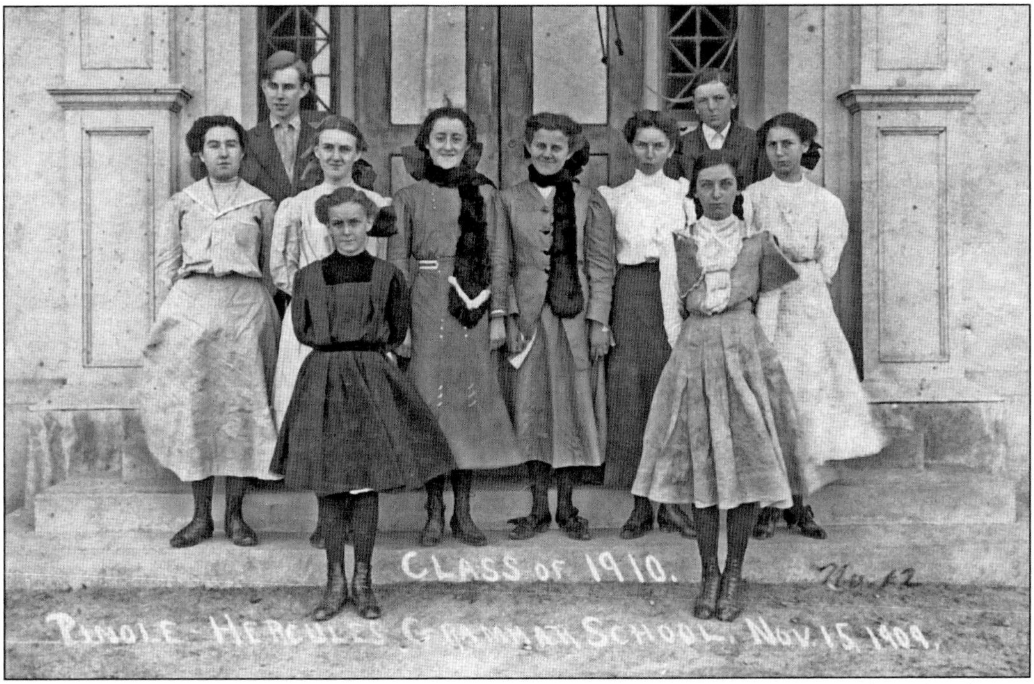

CLASS OF 1910. The graduating class of the Pinole-Hercules School posed on the school steps for a portrait on November 20, 1909. The photographer was the Anchor Studio, located at 41 Market Street, San Francisco. (Courtesy Family of Irene Silcock Dias.)

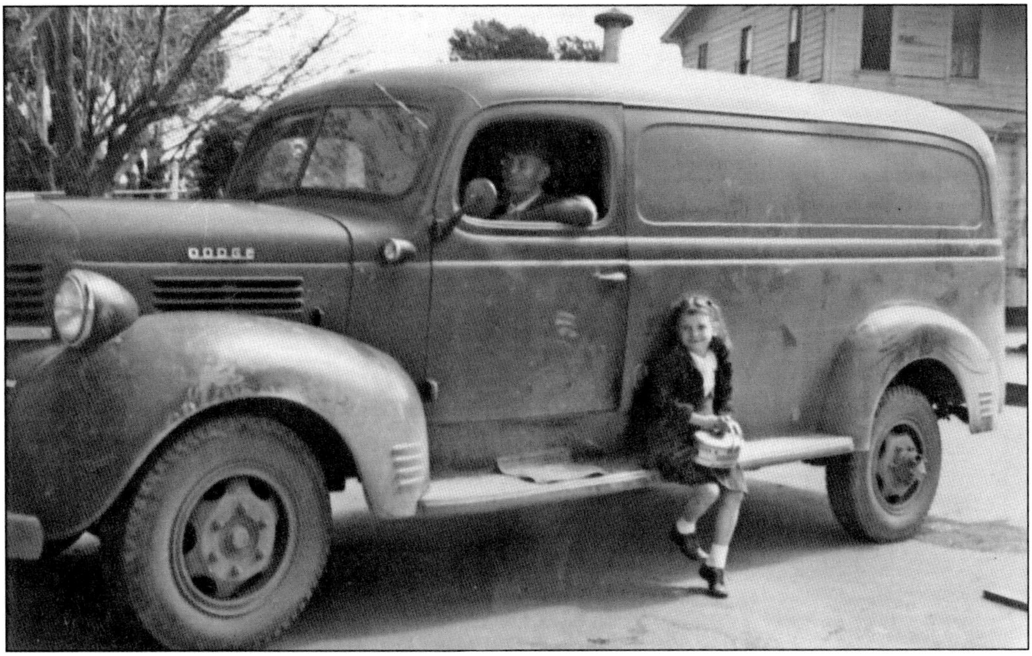

SCHOOL TRANSPORTATION. The tradition of taking children who lived on the Hill to the Pinole-Hercules School continued. In 1948, Anita Wennblom posed on the running board of the orange-colored school bus that took her, Billy and Bobby DeVrey, Danette "Lucky" Bentz, and Elise Bennett to classes. (Courtesy Anita Wennblom Broberg McKee.)

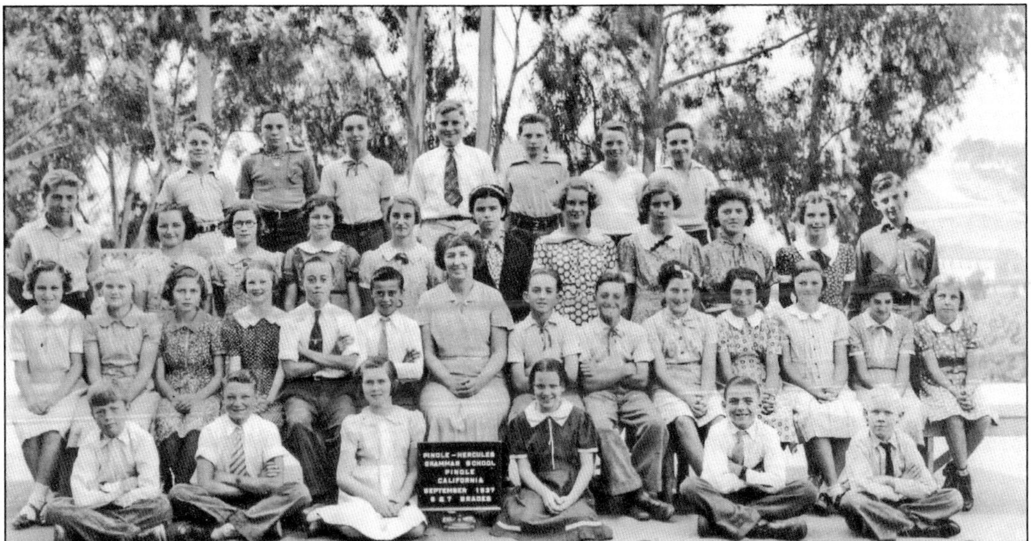

CLASS OF 1937. Those pictured are, from left to right, (first row) James Turner, Tommy Turigliatto, Jeanne Hileman, Jane Silva, Wallace Martin, and Robert Wessman; (second row) Mary Cole, Evelyn Eye, Irene Silcock, Phyllis Townes, Mike Gery, Gene Gery, Caroline Jordan, John Catrino, Orland Catrino, Patricia Malone, Helen Poulos, Anna Weiss, Adeline ?, and Doris Collins; (third row) Manual Ramos, Stella Freitas, Joella Jackson, Laverne Lewis, Ruth Befford, Margaret Faria, and Betty Boyd; (fourth row) Bob Laing, Bruce Buckley, Alfred Catrino, Sterling Kelly, Harry McKoy, Alex Clark, and Joseph Bispo. (Courtesy family of Irene Silcock Dias.)

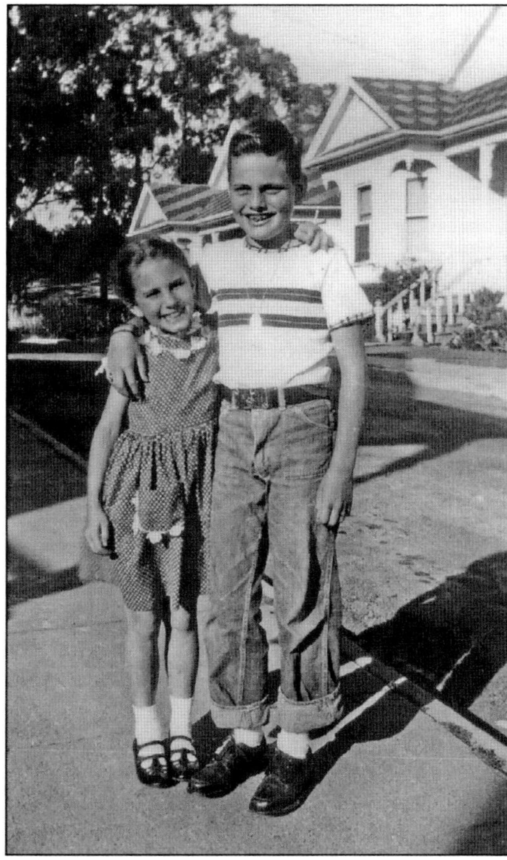

Siblings Nancy and Douglas Williams on Pinole Street. Douglas is shown wearing a school-issued dog tag. During the 1950s Cold War era, civilian preparedness included backyard bomb shelters, duck and cover atomic air raid drills at schools, and dog tags given to children with the implied purpose of identifying them following a nuclear attack. (Courtesy Estate of Ralph and Edna Williams.)

Pinole-Hercules School No. 2. Pictured are, from left to right, (first row, bottom) Louis Chavier, teacher Avanelle Hutchison, and George Parsons; (second row) Betty Beaver, James Woods, Patty Flory, Douglas Williams, Sharon Nelson, Greg Smith, Sue Marshall, Floyd VanOver, and Carol Davis; (third row) Jerry Binkley, Peggy Ashlock, Nowell MacArthur, Barbara Tames, Franz Erskine, Donna Payne, Glen Pumroy, Louise Ledford, and Robert Erbland; (fourth row) Loretta Garrett, Kenny Paules, Judy Smith, Joe Silveira, Karen Binkley, Charles Lewis, Garnet McCash, David Beatty, and Ellen Tedesco. This school opened in the fall of 1950 and was dedicated as the Margaret Collins School in May 1951. (Courtesy Douglas Williams.)

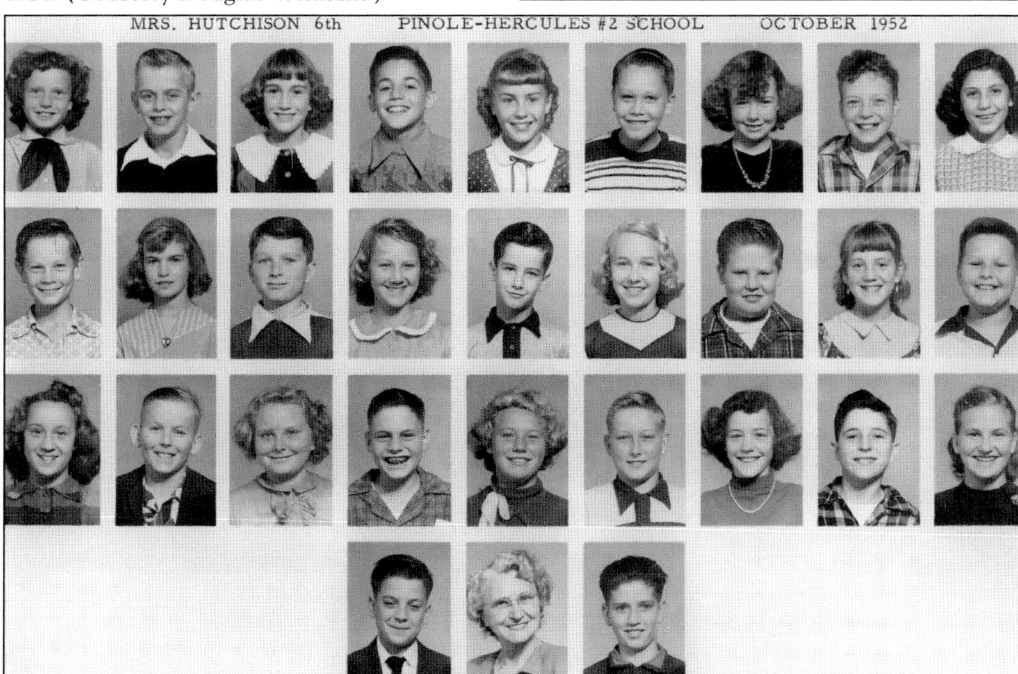

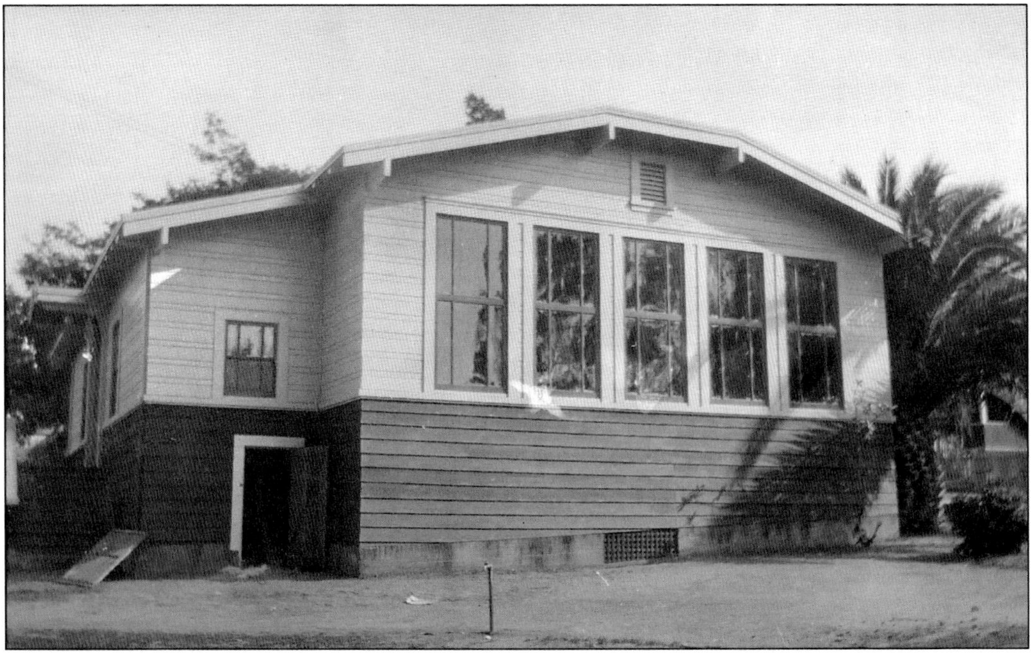

Community Center. The community center at Triangle Park on Park Street was completed in 1918. Dance classes were taught here. It was also used as a polling and meeting place and it housed a kindergarten. The community building was later sold and was moved to Pinole behind St. Joseph's Church, where it now functions as a parish hall. Although the exterior walls have been re-covered with stucco, the building is still recognizable by its clipped gable. (Courtesy Ashland Inc.)

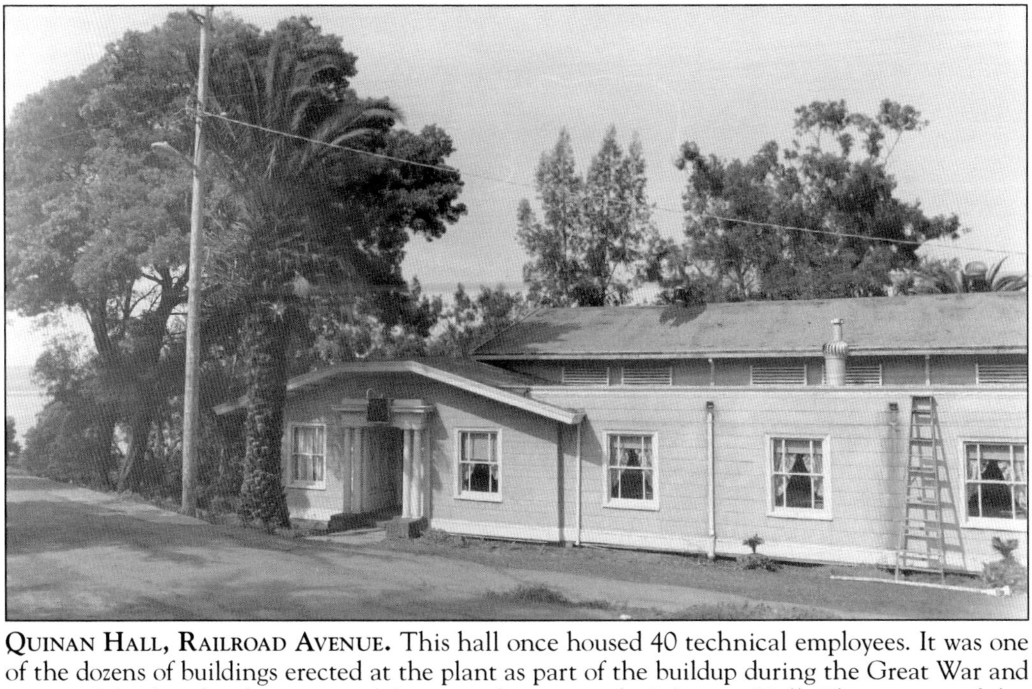

Quinan Hall, Railroad Avenue. This hall once housed 40 technical employees. It was one of the dozens of buildings erected at the plant as part of the buildup during the Great War and is one of the few that has survived. It is now known as the Masonic Hall. The interior of this building is shown on page 55. (Courtesy Dr. Joseph Mariotti.)

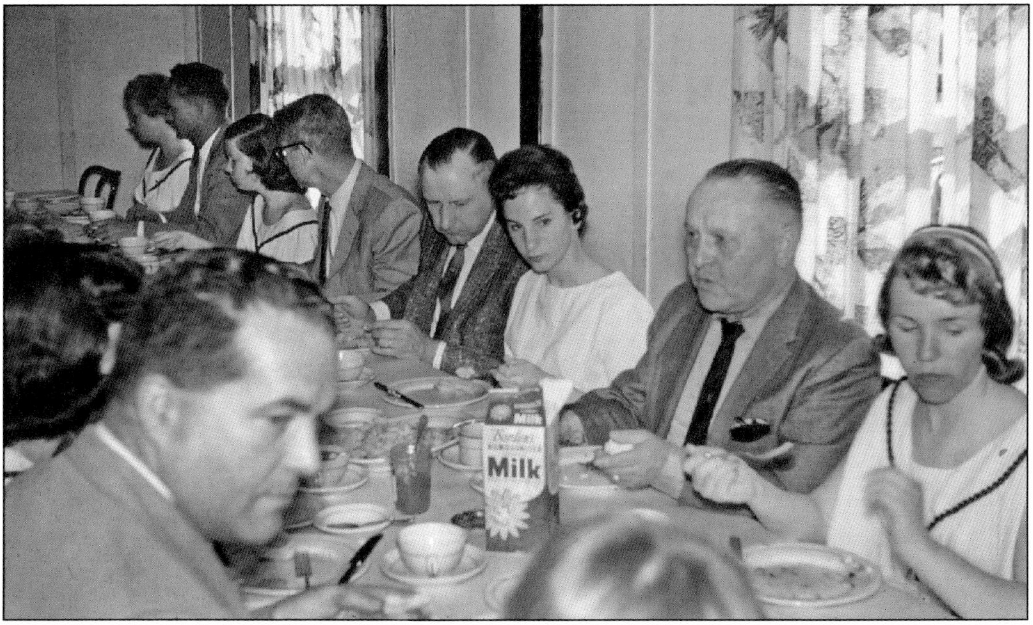

Father and Daughter Luncheon. Job's Daughters Bethel No. 149 enjoyed a meal at the Hercules Masonic Hall. Those identified are Ralph and Nancy Williams, fifth and sixth from left facing the camera, and Joyce Cross at far right. At meetings, the girls wore white togas with purple cords. Job's Daughters is a Masonic youth organization for girls. (Courtesy Estate of Ralph and Edna Williams.)

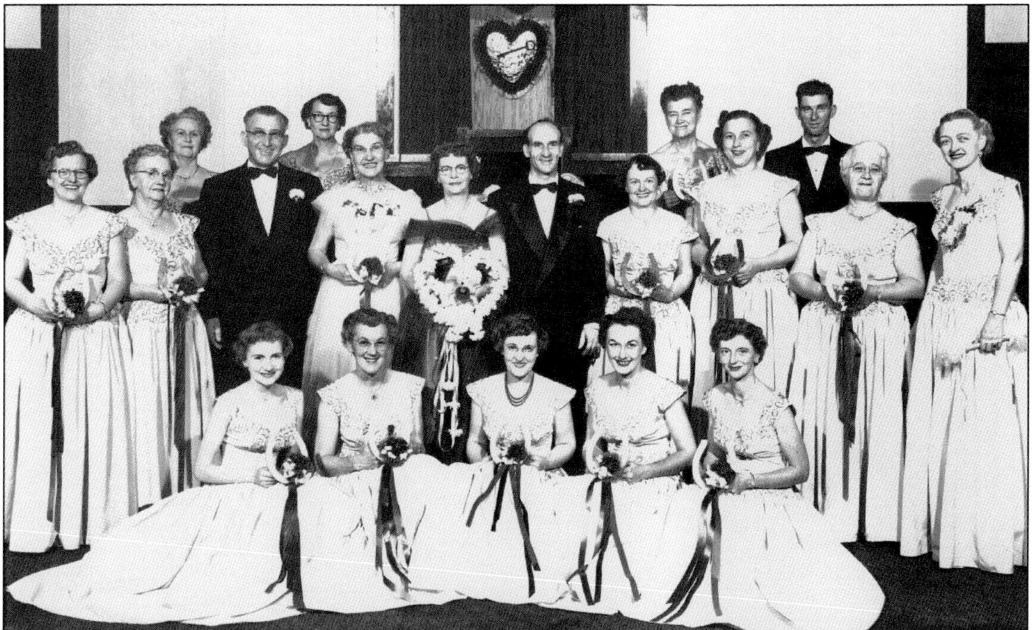

Order of Eastern Star, c. 1954. The OES Chapter No. 220 honors Nellie Mumford, worthy grand matron, who is escorted by her husband, Bill. In 1904, a Masonic organization for men and women was established in Pinole as Chapter No. 220 Order of Eastern Star. The women are celebrating the 50th anniversary of the chapter. (Courtesy Thompson family.)

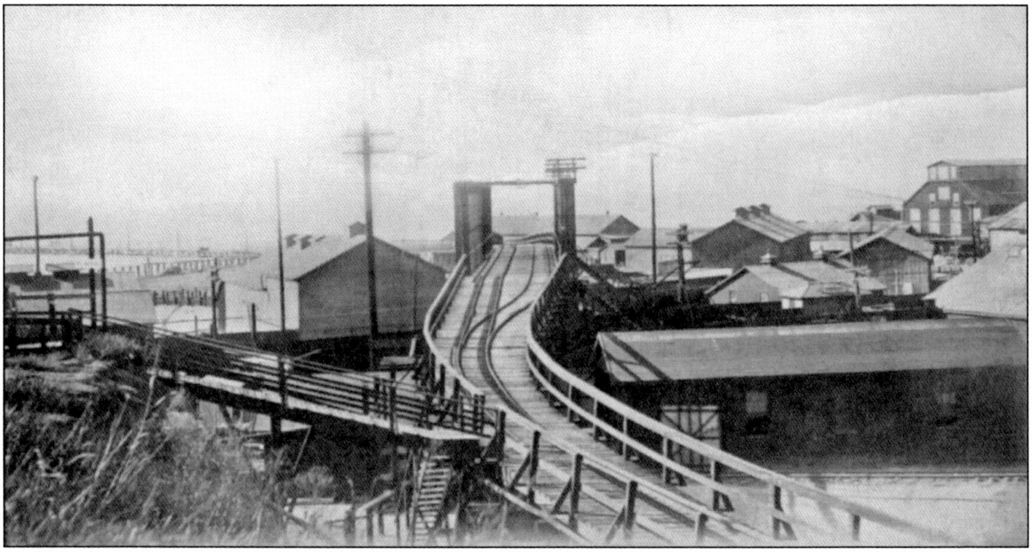

NARROW GAUGE TO WHARF. A 1906 image shows the narrow gauge line to Hercules Point, built to span the tracks. In the background (left) is the 800-foot wharf that extended over the tidelands to San Pablo Bay. At right is the newly constructed acid plant. (Courtesy William Ingalls.)

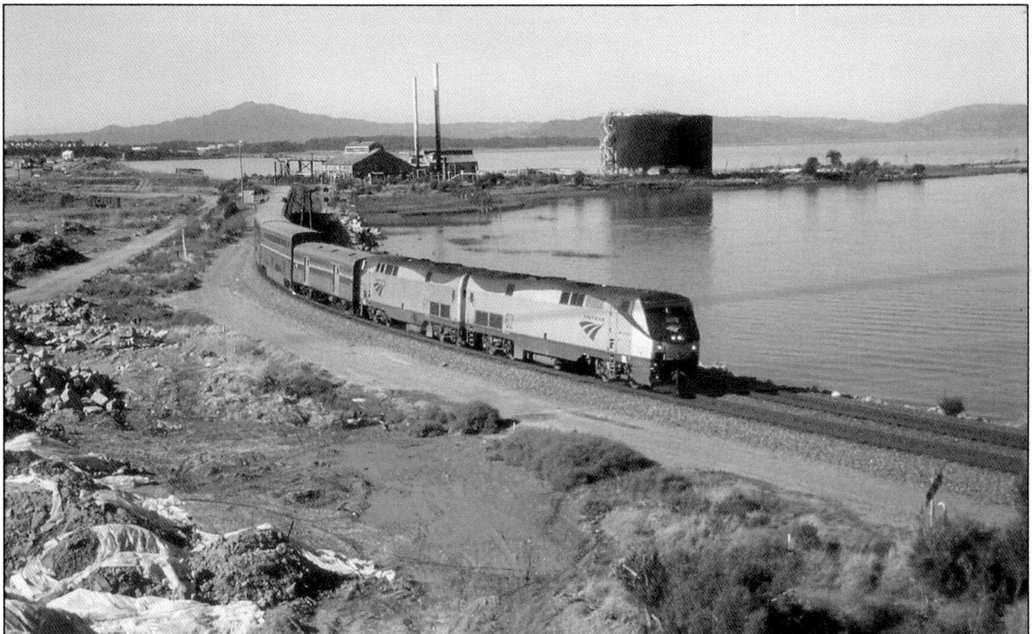

AMTRAK, NOVEMBER 2004. A Capitol Corridor passenger train passes by Hercules Point, site of the old Acid Wharf, near present-day Bayfront Boulevard, the location proposed for a new rail and ferry passenger terminal. In 1996, Union Pacific acquired the Southern Pacific Railroad, including this line. In the background are the remains of the boiler house, with engine and pump room, and a low-pressure ammonia storage tank. (Courtesy Chuck Zeiss.)

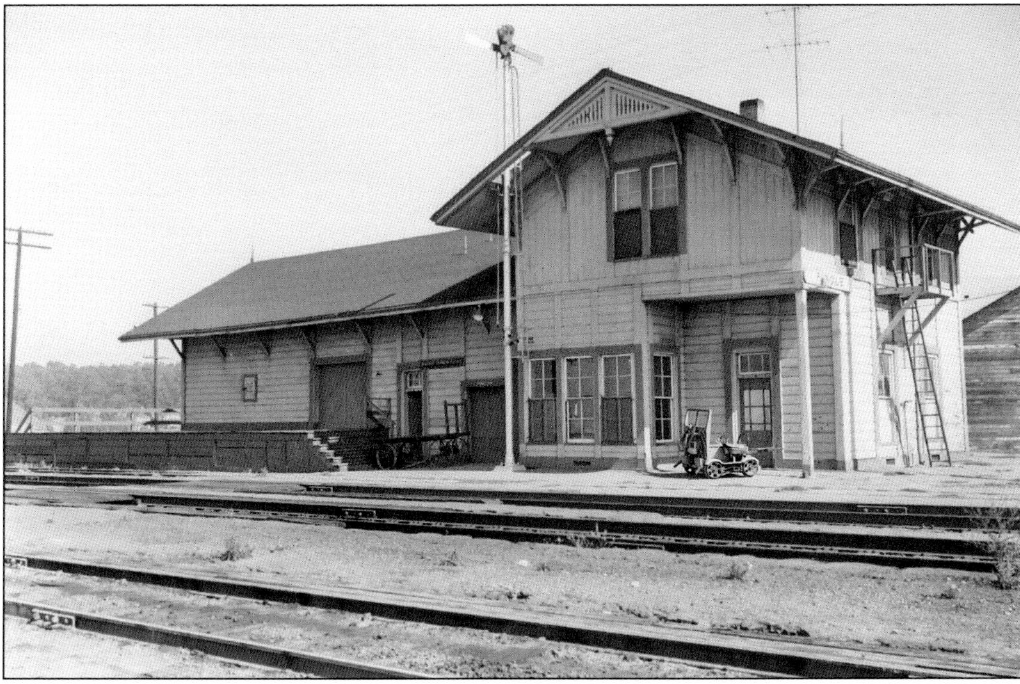

SOUTHERN PACIFIC DEPOT, 1955. The depot at the foot of Tennant Avenue in Pinole dates from the 1880s. A 1907 *Oakland Tribune* editorial criticized the powder works for locating near railroad tracks over which passenger trains operated. In 1958, the depot was demolished. (Courtesy Robert Morris.)

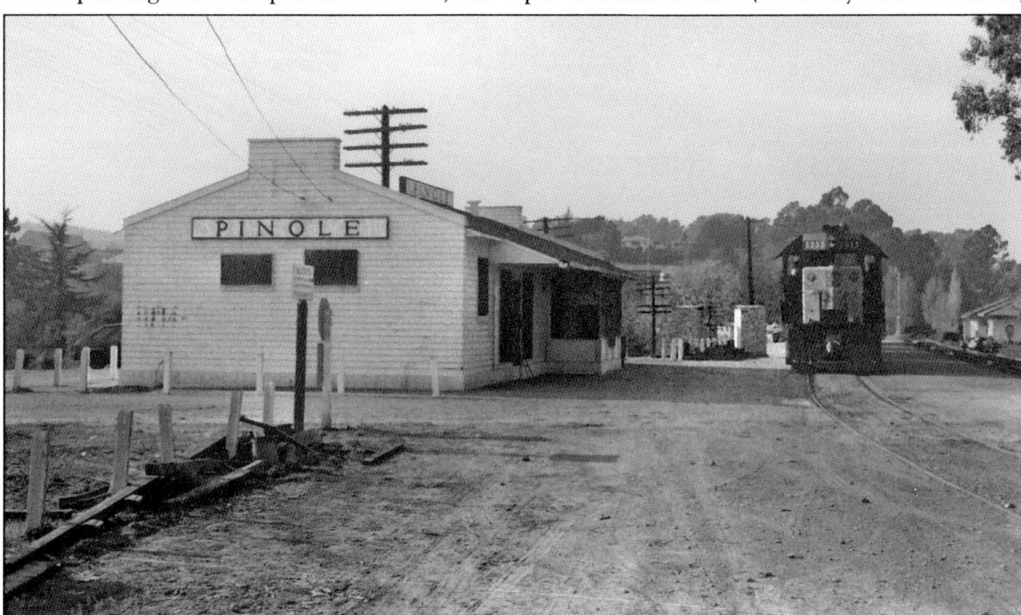

SANTA FE STATION AT PINOLE. This photograph of engine No. 3339 arriving at Pinole was taken on December 29, 1978. The depot was established in 1901, one year after Santa Fe ran its first overland train from the east into Richmond. This building was constructed in 1945 after the first station was destroyed in a fire. It was razed in 1998. The right-of-way is now owned by Burlington Northern Santa Fe. (Courtesy John Harder.)

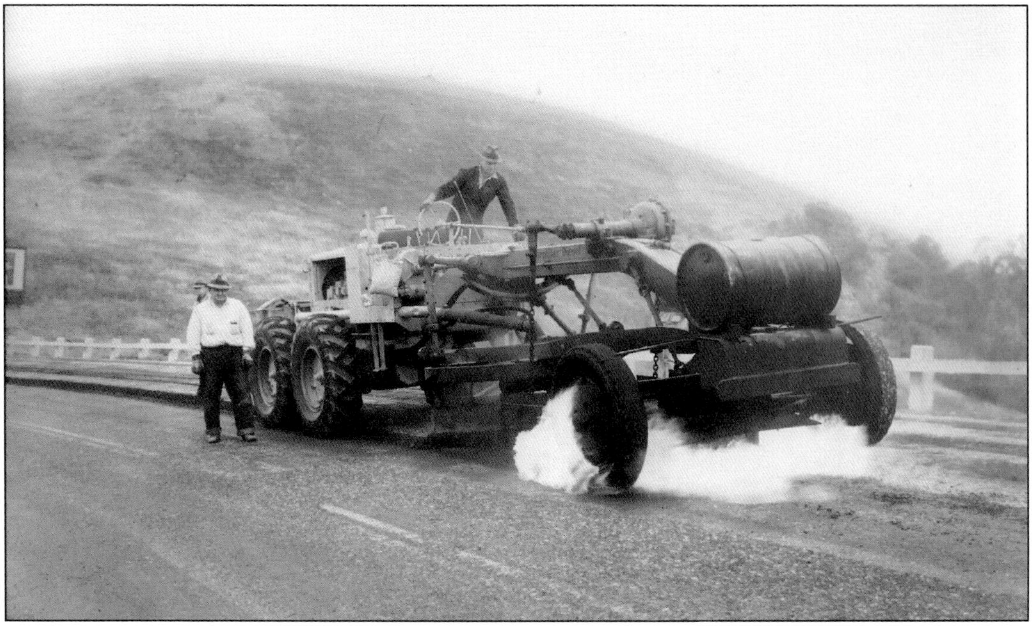

ROAD GRADING, 1939. A Depression-era crew resurfaces Highway 40, also known as San Pablo Avenue. The length within the corporate limits of Hercules is 1.86 miles. In May 1960, the city made a request to the Contra Costa County Board of Supervisors that it maintain the highway, claiming it was "used entirely by through traffic and without benefit to the community." (Courtesy Dr. Joseph Mariotti.)

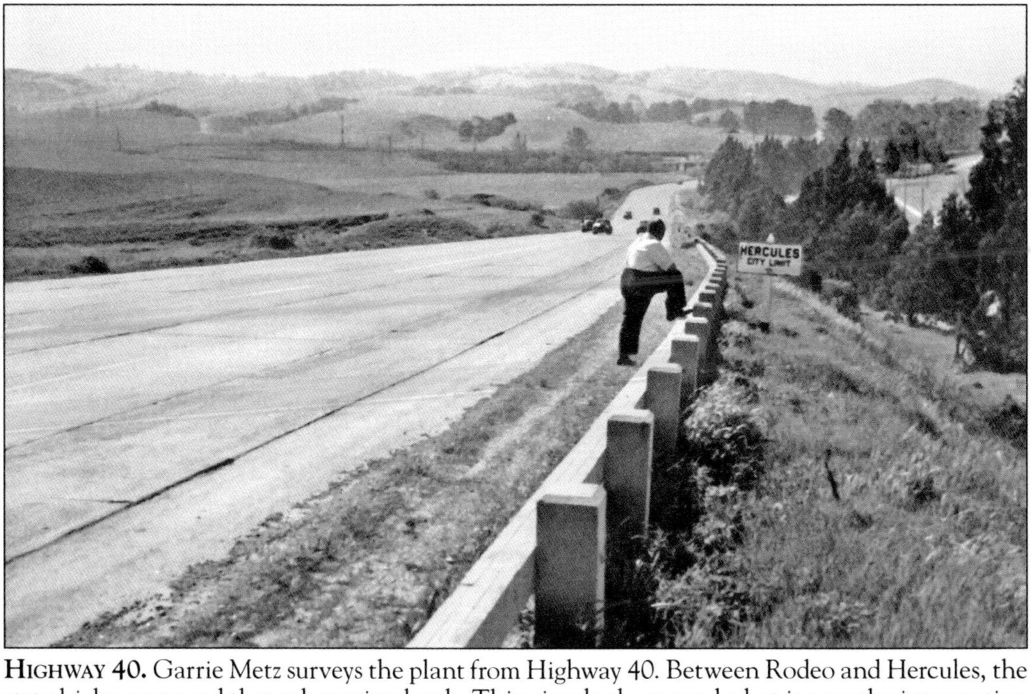

HIGHWAY 40. Garrie Metz surveys the plant from Highway 40. Between Rodeo and Hercules, the state highway wound through grazing lands. This view looks toward what is now the intersection of San Pablo Avenue and Highway 4. The Eastshore Freeway (Interstate 80) had not yet been constructed. (Courtesy Ashland-Hercules, Inc.)

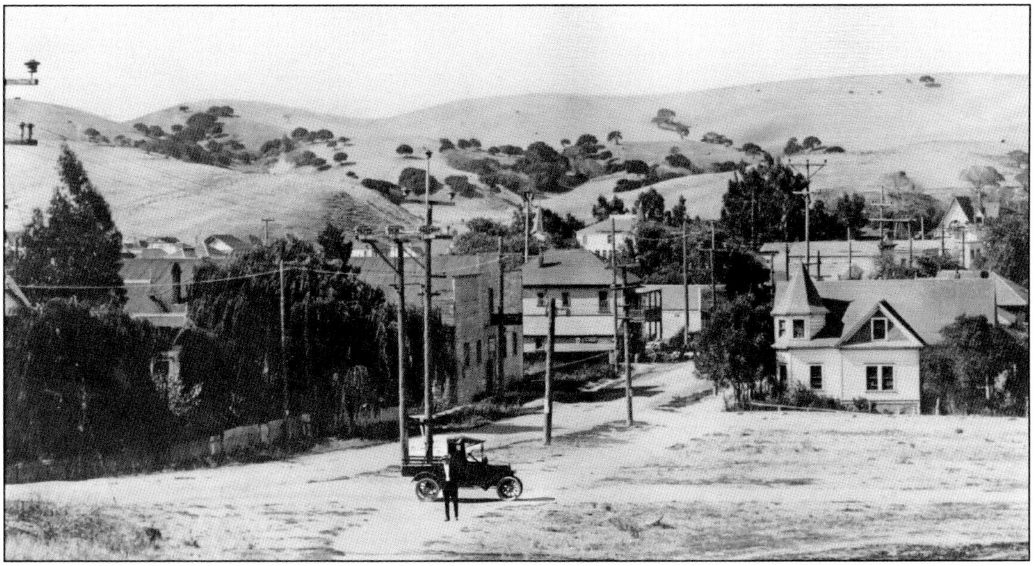

PINOLE BUSINESS DISTRICT. Pinole's business district provided shopping and entertainment opportunities for Hercules plant employees. The view above shows San Pablo Avenue before highway improvements. The house at far right is now known as the Captain's Cottage. At the center of the view below is the intersection of San Pablo and Tennant Avenues prior to the stoplight's installation in 1949. The first St. Joseph's Catholic Church (built in 1881) is at the extreme right. This church was rebuilt in 1951. (Above, courtesy Hercules Historical Society; below, courtesy Crockett Museum.)

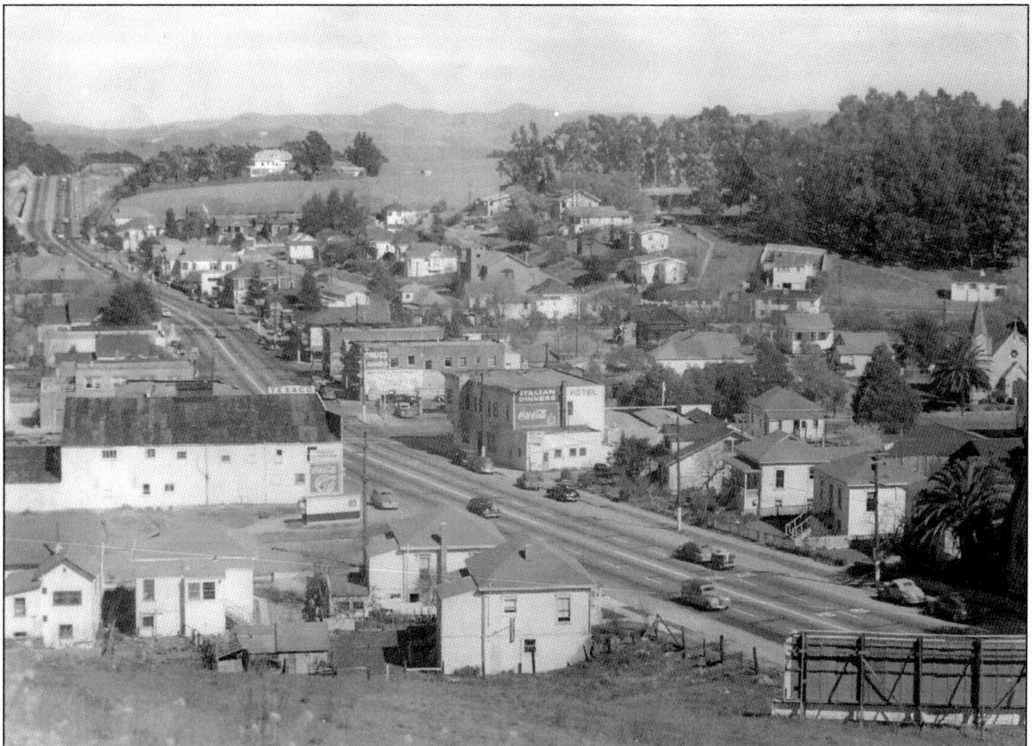

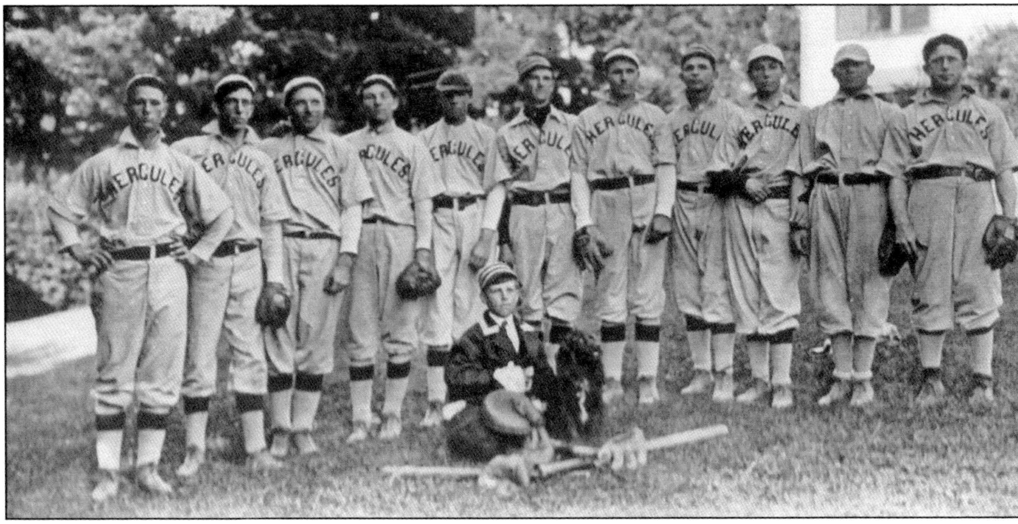

HERCULES BASEBALL, 1910S. The only identified player is Ralph Robison (far right) who played semi-professional ball for 20 years. The club played teams at Port Costa, Concord, and three teams in San Francisco known as the Equitables, Gallagher & March, and Golden Gate. In the early 1900s, steamboat excursions for players and fans were made to games at San Rafael and Napa. Other company-sponsored sports included track and field events. (Courtesy Fred Sill.)

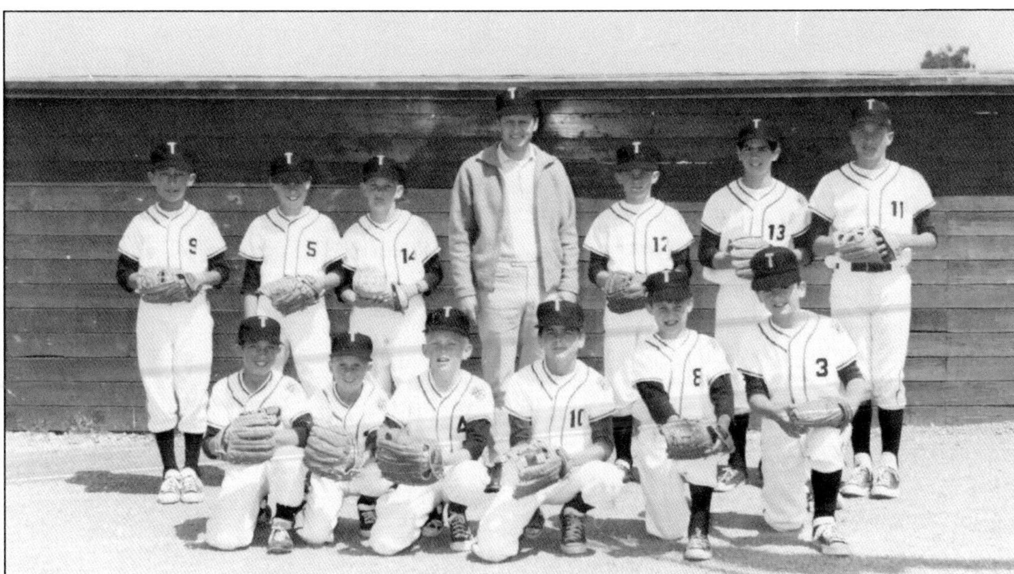

PINOLE HERCULES LITTLE LEAGUE, 1966. George Bradbury, who is standing at the center, coached the "Teamsters," a team of 10- to 12-year-old Pinole Hercules players. In the front row at far left is Mark Ferreira, fourth from left is Mike Foster, and at far right is George Bradbury. In the back at far left is Eddie Frick, with Steve Cook at far right. The other players that year who could not be matched with their uniform numbers are Russ Burns, Dennis Cooper, Greg Dutra, Elray Figurelli, Bruce Marlow, Randy Pool, Don White, Brad Weir, Bob White, and Randy Williams. (Courtesy George Bradbury.)

Ruth Robison, 1920. Robison played tennis at Hercules on a court said to be one of the first lighted tennis courts in the county. After graduating from Richmond High School, Robison earned a college degree and went on to become a physical education teacher at John Swett High School in Crockett. (Courtesy Nancy M. Tooker.)

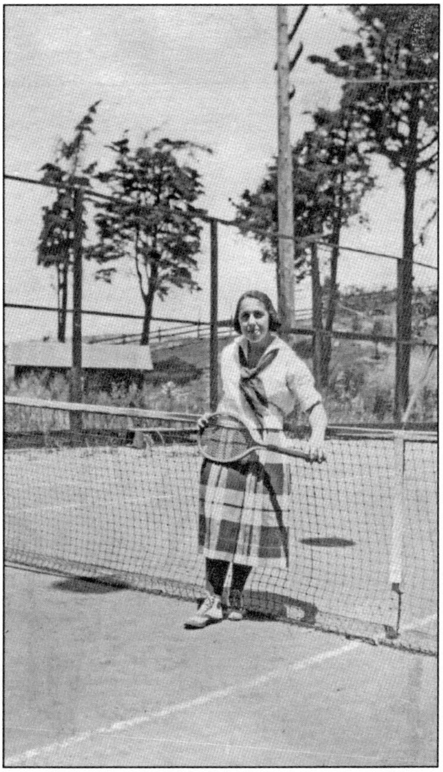

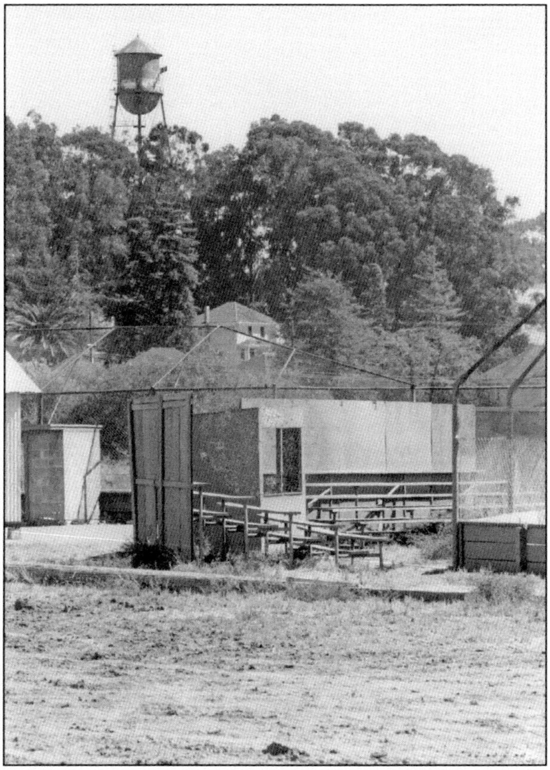

Little League Field, 1978. The fields adjacent to the Southern Pacific tracks and Hercules Avenue were in use for nearly three-quarters of a century. The three fields were the "farm" for six- to seven-year-olds, the "minor field" for the eight-to-nine age group, and the "major field" for 10- to 12-year-old players. Today, the parcel, which is marked by introduced palm trees, has been allowed to return to wetlands. (Courtesy Lynn Fissell.)

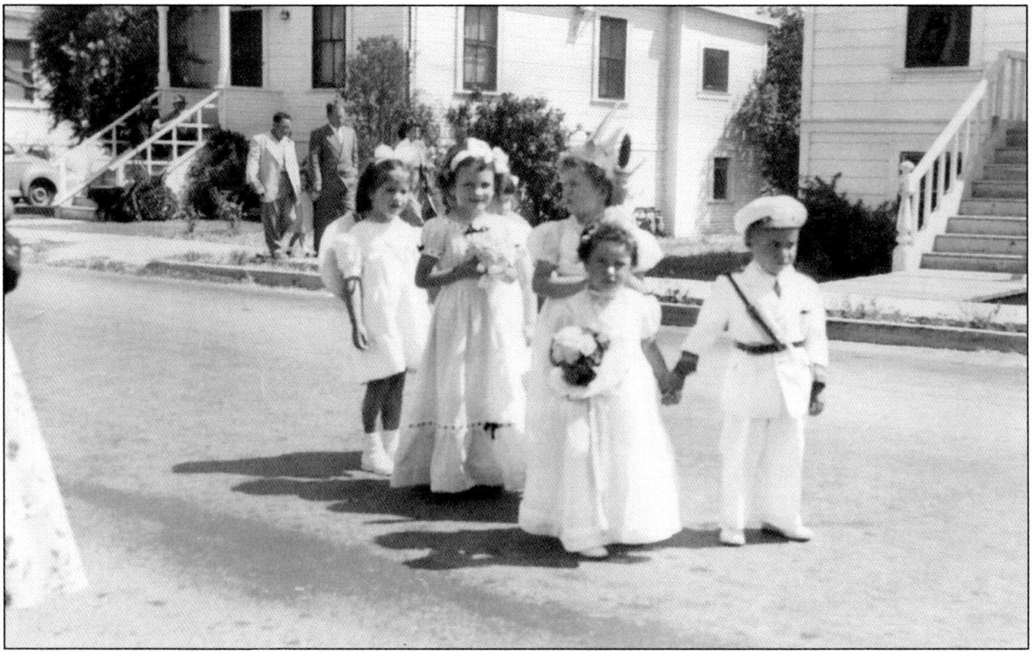

HOLY GHOST PARADE, 1949. The Portuguese tradition of the Holy Ghost festival included an annual procession. Hercules resident Anita Wennbloom, at center holding flowers, and friends assembled for the parade. One girl (rear) added wings to her costume. (Courtesy Anita Wennblom Broberg McKee.)

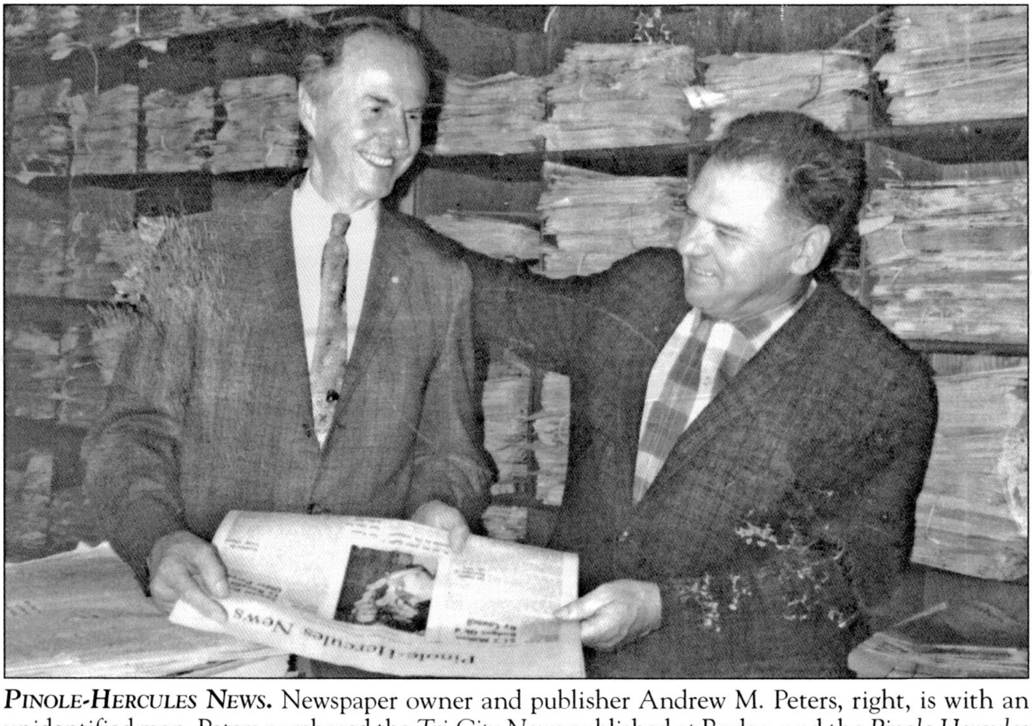

PINOLE-HERCULES NEWS. Newspaper owner and publisher Andrew M. Peters, right, is with an unidentified man. Peters purchased the *Tri-City News* published at Rodeo, and the *Pinole-Hercules News*, founded in the 1946 by Jessie Howe Clark. Both papers carried local news and many personal items. (Courtesy Dr. Joseph Mariotti.)

Six

Hercules Village

Almost from its founding, Hercules Powder diversified its products away from explosives in response to relentless changes in markets and innovations in technology. In the decade after World War II, markets declined sharply for the nitroglycerine-based dynamites produced at the Hercules Works. Production shifted to intermediate chemicals and fertilizers. In 1950, a large anhydrous ammonia facility was installed, and from 1959, new equipment produced methanol and formaldehydes. In 1955, the black blasting powder line was closed. Explosives manufacturing finally ceased in 1964 and the old industrial buildings were demolished. The Hercules Powder Company became Hercules Incorporated in 1968.

By 1966, the Hercules Works consisted of a chemical plant on the bay front, surrounded by large tracts of unused land. Hercules Incorporated briefly considered taking on the task of developing a suburban city on its unused land, but concluded to establish a master plan, then sell large tracts to residential builders. In 1972, the municipality adopted a general plan. In 1973, a new municipal code was adopted, redesignating the town as a city. In 1974, the first homes were built on a subdivided tract on the hills above the upper Refugio Valley.

In 1976, the chemical plant, and much of the lower Refugio Valley, was sold to Valley Nitrogen Producers, a fertilizer cooperative. Additional large tracts were carved out of the remaining lands, including, in 1979, the core bay front site around the old Hercules Station, now merely a siding on the Southern Pacific Railroad's transcontinental line.

In 1980, the remaining 36 buildings on the Hill, in the Village, and the Acid Wharf were listed on the National Register of Historic Places. In 1984, twenty houses in the Village were restored for use as residences. Since then, the city has grown into a transit-oriented, residential suburb with more than 25,000 residents.

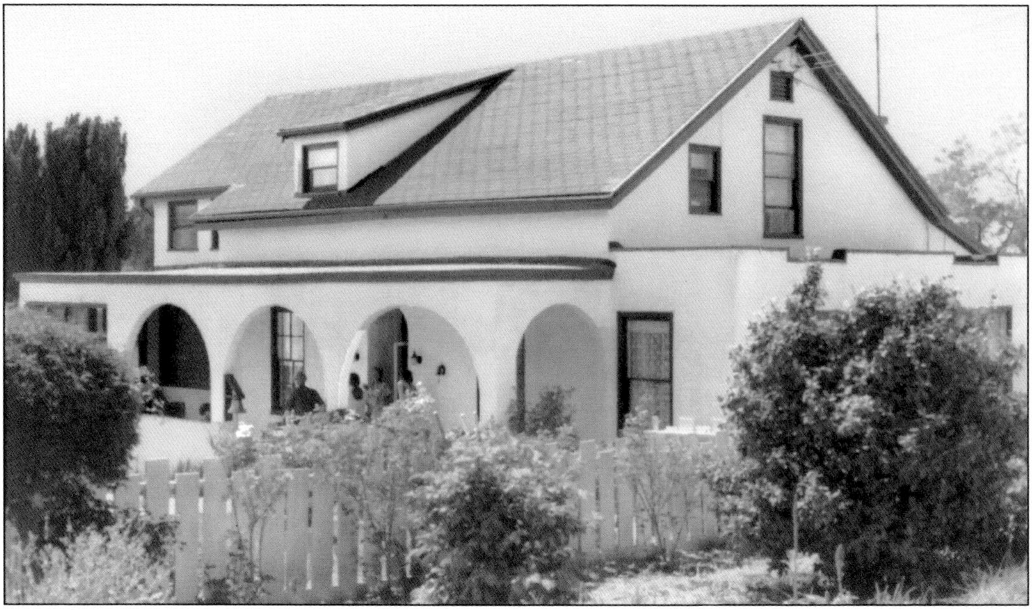

McLeod Ranch, 1978. The ranch, once the site of the only privately owned home in Hercules, is located near the former Santa Fe Railroad station. John and Sara McLeod were the third to occupy the ranch, sold to them by the Ellerhorst family, who had purchased it from Kate Cousins, granddaughter of the original grantee of the Rancho El Pinole, Ignacio Martinez. It was built around 1873. Since then, the exterior of the house has been considerably changed by alterations and additions. The house was included on a tour of old Hercules sponsored by HERC, the Hercules Environmental Resources Committee, in May 1978. Motorized cable cars picked up sightseers at Tennant and San Pablo Avenues, making stops at the clubhouse and houses in the former company town. (Both courtesy Dr. Joseph Mariotti.)

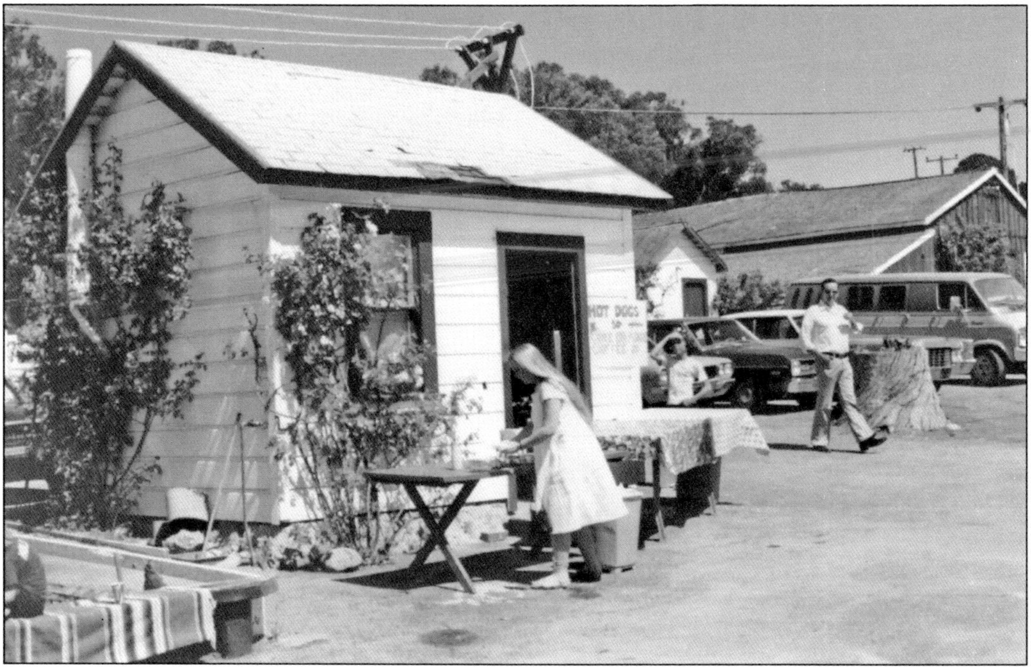

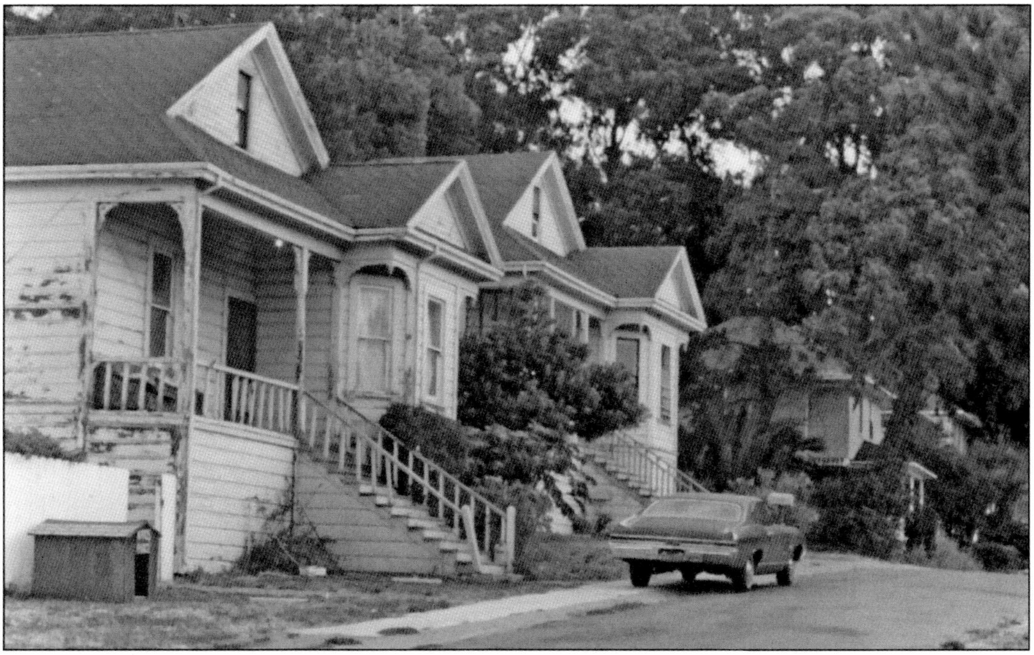

COMPANY-BUILT HOMES. Because there were few rentals in Pinole in the late 1890s, John Bermingham Jr., plant superintendent, ordered the construction of 12 company houses, such as these shown in a 1979 photograph of Pinole Street. They were built for plant foremen and others holding "superior" positions. Later, Bermingham added 50 additional cottages for workmen and their families. (Courtesy Dr. Joseph Mariotti.)

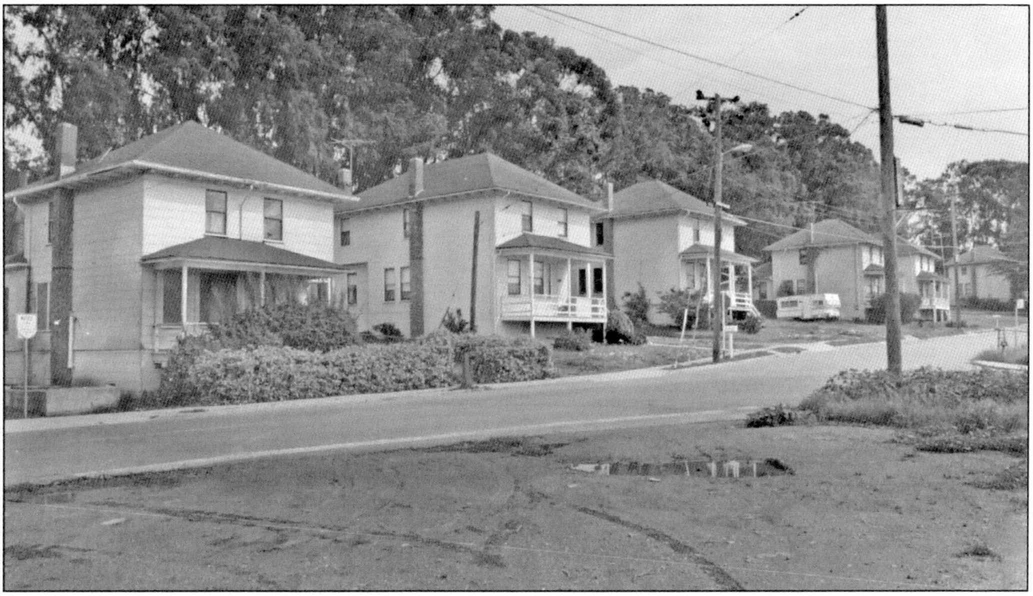

SANTA FE AVENUE, 1979. These two-story pattern book houses, dating from the early 1900s, were among the last occupied when Hercules Incorporated sold the plant and town buildings. In the last years of plant operation, houses fell into disrepair, and as they became vacant, many were torn down. These remaining houses were moved into the historic district and rehabilitated in 1984. (Courtesy Dr. Joseph Mariotti.)

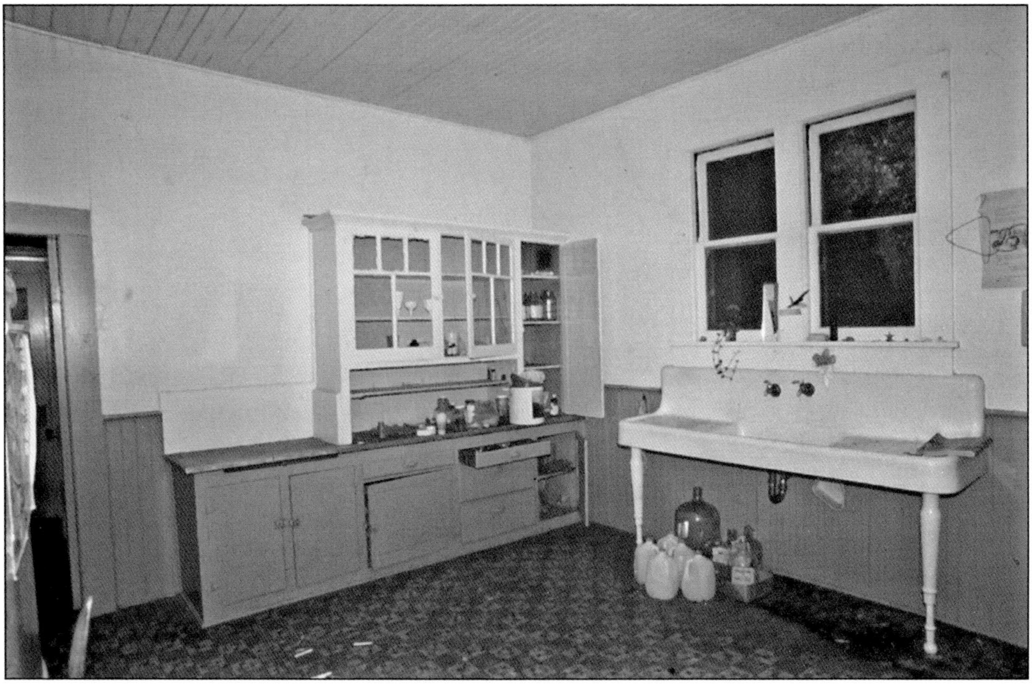

EARLY KITCHEN. This kitchen has a 1920s sink, with a wooden counter top. The floor is linoleum. When the homes were rehabilitated in the early 1980s, the wall to the right of the windows was bumped out. Additional windows were installed, plus new floor coverings, updated appliances and plumbing, and white cabinets that replaced the old built-ins. (Courtesy Aegis Corporation/Drake Property Group.)

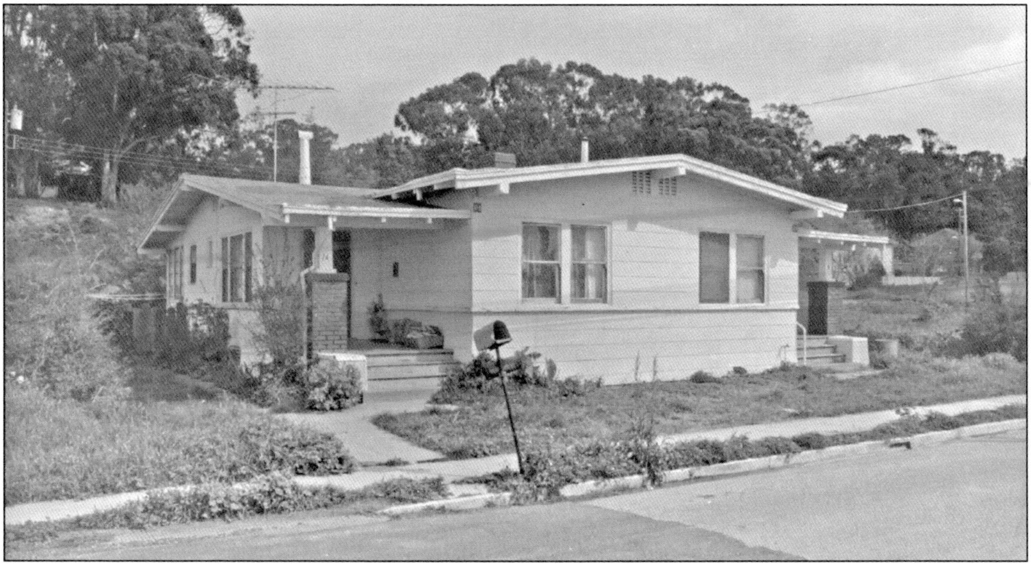

CRAFTSMAN-STYLE DUPLEX. This house at 1A Santa Fe Avenue, photographed in the late 1970s, was once the home of Jessie Buckley, who lived in the village for 30 years after her husband, Rollie, died in a 1948 explosion at the plant. The employee magazine once described the street as "charming with its rows of cozy little bungalows" where "families live in comfort and contentment." (Courtesy Dr. Joseph Mariotti.)

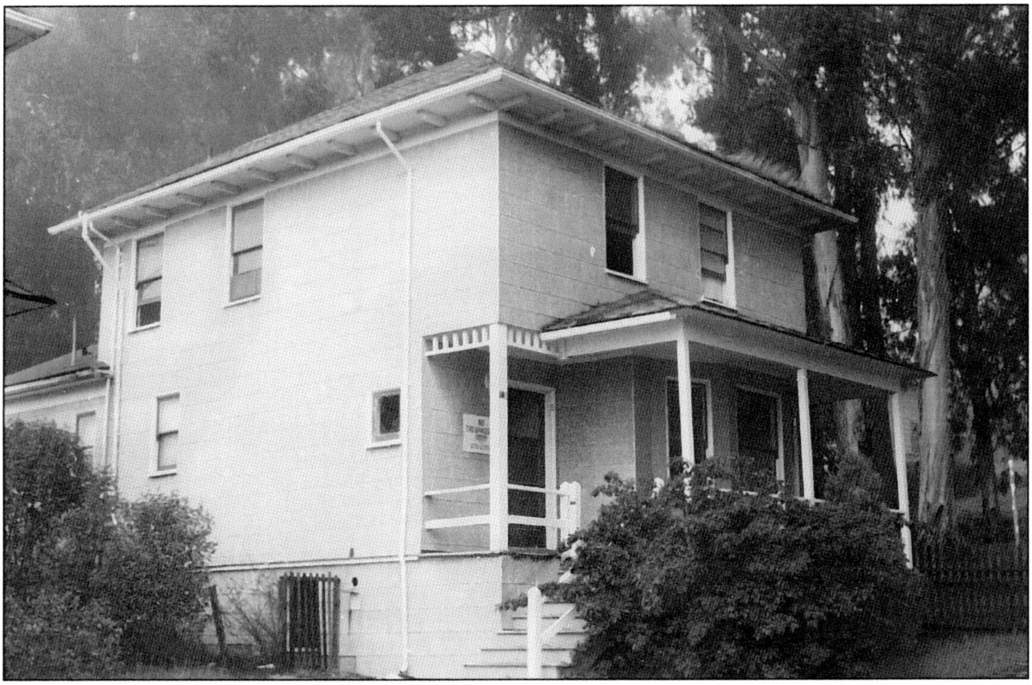

COLONIAL REVIVAL–STYLE DWELLING. The historic village includes 17 buildings in a simplified version of the Colonial Revival style that was popular from about 1895 to 1910. Like this house, all of the residences in the district sit on raised foundations. This two-story house has a hip roof, full-width front porch, and one-story rear service porch with kitchen and pantry. The original siding had been covered by asbestos that was removed during the restoration process. (Courtesy Hercules Historical Society.)

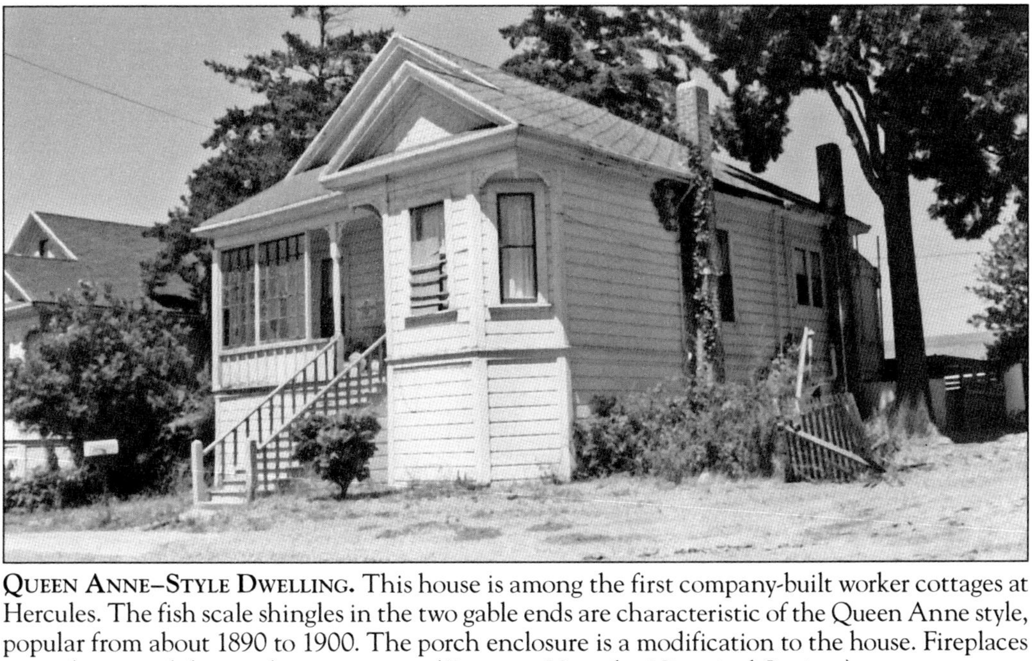

QUEEN ANNE–STYLE DWELLING. This house is among the first company-built worker cottages at Hercules. The fish scale shingles in the two gable ends are characteristic of the Queen Anne style, popular from about 1890 to 1900. The porch enclosure is a modification to the house. Fireplaces were eliminated during the restoration. (Courtesy Hercules Historical Society.)

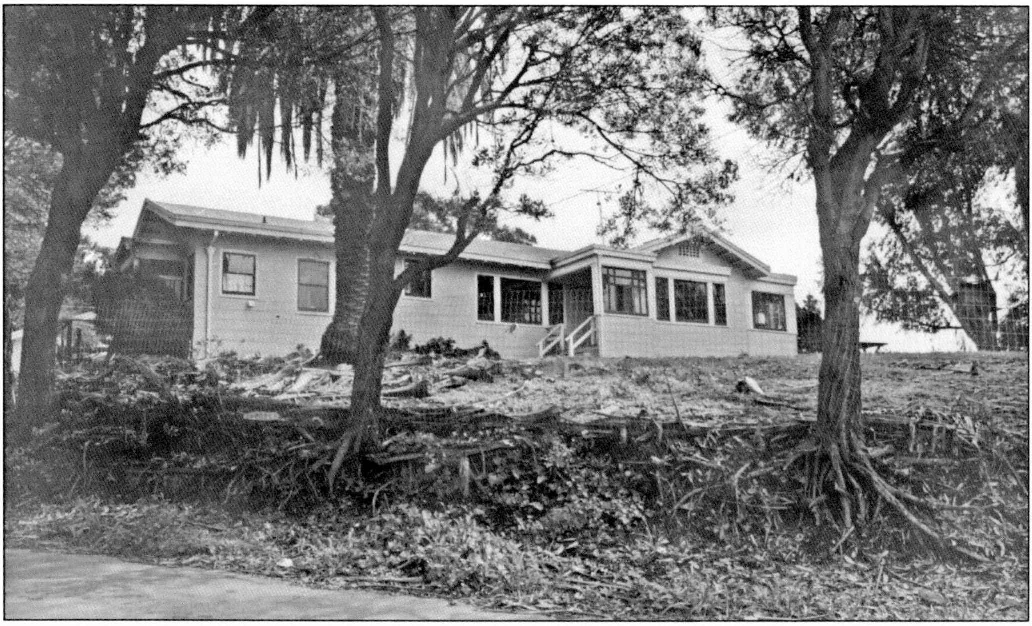

1991 Railroad Avenue, c. 1979. This Craftsman-style bungalow represents the third major style of housing built in the district. Following the plant closure, it was temporarily used for city council meetings. In 1980, the facility was listed on the National Register of Historic Places as part of the Hercules Village. The house, known as the Civic Arts Building, was refurbished in 2008. Site improvements included a parking lot and retaining walls. (Courtesy Dr. Joseph Mariotti.)

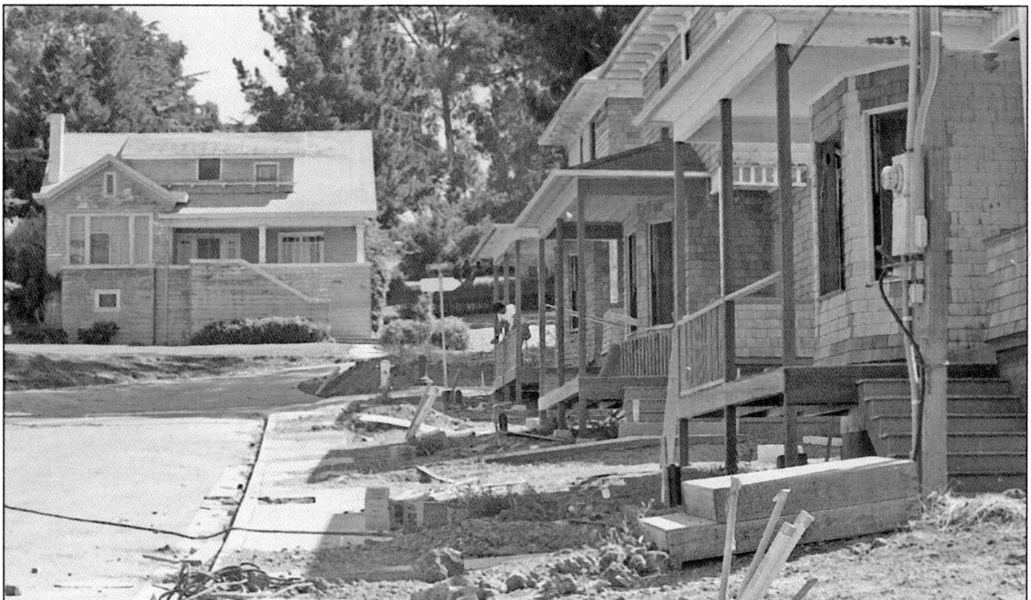

Bay Street Progress, 1984. Porches and basements are being rebuilt at the homes on Bay Street. Care was taken to restore the street-facades to their original appearance. Additions and extensions were made only in the rear and along the alleys behind the houses. At the end of the street is 1 Talley Way. Not part of the historic district, the house was later moved to a nearby location where it awaits its next use. (Courtesy Aegis Corporation/Drake Property Group.)

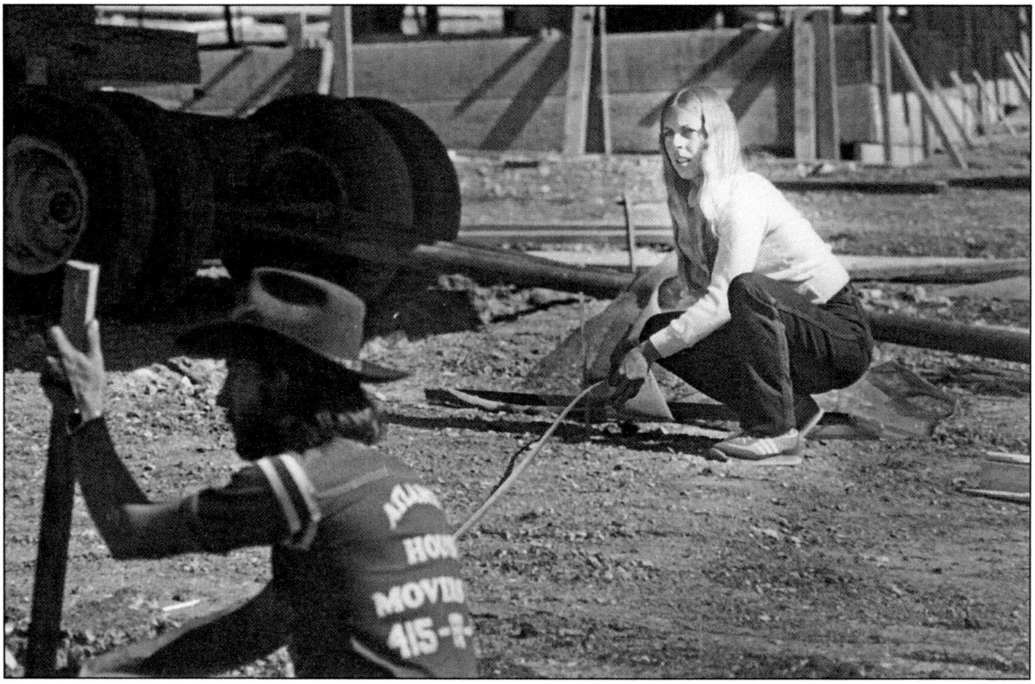

Relocating Houses. In October 1981, Atlantic House Movers of Fremont moved 13 homes, each weighing an estimated 30 tons. The houses were moved from adjacent streets to form a cluster on Bay and Pinole Streets, together with seven other homes on their original sites. According to the developer, there was no precedent for moving houses in a registered historic district. (Both courtesy Hercules Historical Society.)

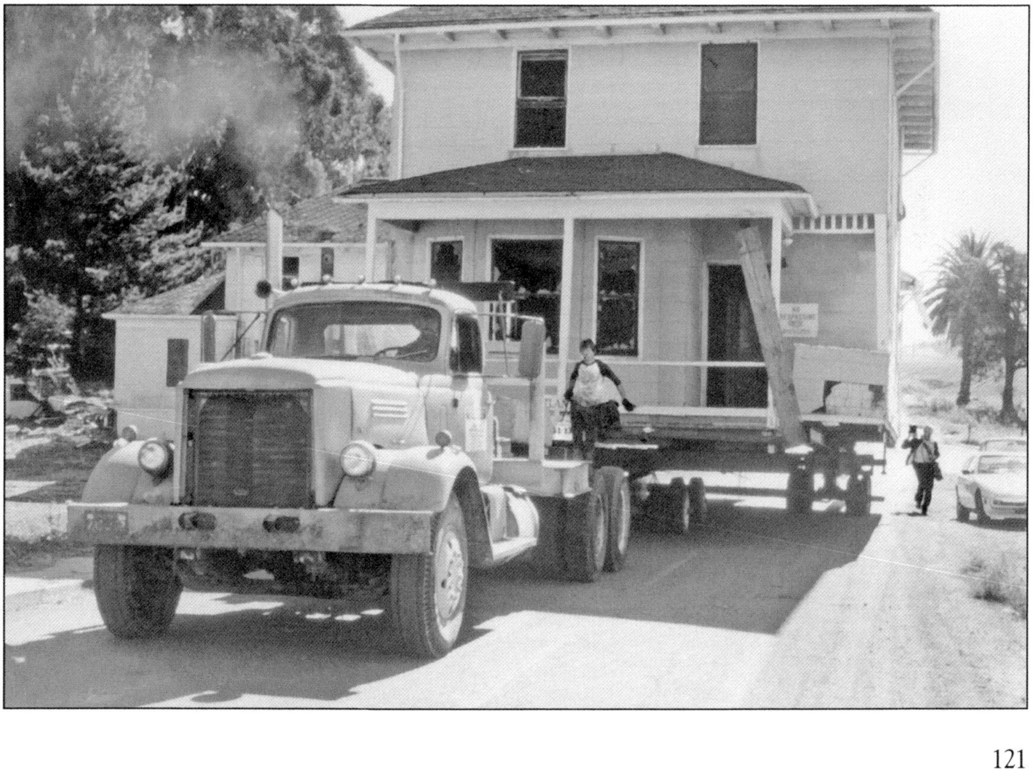

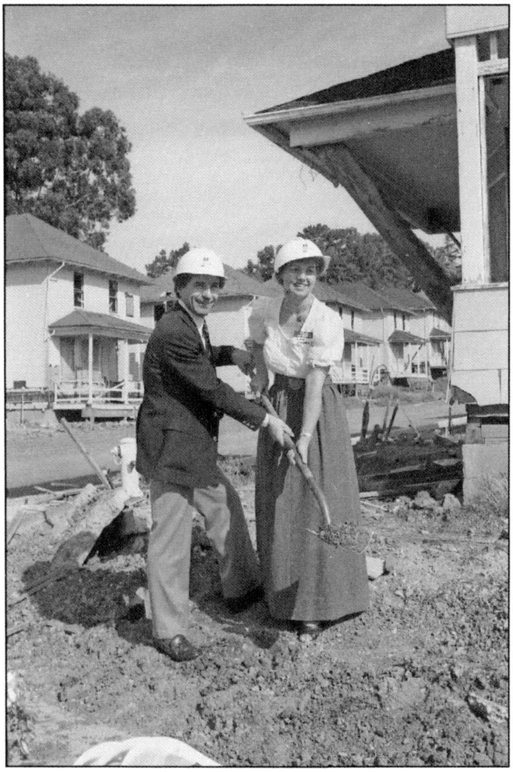

GROUND BREAKING, JANUARY 1984. Peter Supino and then-Hercules mayor Lynn Fissell (formerly Judnich) turn the ceremonial spade of earth, launching Aegis Financial Corporation's project to restore the historic district. Supino's company had worked since 1978 to get permits in place for the project. (Courtesy Aegis Corporation/Drake Property Group.)

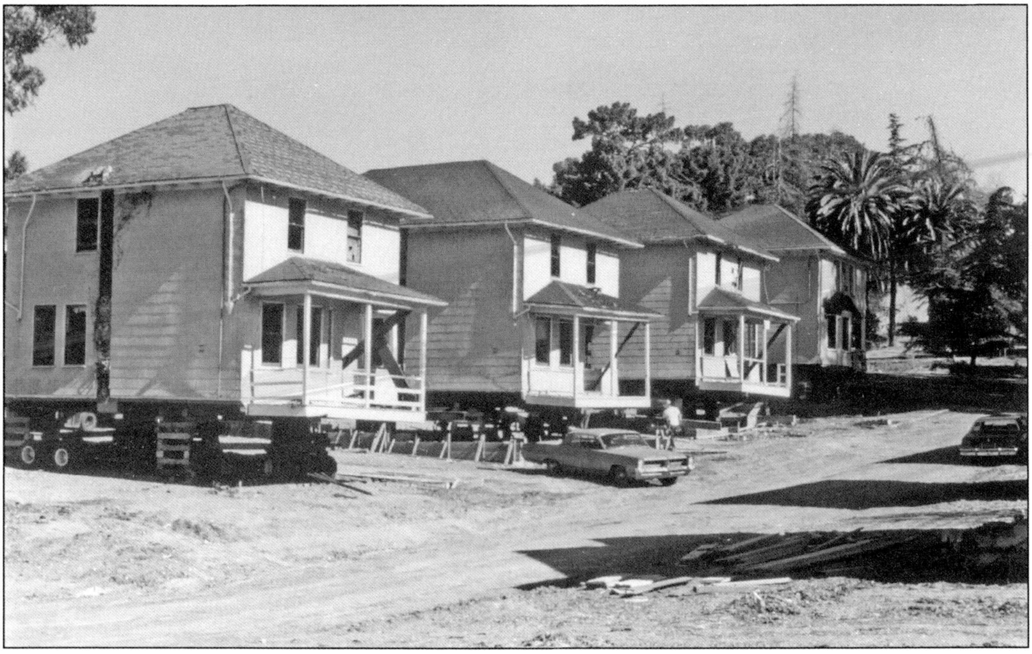

READY FOR NEW FOUNDATIONS. New foundations were built. Front porches, steps, and roofs were reinforced. Nearly 50 percent of the shingles were reused. Design guidelines for historic preservation developed in 2004, and revised in 2006, now govern the alteration or restoration of the homes' exterior features. (Courtesy Aegis Corporation/Drake Property Group.)

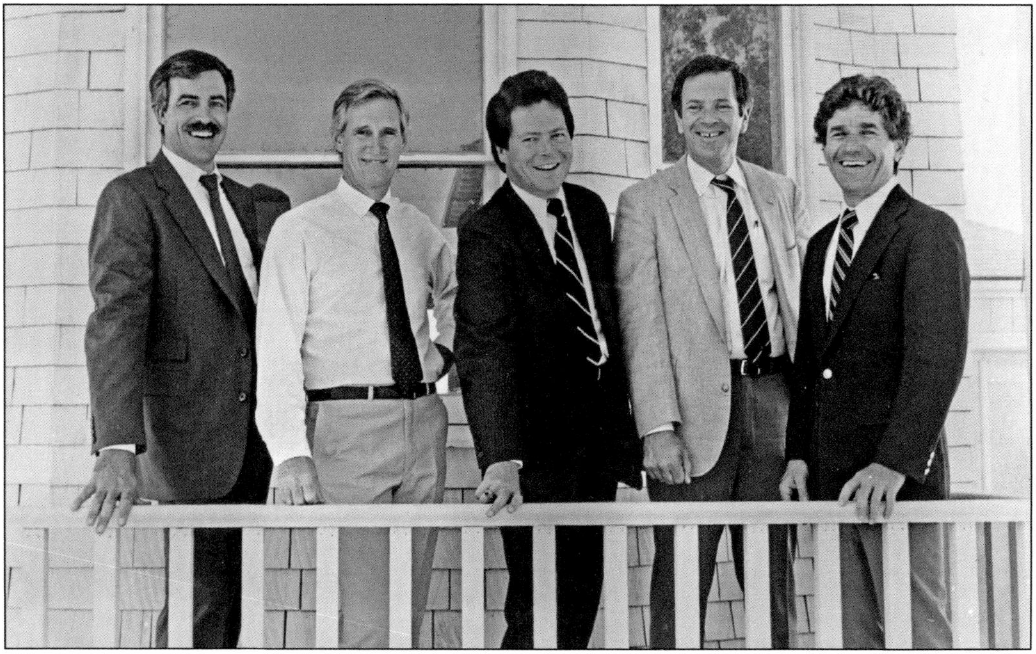

DEVELOPMENT TEAM. From left to right are Roger Nelson, president of Midstate Construction Company; Robert Berner, vice president of Aegis Corporation, former executive director of the San Francisco Heritage Foundation, and current executive director of the Marin Agricultural Land Trust, Point Reyes Station; unidentified; Phillip J. Von Pinnon, former development consultant to Aegis Corporation; and Peter F. Supino, president of Aegis Corporation and now a principal in the Drake Property Group. Developer is Aegis Corporation. Construction contractor Midstate also rehabilitated the clubhouse in 1986. (Courtesy Aegis Corporation/Drake Property Group.)

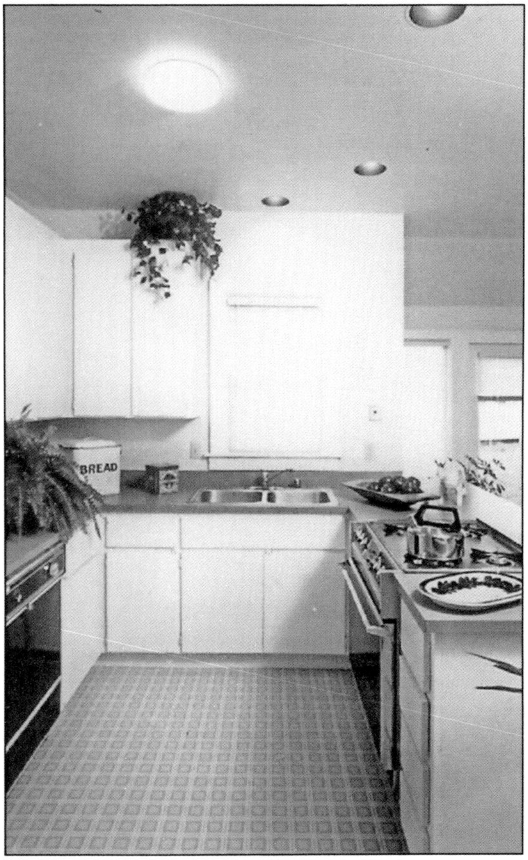

UPDATED KITCHEN. Modernizing touches were added sparingly to create space for kitchen work islands and dining rooms. Contemporary appliances were installed, but vinyl floors were selected that resembled the look of linoleum floor coverings from an earlier period. The rear wall was extended and decks were added to provide additional living area. Second bathrooms were carved out of the existing space. (Courtesy Aegis Corporation/Drake Property Group.)

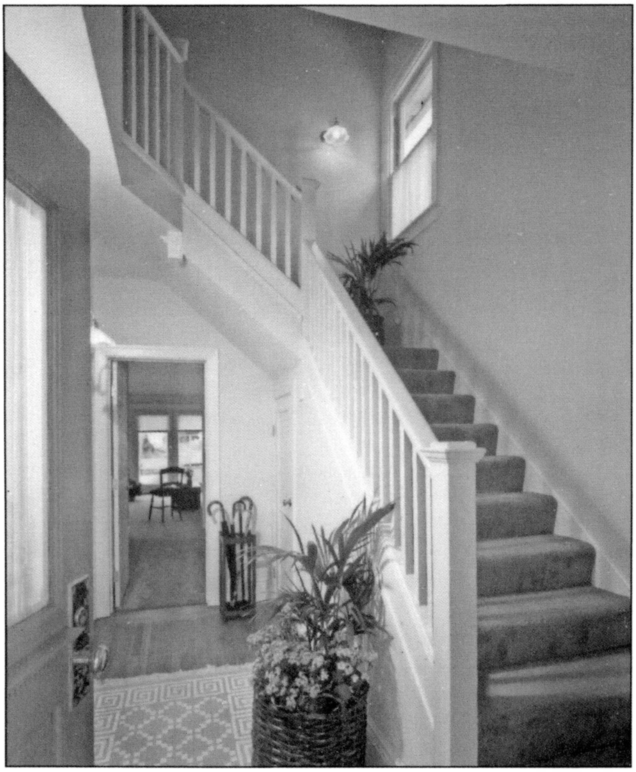

Foyer and Stairway. Inside the houses, updates were kept to a minimum. Stairways, moldings, wood floors, and high baseboards were replicated from the originals. Restoration of the historic district homes earned the Best in the West award from the Pacific Coast Builders Conference and a 1987–1988 Western Home award, co-sponsored by *Sunset* and the American Institute of Architects. (Courtesy Aegis Corporation/ Drake Property Group.)

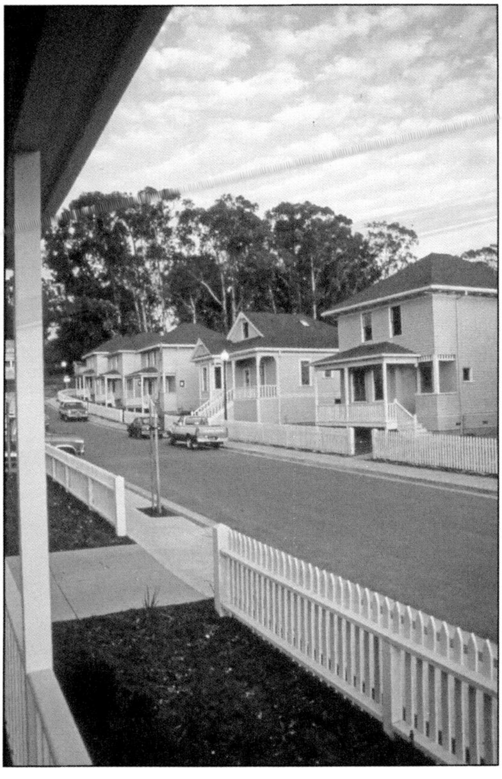

Bay Street Completed, 1984. During the planning, designers debated the style of the picket fences in the district, because the spade top, pointed top, and oval top were all in style when the houses were built. The street was kept at its original width of 25 feet. Each house has a brass plaque near the front door, designating its National Register status. (Courtesy Aegis Corporation/Drake Property Group.)

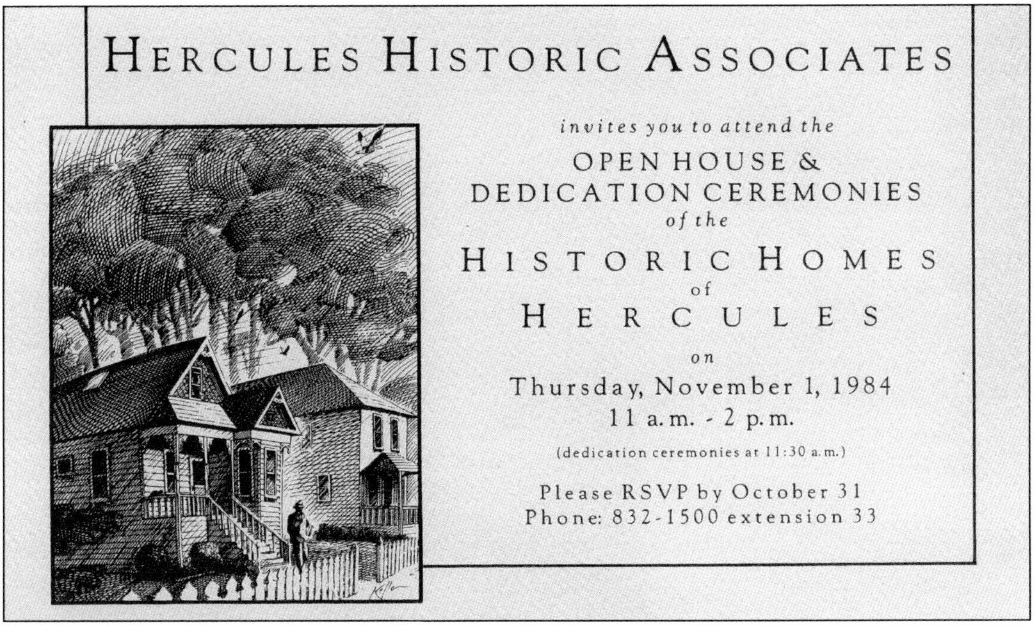

OPEN HOUSE, 1984. Hercules Historic Associates dedicated the 20 restored historic homes of Hercules on November 1, 1984, with an open house and public offering. This image recalls the 1947 photograph of Garrie Metz, hat on head, departing for work (see page 90). The designs of recently built homes in adjacent neighborhoods are influenced by these earlier structures. (Courtesy Aegis Corporation/Drake Property Group.)

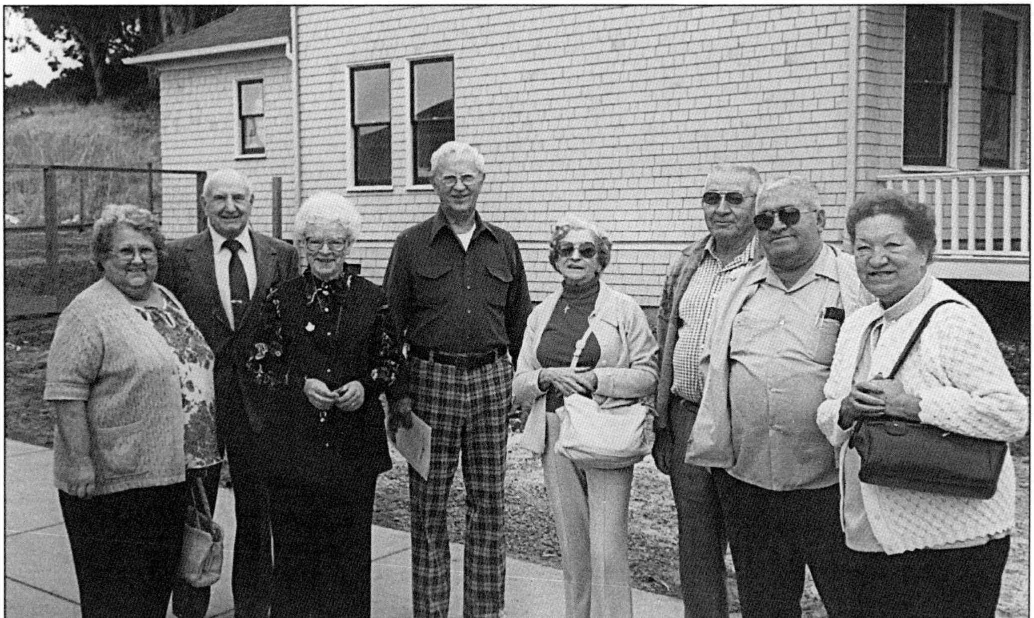

GATHERING OF HERCULITES. Taking a tour of the restored homes are, from left to right, unidentified, Ralph Williams, Maddy McCall, unidentified, Ethyl Staples, Dan McCall, Edwin E. "Bud" Randall, and Marvela Randall. Each of the men worked at the plant for 30 to 40-plus years. (Courtesy Douglas Williams.)

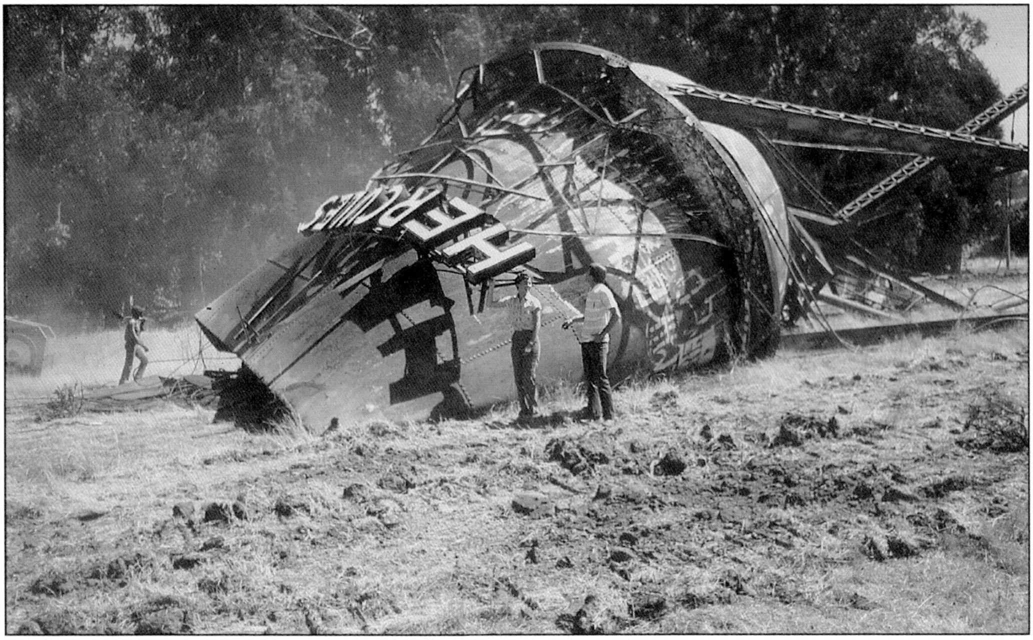

Symbol of the Company Town. The water tower, once located on the north side of Hercules Avenue west of San Pablo Avenue, was razed in 1981 to make way for 310 housing units in the Olympian Hills development. Lynn Fissell and Dave Thomason inspect the fallen tower. The letters are currently in storage. (Courtesy Lynn Fissell.)

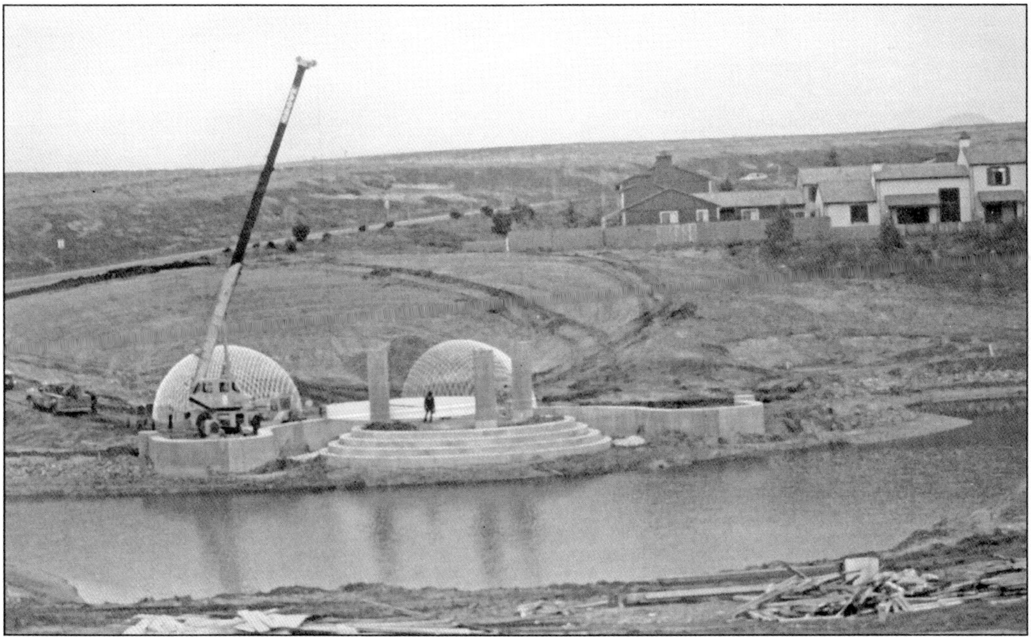

New Landmark. Refugio Valley Park is an icon of today's Hercules. The large park begins at the corner of Refugio Valley Road and Sycamore Avenue and includes a small lake, amphitheater, and large playing field. Today, the "dynamic" city of Hercules has its own retail centers, schools, and parks, with a variety of residential neighborhood styles, and is home to more than 25,000 residents. (Courtesy Hercules Historical Society.)

Bibliography

The California Powder Works: Manufacturers of Hercules Powder. Pinole, Contra Costa County, CA: Hercules Powder Works, San Francisco Office, 1897.

Dyer, Davis and David. B. Silica. *Labors of a Modern Hercules: Evolution of a Chemical Company.* Boston: Harvard Business School Press, 1990.

Emanuels, George. *California's Contra Costa County: An Illustrated History.* Fresno, CA: Panorama West, 1986.

Fridell, Lee D. *The Story of Richmond: El Cerrito – San Pablo – Pinole –Hercules.* Richmond, CA: Board of Trustees, Richmond Union High School District.

The Giant Powder Co: Dynamite, Gelatine, Gelatin Dynamite and Judson Powder. San Francisco: Bandmann, Nielsen and Co.

Hercules Powder Company. *The Hercules Mixer.* 1.1–37.1. Wilmington, DE: March 1919–December 1955.

Hulaniski, F.J. *The History of Contra Costa County.* Berkeley, CA: Elms Publishing, 1917.

McGrath, Kevin and Cori Ojala. Dorway-Worley, Pamela, ed. and Patricia M. Perkins, associate ed. *Remembering Days Past: Hercules, California 1879 to 1979.* Spring 1980.

Purcell, Mae Fisher. *History of Contra Costa County.* Berkeley, CA: Gillick Press, 1940.

Salley, Harold E. *History of California Post Offices, 1849–1976.* La Mesa, CA: Postal History Associates, c. 1977.

Tatum, Robert Daras. *Old Times In Contra Costa: A Journey to the Past.* Pittsburg, CA: Highland Publishers, 1993.

VanGelder, Arthur Pine and Hugo Schlatter. *History of the Explosives Industry in America.* New York: Columbia University Press, 1927.

Woodbridge, Sally B. *Hercules: Architectural and Historical Survey of Buildings and Landscape Elements.* Unpublished manuscript, May 6, 1979.

Consistent with our mission to preserve history on a local level, this book was printed in South Carolina on American-made paper and manufactured entirely in the United States. Products carrying the accredited Forest Stewardship Council (FSC) label are printed on 100 percent FSC-certified paper.

MADE IN THE USA